D0175997

# COMPREHENSIVE GLOSSARY OF PSYCHIATRY AND PSYCHOLOGY

REFERENCE ONLY

QUIMBY MEMORIAL LIBRARY
Southwestern College
P.O. Box 4788
Santa Fe, New Mexico 87502

SENIOR CONTRIBUTING EDITOR

## Robert Cancro, M.D., MeD.D.Sc.

Professor and Chairman, Department of Psychiatry,
New York University School of Medicine;
Director, Department of Psychiatry, Tisch Hospital, the University
Hospital of New York University Medical Center;
Director, Nathan S. Kline Institute for
Psychiatric Research, Orangeburg, New York

QUIMBY MEMORIAL LIBRARY

# COMPREHENSIVE
## GLOSSARY
## OF
# PSYCHIATRY
## AND
# PSYCHOLOGY

## Harold I. Kaplan, M.D.

Professor of Psychiatry, New York University School of Medicine
Attending Psychiatrist, Tisch Hospital, the University
Hospital of New York University Medical Center
Attending Psychiatrist, Bellevue Hospital
New York, New York

## Benjamin J. Sadock, M.D.

Professor and Vice Chairman, Department of Psychiatry,
New York University School of Medicine,
Attending Psychiatrist, Tisch Hospital, the University
Hospital of New York University Medical Center
Attending Psychiatrist, Bellevue Hospital
New York, New York

QUIMBY MEMORIAL LIBRARY
Southwestern College
P.O. Box 4788
Santa Fe, New Mexico 87502

616
.89
KAP

### Williams & Wilkins

BALTIMORE • PHILADELPHIA • HONG KONG
LONDON • MUNICH • SYDNEY • TOKYO

A WAVERLY COMPANY

*Editor:* William R. Hensyl
*Associate Editor:* Julie D. Rodowski
*Copy Editor:* Thomas Lehr
*Designer:* Saturn Graphics
*Production Coordinator:* Charles E. Zeller
*Cover Design:* Dan Pfisterer

Copyright © 1991
Williams & Wilkins
428 East Preston Street
Baltimore, Maryland 21202, USA

All rights reserved. This book is protected by copyright. No part of this book may be reproduced in any form or by any means, including photocopying, or utilized by any information storage and retrieval system without written permission from the copyright owner.

Accurate indications, adverse reactions, and dosage schedules for drugs are provided in this book, but it is possible that they may change. The reader is urged to review the package information data of the manufacturers of the medications mentioned.

*Printed in the United States of America*

**Library of Congress Cataloging-in-Publication Data**

Kaplan, Harold I., 1927–
    Comprehensive glossary of psychiatry and psychology / Harold I. Kaplan, Benjamin J. Sadock.
        p.   cm.
    ISBN 0-683-04527-X
        1. Psychiatry—Dictionaries.    2. Psychology—Dictionaries.
    I. Sadock, Benjamin J., 1933–    .  II. Title.
    RC437.K36   1991
    616.89′003—dc20                                                                90-22810
                                                                                            CIP


                                                                                    94   95
                                                                5   6   7   8   9   10

*Dedicated*
*to our wives,*
*Nancy Barrett Kaplan*
*and*
*Virginia Alcott Sadock,*
*without whose help and sacrifice*
*this book would not have been possible*

# Preface

The need for a comprehensive glossary of psychiatric and psychological terms has never been more pressing. Within the past few years there have been tremendous advances in the behavioral sciences, psychiatry, psychology, and social work, as well as in the neural sciences such as neurochemistry, neuroimmunology, and neurophysiology. The resulting increase in knowledge has been accompanied by so many new scientific terms that greater precision in the use of language is necessary to keep up with the continuous change and refinements in these fields.

The authors have attempted to provide definitions in a concise, simple, and lucid manner and, when necessary, to include clinical examples and facts to make definitions as meaningful as possible. In addition, cross-references are often used to refer the reader to other entries as an aid to fuller comprehension and understanding. The authors intend to have this glossary undergo frequent revisions to keep it as up-to-date as possible.

This glossary can serve as an excellent study guide to the busy student or clinician who requires a quick and ready reference to both classical and innovative terms in the psychiatric and psychological literature. It will also be useful to mental health professionals, scientific writers, nurses, members of the legal profession, and others who need to be knowledgeable of the terms used by psychiatrists and psychologists.

The terms defined in this glossary come from a variety of sources, especially Kaplan and Sadock's *Comprehensive Textbook of Psychiatry* and their *Synopsis of Psychiatry*. The user who wishes more information is referred to those books, which form part of an educational system devised by the authors. We want to thank Robert J. Campbell, M.D., and his publishers for giving us permission to derive some of the definitions in this text from his book, the sixth edition of *Psychiatric Dictionary*, published by Oxford University Press, to which the reader is also referred. The terms used herein are consistent with the revised third edition of the American Psychiatric Association's *Diagnostic and Statistical Manual of Mental Disorders* (DSM-III-R). The various diagnostic categories of mental illness listed in DSM-III-R are printed on the inside front and back covers for easy reference. The authors have also included appendices covering psychotherapeutic drugs used in psychiatry, including a list of drugs that are commonly abused. A unique feature of this book is the Psychotherapeutic Drug Identification Guide, four pages of colored plates indicating both the forms in which these drugs are commercially available and their dose ranges to help in conveniently recognizing and prescribing these medications. The glossary also incorporates relevant research, neurologic, and statistical terms as well as information about the different psychoanalytic schools of psychiatry and psychology.

Several persons helped in the preparation of this book. Lynda Abrams, M.A., Educational Coordinator in the Department of Psychiatry at the New York University School of Medicine, served as Project Editor, for which we are most grateful; Laura Marino was involved in the complex preparation of the manuscript and worked most efficiently. Others who helped were Norman Sussman, M.D., Rebecca Jones, M.D., Robin Segal, M.D., Peter Kaplan, M.D., and Phillip Kaplan, M.D., James Sadock, Victoria Sadock, Nancy Kaplan, and Jennifer Kaplan D'Addio offered helpful advice.

We especially wish to thank Virginia Sadock, M.D., Clinical Professor of Psychiatry and Director of Graduate Education in Human Sexuality at the NYU School of Medicine, for her collaboration and her help in providing the definitions for terms particularly in the area of sexology.

Robert Cancro, M.D., Professor and Chairman of the Department of Psychiatry at the NYU School of Medicine, deserves special thanks for his role as Senior Contributing Editor of this volume and for his unwavering support in all our efforts.

Harold I. Kaplan, M.D.
Benjamin J. Sadock, M.D.

# Explanatory Notes

*Comprehensive Glossary of Psychiatry and Psychology* uses familiar lexicographic conventions in the organization and format of its vocabulary. Users of the glossary who familiarize themselves with these features will not only benefit from time saved through an efficient search for information but also will increase the amount of information obtained.

Entry words, terms, and abbreviations are alphabetized letter by letter as spelled, in standard dictionary sequence. Prepositions, conjunctions, articles, punctuation, Greek letters, numbers, and spaces are disregarded. Biographical entries are listed by surname.

Each entry consists of two parts: the **boldface** entry word or term, followed by its abbreviation (if any), and its definition in lightface. If there is more than one definition, each is numbered in boldface. Synonyms are listed at the end of the definition, preceded by "Also called," and also are listed as boldface cross-reference entries. Cross-references follow the synonyms.

An abbreviation as an entry word has only its spelled-out form as the definition, thus serving as a cross-reference to that entry, where a complete definition is given. In cases where the abbreviation is more widely used than the spelled-out form, the latter entry is the cross-reference.

A synonym entry functions as a cross-reference to its defined synonymous entry word or term, its definition consisting solely of the latter set in SMALL CAPITALS. The complete definition of the synonym is given at the referred-to entry.

Cross-references are prefaced by *See, See also,* and *Compare.* A *See* cross-reference functions as a locator to show where the definition or information about the entry word or term can be found. *See also* directs the user to related or associated entries for additional relevant information. *Compare* serves to point out entries related by contrast or opposition.

# Contents

# A

**AA**   Alcoholics Anonymous.

**AACAP**   American Academy of Child and Adolescent Psychiatry.

**AACDP**   American Association of Chairmen of Departments of Psychiatry.

**AADPRT**   American Association of Directors of Psychiatric Residency Training, Inc.

**AAMC**   Association of American Medical Colleges.

**ability**   Capacity or competence to perform an act without previous training. *Compare* aptitude.

**ablation**   Excision of part of the body, as in lobotomy or topectomy.

**ablutomania**   Excessive interest in bathing and cleaning oneself; commonly observed in obsessive-compulsive disorder.

**abnormal**   Term subject to considerable variability in definition and usage, roughly the equivalent of "psychopathological," and defined according to several criteria: **1.** *Normative or statistical approach,* considers abnormal any mental or behavioral activities that deviate from culturally determined averages or norms. **2.** *Subjective approach,* regards as abnormal or psychopathological those phenomena that cause pain or suffering or induce a person to seek help. **3.** *Theoretical approach,* considers as abnormal any deviations from a theoretical concept of normal functioning that are indicative of psychiatric illness.

**abortion**   Spontaneous or induced expulsion of an embryo or fetus before it has reached the stage of viability, i.e., before about 20 weeks gestation.

**ABPN**   American Board of Psychiatry and Neurology.

**abreaction**   A process by which repressed material, particularly a painful experience or a conflict, is brought back to consciousness; in this process, the person not only recalls but relives the repressed material, which is accompanied by the appropriate affective response. *See also* catharsis.

**absolute threshold**   Minimum amount of stimulus needed to produce a response.

**absence**   PETIT MAL EPILEPSY.

**abstinence**   The act of refraining voluntarily from some activity or from the use of certain substances, such as food or drugs; in psychoanalysis, refers to refraining from sexual intercourse.

**abstinence syndrome**   WITHDRAWAL SYNDROME.

**abstract attitude**   ABSTRACT THINKING.

**abstraction**   The process whereby thoughts or ideas are generalized and dissociated from particular concrete instances or material objects; concreteness in proverb interpretation suggests an impairment of abstraction, as in schizophrenia.

**abstract thinking**   Thinking characterized by the ability to assume a mental set voluntarily, to shift voluntarily from one aspect of a situation to another, to keep in mind simultaneously various aspects of a situation, to grasp the essentials of a whole and to break a whole into its parts, to discern common properties, to plan, to assume make-believe attitudes, and to think or act symbolically. The capacity for abstract thinking is frequently impaired in patients with organic mental disorders and schizophrenia. Also called abstract attitude; categorical attitude. *Compare* concrete thinking.

**abulia**   Inability to make decisions; lack of will.

**abuse**   To attack or injure physically or psychologically, most commonly children, the elderly, and marital partners. *See also* battered child syndrome.

**acalculia**   Learning or speech disorder characterized by the inability to perform simple arithmetic operations.

**acarophobia**   Abnormal fear of minute animate (insects, worms) or inanimate (pins, needles) objects.

**acatalepsia**   Severe mental deficiency characterized by the inability to reason or comprehend.

**acataphasia**   Disordered speech in which statements are incorrectly formulated. Patients may express themselves with words that sound like the ones intended but that are not appropriate to the thoughts, or they may use totally inappropriate expressions.

**acathexis**   Lack of feeling associated with an ordinarily emotion-charged subject; in psychoanalysis, denotes the patient's detaching or transferring of emotion from thoughts and ideas. Also called decathexis. *Compare* cathexis.

**accelerated interaction**   Alternate term for marathon group session.

**accident proneness**   Tendency to have accidents as a result of psychological causes.

**accreditation**   A voluntary process by which standards for hospitals and health facilities are approved by the Joint Commission on Accreditation of Healthcare Organizations (JCAHO); may also refer to being credentialed by the American Board of Psychiatry and Neurology (ABPN). *See also* board certified psychiatrist.

**acenesthesia**   Loss of sensation of physical existence.

**acetylcholine**   A neurotransmitter that causes cardiac inhibition, vasodilation, gastrointestinal peristalsis, and other parasympathetic effects; plays a critical role in memory, sleep, and the regulation of mood.

**achluophobia**   Abnormal fear of the dark.

**acid**   Slang for lysergic acid diethylamide (LSD). *See* Appendix 2.

**ACP**   American College of Physicians.

**acquired immunodeficiency syndrome (AIDS)**   According to the U.S. Centers for Disease Control, "a disease, at least moderately predictive of a defect in cell-mediated immunity, occurring in a person with no known cause for diminished resistance to that disease. Such diseases include Kaposi's sarcoma (KS), *Pneumocystis carinii* pneumonia (PCP), and other serious opportunistic infections." The disease is caused by the human immunodeficiency virus type 1 (HIV-1). *See also* AIDS dementia complex.

**acromegaly**   Disorder marked by hypersecretion of growth hormone by the anterior pituitary resulting in characteristic enlargement of certain body structures, such as the head, hands, feet, lips, and jaw; often associated with somnolence, moodiness, and decreased libido.

**acrophobia**   Abnormal fear of high places.

**acting out**   Behavioral response to an unconscious drive or impulse that brings about temporary partial relief of inner tension; relief is attained by reacting to a present situation as if it were the situation that originally gave rise to the drive or impulse.

**activity group psychotherapy**   Type of group therapy, introduced and developed by S. R. Slavson, designed for children and young adolescents, with emphasis on emotional and active interaction in a permissive, non-threatening atmosphere; the therapist interprets behavior and stresses reality testing.

**actualization**   Realization of one's full potential. *See also* individuation.

**aculalia**   Nonsense speech associated with marked impairment of comprehension.

**acute schizophrenia** Term commonly used to refer to the sudden onset of schizophrenic signs and symptoms. Since a 6-month duration of illness is required for the diagnosis, there is no acute type of schizophrenia listed as an official diagnosis in DSM-III-R.

**acute situational** or **stress reaction** Severe emotional reaction resulting from extreme environmental stress such as the death of a loved one, a disaster, or a catastrophic life situation. Called post-traumatic stress disorder in DSM-III-R.

**ADAMHA** Alcohol, Drug Abuse, and Mental Health Administration.

**adaptation** Process of fitting or conforming to the environment by behavioral or psychic changes that promote an optimal level of functioning.

**adaptational approach** In analytic therapy, consonant with Sandor Rado's formulations on adaptational psychodynamics, therapy focusing on the maladaptive patterns used by patients in the treatment sessions, on how those patterns developed, and on what the patients must do to overcome them and stabilize their functioning at self-reliant, adult levels. *See also* social adaptation.

**adaptive behavior** Any behavior that increases an organism's ability to adjust to a specific environment or situation.

**addiction** Repeated and increased use of a drug or chemical substance, the deprivation of which gives rise to symptoms of distress and an irresistible urge to use the agent again; leads to deterioration of physical and mental health. *See also* drug dependence.

**ADHD** Attention deficit hyperactivity disorder.

**adiadochokinesis** Inability to perform rapid alternating movements.

**adjustment** A person's relation to the environment and to his or her inner self. *See also* adaptation.

**adjustment disorder** Maladaptive reaction to identifiable circumstances or life events that is expected to remit when the stress ceases.

**Adler, Alfred** (1870–1937) Viennese psychiatrist and one of Freud's original followers who broke with him and introduced and developed the concepts of individual psychology, inferiority complex, and overcompensation. *See also* masculine protest.

**adlerian** Attributed to or described by Alfred Adler.

**administrative psychiatry**   Psychiatry concerned with public affairs, policy-making, executive decisions, and the duties of persons in executive positions.

**adolescence**   Period of growth from puberty to maturity. Its beginning is marked by the appearance of secondary sexual characteristics, usually at about age 12; termination is marked by the achievement of sexual maturity at about age 20. *See also* psychosexual development.

**adolescent mania**   Signs of mania occurring in an adolescent as the result of substance abuse (including alcohol) or of antisocial behavior but not as the result of a true bipolar disorder.

**adrenaline**   EPINEPHRINE.

**adrenergic   1.** Relating to nerve fibers, tracts, or pathways in which synaptic transmission is mediated by norepinephrine (e.g., the sympathetic division of the autonomic nervous system); more generally, to processes activated by epinephrine or norepinephrine. **2.** Relating to drugs (catecholamines) that mimic the actions of the sympathetic nervous system.

**adrenergic system**   Nerve cells or fibers of the autonomic nervous system that employ norepinephrine as their neurotransmitter.

**adventitious reinforcement**   Responses that are reinforced accidentally by the coincidental pairing of response and reinforcement; such events may have clinical implications in the development of phobias or other neurotic behavior.

**adverse effects**   Secondary, unfavorable reactions or results; usually referring to side effects of drugs.

**adynamia**   Weakness and fatigability, a characteristic of asthenic personality and depression.

**adynamic ileus**   PARALYTIC ILEUS.

**aerophagia**   Excessive swallowing of air.

**affect**   The subjective and immediate experience of emotion attached to ideas or mental representations of objects. Affect has outward manifestations that may be classified as restricted, blunted, flattened, broad, labile, appropriate, or inappropriate. *See also* mood.

**affect-fantasy**   Jung's term for an emotional-laden fantasy.

**affectionate transference**   *See* transference.

**affective disorder**   MOOD DISORDER.

**affective hallucination**   Hallucination in which the content is either grandiose or self-deprecatory or involves other features common to a depressive syndrome such as guilt, disease, or poverty.

**affective interaction**   Interpersonal experiences and exchanges that are emotionally charged.

**aftercare**   After hospitalization, a continuing program of rehabilitation designed to reinforce the effects of therapy and to help patients adjust to their environment.

**ageism**   Prejudice or discrimination against a particular age-group, especially the elderly.

**ageusia**   Lack or impairment of the sense of taste; may be seen in depression.

**aggression**   Forceful behavior, verbal or physical, usually directed against another person.

**aggressive drive**   One of the two primal drives or instincts (the other is the sexual drive) in Freud's dual-instinct psychoanalytic theory. It is conceived of as an unconscious destructive drive or an impulse directed at oneself or another that aims toward dissolution and death and operates on the repetition-compulsion principle, in contrast to the sexual drive, which follows the pleasure-pain principle. Also called death instinct; Thanatos.

**aging**   The process of growing old; in human physiology, aging is said to occur when there is a failure to replace cells in sufficient numbers to maintain full functional capacity.

**agitated depression**   Major depressive disorder with psychomotor agitation as a primary sign and symptom, characterized by restlessness, increased motor activity, and racing thoughts.

**agitation**   State of anxiety associated with severe motor restlessness.

**agnosia**   Inability to understand the import or significance of sensory stimuli; cannot be explained by a defect in sensory pathways or sensorium. In strict usage, diagnosis of agnosia implies an organic cerebral lesion; however, the term has also been used to refer to the selective loss or disuse of knowledge of specific objects due to emotional circumstances, as seen in certain schizophrenic, hysteric, and depressed patients. For types of agnosia, see the specific term.

**agonist**   In pharmacology, a substance that excites the receptor sites of the cell and promotes or enhances a biologic response. *Compare* antagonist.

**agoraphobia**   Morbid fear of open places or of leaving the familiar setting of the home; may be present with or without panic attacks.

**agraphia**   Loss or impairment of a previously possessed ability to write.

**AHD**   Attention-deficit hyperactivity disorder.

**aichmophobia**   Abnormal fear of pointed objects.

**AIDS**   Acquired immunodeficiency syndrome.

**AIDS dementia complex**   Neurologic complication of AIDS characterized by confusion, impaired judgment, impulsive behavior, and psychosis. Also called AIDS encephalopathy.

**ailurophobia**   Abnormal fear of cats.

**akathisia**   State of motor restlessness manifested by a compelling need to be in constant movement; may be seen as an extrapyramidal side effect of phenothiazine or other antipsychotic medication.

**akinesia**   Lack of physical movement, as in the extreme immobility of catatonic schizophrenia; may also occur as an extrapyramidal effect of antipsychotic medication.

**akinetic mutism**   Absence of voluntary motor movement or speech in a patient who is apparently alert (as evidenced by following eye movements).

**Al-Anon**   Organization of relatives of alcoholics, patterned after Alcoholics Anonymous, that promotes the discussion and resolution of common problems.

**alarm reaction stage**   *See* general adaptation syndrome.

**Alateen**   Organization directed to children of alcoholics, through group support, so that they may better understand their parents' alcoholism. *See also* Alcoholics Anonymous.

**alcohol abuse and dependence**   DSM-III-R term for alcoholism.

**alcohol amnestic disorder**   DSM-III-R term for Korsakoff's psychosis.

**alcohol dementia**   WERNICKE'S SYNDROME.

**Alcohol, Drug Abuse, and Mental Health Administration (ADAMHA)**   An agency of the U.S. government that is part of the National Institutes of Health within the Department of Health and Human Services. It administers grant programs supporting research, training, and service programs in alcoholism, drug abuse, and mental health. Individual institutes within the agency are the National Institute on Alcohol Abuse and Alcoholism (NIAAA), the National Institute of Drug Abuse (NIDA), and the National Institute of Mental Health (NIMH).

**alcoholic blackout**   Amnesia experienced by alcoholics concerning behavior during drinking bouts; usually indicates that reversible brain damage has occurred.

**alcoholic deterioration**  Dementia and mental deterioration associated with chronic excessive alcohol use. Called dementia associated with alcoholism in DSM-III-R.

**alcoholic hallucinosis**  Occurrence of hallucinations with a clear sensorium in a person with a history of heavy drinking and alcohol dependence; usually follows a prolonged drinking bout. *See also* Delirium tremens.

**alcoholic psychosis**  Mental disorder that results from alcoholism and that involves organic brain damage, as in delirium tremens and Korsakoff's psychosis.

**Alcoholics Anonymous (AA)**  An organization of alcoholics formed in 1935 that uses certain group methods, such as inspirational-supportive techniques, to help rehabilitate chronic alcoholics.

**alcohol idiosyncratic intoxication**  DSM-III-R term for a syndrome of marked alcohol intoxication with subsequent amnesia for the period of intoxication produced by the ingestion of quantities of alcohol that would be insufficient to induce intoxication in most people. Also called pathological intoxication.

**alcohol intoxication**  Constellation of specific neurological, psychological, and behavioral effects produced by the recent ingestion of alcohol; characteristically, the effects include slurred speech, motor ataxia, disinhibition of sexual or aggressive impulses, lability of mood, impairment of attention or memory, and impairment of judgment. *See also* intoxication.

**alcoholism**  Excessive dependence on or addiction to alcohol, usually to the point that the person's physical and mental health is threatened or harmed; may be episodic or continuous. Called alcohol abuse and dependence in DSM-III-R.

**alcohol withdrawal delirium**  DSM-III-R term for delirium tremens.

**alcohol withdrawal syndrome**  Symptom complex resulting from the cessation or reduction in alcohol intake in a person who has been drinking heavily; includes tremulousness, seizures (rum fits), hallucinations, and autonomic hyperactivity (delirium tremens). *See also* withdrawal syndrome.

**Alexander, Franz** (1891–1964). Hungarian psychoanalyst who founded the Chicago Institute for Psychoanalysis, developed the concept of corrective emotional experience and specificity hypothesis in psychosomatic disorders, and, in collaboration with

Thomas French in 1946, identified most of the basic characteristics of brief dynamic psychotherapy.

**alexia**  Loss of the power to understand the meaning of written or printed words and sentences. *Compare* dyslexia.

**alexithymia**  Inability or difficulty in describing or being aware of one's emotions or moods; associated with depression, substance abuse, and post-traumatic stress disorder.

**algophobia**  Abnormal fear of pain.

**algorithm**  Graphic representation used as a set of instructions for solving diagnostic or clinical problems. Also called decision tree.

**alienation**  In psychiatry, used to describe a person's feelings of detachment from self or society, to denote one's avoidance of emotional experiences, or to describe efforts to estrange oneself from one's own feelings. *Compare* relatedness. *See also* isolation.

**alienist**  Obsolete term for a psychiatrist who offers expert opinion about a person's mental health or sanity.

**allergic jaundice**  Relatively rare, unpredictable, non-dose-dependent hypersensitivity reaction after treatment with some phenothiazines; generally appears during the second to fourth week of therapy, resulting in hyperbilirubinemia and deposition of bile pigment in the skin and mucous membranes which causes a yellow appearance of the patient; an obstructive (cholestatic) type of jaundice manifested by predominantly conjugated (direct-reacting) hyperbilirubinemia, the presence of bilirubin in the urine, and an abnormally high plasma alkaline phosphatase.

**alliance**  *See* therapeutic alliance.

**allied health professional**  *See* paraprofessional.

**alloplasty**  Adaptation to stress by attempting to change the environment. *Compare* autoplasty.

**Allport's group relations theory**  Theory developed by Gordon W. Allport that a person's behavior is influenced by his or her personality and the need to conform to social forces; illustrates the interrelationship between group therapy and social psychology.

**alpha (α) error**  TYPE 1 ERROR.

**alpha waves**  As measured by an electroencephalogram (EEG), brain waves that are 8–13 Hz, indicating a relaxed, waking state.

**ALS**  Amyotropic lateral sclerosis.

**alternating role**  Pattern characterized by periodic switching from one type of behavior to another.

**altruism** Regard for and dedication to the welfare of others; a term originated by the French philosopher Auguste Comte (1798–1857). In psychiatry, the term is closely linked with ethics and morals; Freud recognized altruism as the only basis for the development of community interest; Bleuler equated it with morality.

**Alzheimer's disease** PRIMARY DEGENERATIVE DEMENTIA OF THE ALZHEIMER TYPE.

**AMA** American Medical Association.

**ambivalence** Presence of strong and often overwhelming simultaneous contrasting attitudes, ideas, feelings, and drives toward an object, person, or goal; term coined by Bleuler, who differentiated three types: affective ambivalence, intellectual ambivalence, and ambivalence of the will.

**ambulatory schizophrenia** Schizophrenic mental illness that is sufficiently well compensated so as not to require continuous hospitalization.

**amentia** Lack of intellectual development as a result of inadequate brain tissue. *Compare* dementia.

**American Academy of Child and Adolescent Psychiatry (AACAP)** Organization of child and adolescent psychiatrists, founded in 1953, whose objectives are to study and to advance medical contributions to the knowledge and treatment of psychiatric illnesses of children and adolescents.

**American Association of Chairmen of Departments of Psychiatry (AACDP)** Organization of chairpersons of departments of psychiatry, founded in 1967, that concentrates on promoting medical education, research, and patient care, especially as they relate to psychiatry; prompting the growth and development of psychiatry; and providing a forum for discussion among chairpersons.

**American Association of Directors of Psychiatric Residency Training, Inc. (AADPRT)** Organization of training directors of U.S. psychiatric residency programs, founded in 1973, whose mandate is to oversee standards of approved residency criteria and to further psychiatric education.

**American Board of Psychiatry and Neurology (ABPN)** Group, founded in 1934, that sets the standards for teaching and training in psychiatry and neurology in American hospitals and training centers. Its members are from the American Medical Association, American Psychiatric Association, and American Neurological Association. It conducts periodic examinations of those who have satisfactorily completed their training; upon passing the examination, candidates are certified to practice the specialty of psychiatry and/or neurology and/or child psychiatry.

**American College of Physicians (ACP)**   Honorary organization of internists and related medical specialists, founded in 1915, that sponsors postgraduate courses for physicians as well as teaching and research scholarships.

**American College of Psychiatrists (ACP)**   Honorary organization of senior psychiatrists, founded in 1963, established to honor persons who have made a significant contribution to the study and development of psychiatry in the U.S.

**American Law Institute formulation of insanity**   Legal definiton of insanity whereby a person is absolved of criminal responsibility if, as a result of a mental disorder, he "lacks substantial capacity either to appreciate the wrongfulness of his conduct or to conform his conduct to the requirements of law." *See also* Durham rule; M'Naghten rule.

**American Medical Association (AMA)**   National organization of medical doctors of all specialties, founded in 1847, whose mandate is to monitor the educational, training, and research concerns of the medical profession; plays an advisory role in national legislation related to health care and disseminates medical information.

**American Neurological Association (ANA)**   National organization of neurologists, founded in 1875, that conducts research and educational programs; also elects members to the American Board of Psychiatry.

**American Psychiatric Association (APA)**   Most important and largest professional organization of American physicians who specialize in the practice of psychiatry. The organization was founded in 1844 by 13 superintendents ("original thirteen") as the Association of Medical Superintendents of American Institutions for the Insane; in 1891, the name was changed to the American Medico-Psychological Association and in 1921 to its present name. Its purpose is to advance the development of psychiatric education, research, and practice in the U.S.

**American Psychoanalytic Association (APA)**   National organization of graduates of various psychoanalytic training programs, founded in 1911, mandated to establish and maintain standards for the field of psychoanalysis and the training of psychoanalysts and to encourage research; historically represents orthodox schools of classical psychoanalysis derived from Freudian theory.

**American Psychological Association**  Founded in 1892, largest and most important organization of American psychologists who specialize in experimental, clinical, research, and educational psychology, and many other subspecialties in psychology; sometimes known as the "big APA" to distinguish it from the smaller American Psychiatric Association.

**amimia**  Lack of ability to make gestures or to comprehend those made by others.

**amines**  Organic compounds derived from ammonia by replacing hydrogen atoms with organic groups, such as the catecholamines.

**amino acid**  Organic acid in which one of the CH hydrogen atoms has been replaced by $NH_2$; structured building blocks of proteins that function as neurotransmitters similar to the biogenic amines, probably in 60–70% of the synapses in the brain.

**amnesia**  Disturbance in memory manifested by partial or total inability to recall past experiences. For types of amnesia, see the specific term.

**amnestic aphasia, amnesic aphasia**  Disturbed capacity to name objects, even though they are known to the patient. Also called anomic aphasia.

**amnestic syndrome**  Organic mental syndrome in which impairment of memory is the predominant cognitive defect.

**amok**  Condition, usually associated with Malayan men, characterized by a sudden, unprovoked outburst of wild rage usually culminating in homicide.

**amphetamine**  Central nervous system stimulant with a chemical structure and action closely related to the sympathomimetic amines; used to treat depression, attention-deficit hyperactivity disorder, hypersomnia, and narcolepsy; may be abused to prolong wakefulness and attentiveness.

**amygdala**  Part of the basal ganglia complex in the dorsomedial portion of the temporal lobe; it and the hippocampus are major components of the limbic system and have been implicated in the production of memory, emotions, and violent behavior.

**amyotropic lateral sclerosis (ALS)**  Degenerative neuromuscular disease, caused by a slow virus, with an insidious onset beginning between the ages of 50 and 70; wasting begins in upper limbs, eventually spreading to the tongue, mouth, and palate. Degeneration of both pyramidal tracts above the medulla produces pseudobulbar palsy, which, when severe, results in impaired voluntary control of emotional reactions, which consequently may be exaggerated, explosive, and quite inappropriate. Also called Lou Gehrig's disease.

**Amytal interview** Psychiatric interview conducted with the patient having received an intravenous infusion of amobarbital (Amytal), which produces an altered state of consciousness during which repressed memories and feelings may be recalled or reexperienced; used in the treatment of dissociative states, psychogenic amnesia, and conversion disorder.

**ANA** American Neurological Association.

**anaclitic** Depending on others, especially as the infant on the mother; anaclitic depression in children results from an absence of mothering.

**anaclitic therapy** Psychotherapy characterized by allowing the patient to regress; used mainly in the treatment of psychosomatic disorders.

**anal character** Freud's term to describe persons who are perfectionistic, parsimonious, punctual, and stubborn.

**analeptic** PSYCHOMOTOR STIMULANT.

**anal erotism** Pleasurable experience felt by a child in the anal area during the anal phase of psychosexual development.

**analgesia** State in which one feels little or no pain.

**anal phase** Second stage in psychosexual development, occurring when a child is between the ages of 1 and 3 years. During that period, activities, interests, and concerns are centered on the anal zone, and the pleasurable experience felt in that area is called anal erotism. *See also* infantile sexuality; psychosexual development.

**analysand** In psychiatry, the one who is being analyzed.

**analysis in depth** PSYCHOANALYSIS.

**analysis of variance (ANOVA)** Statistical technique designed to compare two or more groups of observations by which sets of measurements are investigated to find out to what extent they are determined by experimental influences or chance influences. *See also* variance.

**analytic psychology** Jung's system of psychology, characterized by a belief in the collective unconscious or objective psyche, the archetype, and the complex.

**anamnesis** Medical history of a patient, particularly used in connection with the patient's own recollections.

**anancasm** Repetitious or stereotyped behavior or thought usually used as a tension-relieving device.

**anankastic personality** OBSESSIVE-COMPULSIVE PERSONALITY.

**ancillary care** Auxiliary, accessory, or secondary services provided in the treatment or rehabilitation of patients.

**androgen** Hormone that is produced in the testes and the adrenal glands and that stimulates activity of the accessory male sex organs, promotes development of male sex characteristics, or prevents changes in the latter following castration; e.g., testosterone. *Compare* estrogen.

**androgyny** Combination of female and male characteristics in one person. *See also* bisexuality.

**androphobia** Irrational fear of men.

**anergic schizophrenic** BURNED-OUT SCHIZOPHRENIC.

**anesthesia** Absence of sensation. *See also* hysterical anesthesia.

**angel dust** Street term for phencyclidine (PCP). *See* Appendix 2.

**anhedonia** State of being unable to experience pleasure. *Compare* hedonism.

**anima** According to jungian psychology, the person's inner self, as opposed to the self that one presents to the outside world (persona).

**Anna O** A patient of Joseph Breuer and Sigmund Freud whose arm became paralyzed whenever she was unconsciously reminded of her feelings for her father (she had been sitting at his bedside with her arm pressed against the side of his bed at the time of his death). The motor disturbance represented an action that was associated with an objectionable infantile sexual impulse.

**anniversary reaction** Behavior, symptoms, or dreams that occur at the same time of year as a significant past event.

**anomia** Inability to recall the names of objects.

**anomic aphasia** AMNESTIC APHASIA.

**anomie** Term, popularized by Émile Durkheim as a major cause for suicide, referring to a sense of alienation and despair resulting from the loss or weakening of previously valued norms, ideals, or goals.

**anorexia nervosa**   Serious and sometimes life-endangering condition characterized by a disturbed body image and self-imposed severe dietary limitation, usually resulting in serious malnutrition.

**anorgasmia**   Inability to achieve orgasm in the female. *See also* frigidity.

**anosognosia**   Unawareness or nonacceptance of a neurological deficit.

**ANOVA**   Analysis of variance.

**antagonist**   In pharmacology, a substance that reduces or blocks the action of another; e.g., naloxone (Narcan) is used in the treatment of opioid overdose because it is reverses the effects of narcotics. *Compare* agonist.

**anterograde amnesia**   Loss of memory for events subsequent to the onset of the amnesia. *Compare* retrograde amnesia.

**anthropology**   Study of humans in relation to distribution, origin, classification, and relationship of races, physical characteristics, environmental and social relations, and culture.

**antianxiety drug**   ANXIOLYTIC.

**anticholinergic effect**   Effect, such as a dry mouth and blurred vision, due to a blockade of the cholinergic (especially the parasympathetic) nerves; often seen as a side effect of therapy with phenothiazine and tricyclic antidepressant drugs.

**anticipation**   Term implying careful planning or worrying, and premature but realistic expectation of dire and potentially dreadful outcomes, in goal-directed inner discomfort.

**anticonvulsant**   Any drug with the ability to prevent the excessive discharge of neurons in the brain and thus lower the threshold for convulsions or seizures. Also called antiepileptic drug.

**antidepressant drug**   Any of a class of psychotherapeutic drugs used in the treatment of pathological depression. Two main categories are the cyclic antidepressants and the monoamine oxidase inhibitors; more recently, serotonergic agents such as fluoxetrine. Lithium carbonate also has antidepressant activity in certain patients. *See also* Appendix 1.

**antiepileptic drug**   ANTICONVULSANT.

**antimanic drug**   Drug used to alleviate the symptoms of mania; lithium is particularly effective in preventing relapses in bipolar disorder. *See* Appendix 1.

**antiparkinsonism drug**   Drug that relieves the symptoms of parkinsonism and is effective in countering the extrapyramidal side effects often induced by antipsychotic drugs by acting on the central nervous system to diminish skeletal muscle tone and involuntary movements. Levodopa, the agent of choice for Parkinson's disease, does not antagonize' the extrapyramidal effects of antipsychotic drugs. Anticholinergic agents, such as benztropine and trihexyphenidyl, effectively counteract drug-induced parkinsonism but are now secondary drugs in the treatment of Parkinson's disease.

**antipsychotic**    Any of a class of psychotherapeutic drugs used to treat psychosis, particularly schizophrenia; includes the phenothiazine, thioxanthene, and butyrophenone derivatives and the dihydroindolones. Also called neuroleptic; major tranquilizer; ataractic drug. *See also* Appendix 1.

**antisocial behavior**    Behavior pattern of such marginal criminal types as racketeers, prostitutes, and illegal gamblers. Formerly called sociopathic behavior. *See also* antisocial personality disorder.

**antisocial personality disorder**    Disorder characterized by an inability to get along with other members of society and by repeated conflicts with individual persons and groups; common attributes include impulsiveness, egocentricity, hedonism, low frustration tolerance, irresponsibility, inadequate conscience development, exploitation of others, and rejection of authority and discipline. *See also* antisocial behavior.

**Anton's syndrome**    Disorder caused by a lesion in the occipital lobe of the brain that causes blindness which the patient denies experiencing.

**anxiety**    Unpleasurable emotional state associated with psychophysiological changes in response to an intrapsychic conflict; in contrast to fear, the danger or threat in anxiety is unreal. Psychological changes consist of an uncomfortable feeling of impending danger, an overwhelming awareness of being powerless, inability to perceive the unreality of the threat, prolonged feeling of tension, and exhaustive readiness for the expected danger; physiological changes consist of increased heart rate, disturbed breathing, trembling, sweating, and vasomotor changes. *Compare* fear.

**anxiety disorder**    Disorder in which anxiety is the most prominent disturbance or in which patients experience anxiety if they resist giving in to their symptoms. In DSM-III-R, anxiety disorders include phobic disorder, panic disorder with agoraphobia, agoraphobia without history of panic disorder, social phobia, simple phobia, generalized anxiety disorder, obsessive-compulsive disorder, and post-traumatic stress disorder.

**anxiety disorders of childhood or adolescence** Disorders characterized by chronic anxiety, unrealistic fears, hypersensitive autonomic responses, or fear of leaving home; patients are usually immature, inhibited, timid, approval-seeking, and apprehensive in new situations or places. In DSM-III-R, anxiety disorders of childhood or adolescence include separation anxiety disorder, avoidant disorder of childhood or adolescence, and overanxious disorder.

**anxiety hysteria** PHOBIC DISORDER.

**anxiety neurosis** As initially described by Sigmund Freud, a syndrome characterized by general irritability, anxious expectation, pangs of conscience, anxiety attacks, and phobias. Called generalized anxiety disorder in DSM-III-R.

**anxiety state** Disorder characterized by panic and anxious overconcern; somatic symptoms are often prominent.

**anxiolytic** Any of a class of psychotherapeutic drugs used to treat pathological anxiety and its related symptoms; includes the benzodiazepines and buspirone. Also called antianxiety drugs; minor tranquilizers. *See also* Appendix 1.

**APA** Americal Psychiatric Association; American Psychoanalytic Association; American Psychological Association.

**apathetic withdrawal** *See* withdrawal.

**apathy** Want of feeling or affect, a lack of interest and emotional involvement in one's surroundings; observed in certain types of schizophrenia and depression.

**Apgar scores** Measurements taken 1 and 5 minutes after birth to determine physical normality in the neonate; scores are based on color, respiratory rate, heart beat, reflex action, and muscle tone.

**aphasia** Any disturbance in the comprehension or expression of language due to a brain lesion. For types of aphasia, see the specific term.

**aphonia** Loss of voice.

**apoplexy** Old classical term for cerebrovascular accident.

**apperception** Awareness of the meaning and significance of a particular sensory stimulus as modified by one's own experiences, knowledge, thoughts, and emotions. *See also* perception.

**appetitive phase** First stage in the sexual response cycle, as described by Masters and Johnson, characterized by sexual fantasies and the desire to have sex.

**appropriate affect** Emotional tone in harmony with the accompanying idea, thought, or speech.

**apraxia** Inability to perform a voluntary purposeful motor activity; cannot be explained by paralysis or other motor or sensory impairment. In constructive apraxia, a patient cannot draw two-or three-dimensional forms.

**aptitude** Potential to acquire competence or skill if trained. *Compare* ability.

**archetype** Jung's term for the symbols used by individuals to express the collective experience of the human race. *See also* collective unconscious.

**arithmetic disorder** DEVELOPMENTAL ARITHMETIC DISORDER.

**arteriosclerosis** Degenerative condition marked by loss of elasticity, hardening, and thickening of the arteries, with progressive narrowing of their lumina and gradual obstruction to blood flow; organic mental disorder may develop when cerebral arteries are involved in the degenerative process.

**artificial intelligence** Computer production of a pattern of output that would be considered intelligent if displayed by human beings.

**art therapy** Treatment procedure that uses the spontaneous creative work of the patient; e.g., persons make and analyze drawings, which are often expressions of their underlying emotional problems.

**asceticism** Defense mechanism directed against all consciously perceived base pleasure by elimination of the pleasurable effects of experiences; there is a moral element in assigning values to specific pleasures, and gratification is derived from renunciation.

**asociality** Indifference to social values or customs, withdrawal from society, as seen in a recluse or a regressed schizophrenic person.

**assertiveness training** Behavior therapy that involves teaching frank and direct interpersonal expression of feelings and ideas.

**assimilation** Subjective process that involves filtering the world through one's own system of knowledge, i.e., taking in of new experience through one's established mental structure.

**association**  Relation between ideas or feelings. *See* clang association; loosening of associations.

**Association of American Medical Colleges (AAMC)**  Organization of American medical schools and teaching hospitals, founded in 1876, concerned with the advancement and improvement of medical education, biomedical research, and health care in the U.S.

**astasia-abasia**  Inability to stand or walk in a normal manner, even though normal leg movements can be performed in a sitting or lying down position; seen in conversion disorder.

**astereognosis**  Inability to identify familiar objects by touch; cannot be explained by an impairment of elementary sensory pathways or a depressed sensorium. *See also* neurological amnesia.

**asthenic personality**  Disorder characterized by lack of enthusiasm, fatigability, lack of capacity for enjoyment, and low tolerance for stress; omitted from DSM-III and DSM-III-R. *See also* adynamia; anhedonia.

**astraphobia, astrapophobia**  Abnormal fear of thunder and lightning.

**asyndesis**  Disorder of language, commonly seen in schizophrenia, in which the patient combines unconnected ideas and images.

**ataractic drug**  ANTIPSYCHOTIC.

**ataxia**  Lack of coordination, either physical or mental. **1.** In neurology, refers to loss of muscular coordination. **2.** In psychiatry, the term "intrapsychic ataxia" refers to lack of coordination between feelings and thoughts; seen in schizophrenia and in severe obsessive-compulsive disorder.

**athetosis**  Movement disorder characterized by involuntary, slow, writhing, worm-like movements of the fingers and extremities; a form of extrapyramidal dyskinesia.

**atonia**  Lack of muscle tone.

**attachment**  According to John Bowlby, the affective tie between infant and mother or primary caregiver, the disruption of which heightens vulnerability to depression or anxiety. *See also* bonding.

**attachment disorder of infancy**  Absence or disruption of behaviors that serve to anchor the infant to its mother or primary caregiver and that produce abnormal reactions in the infant's behavior.

**attachment learning**  Theory that learning is enhanced in the presence of the person to whom one is attached or affiliated; applies especially to infant learning.

**attention** Concentration; the aspect of consciousness that relates to the amount of effort exerted in focusing on certain aspects of an experience, activity, or task.

**attention-deficit hyperactivity disorder (ADHD)** DSM-III-R diagnosis for a childhood mental disorder characterized by developmentally inappropriate short attention span, hyperactivity, and poor concentration. The category subsumes abnormal behavior patterns that had been referred to by a variety of names, including hyperkinetic syndrome, hyperactive child syndrome, and minimal brain dysfunction.

**attitude** Preparatory mental posture with which one receives stimuli and reacts to them.

**attributable risk** Absolute incidence of a disease in exposed individuals that can be attributed to the exposure.

**atypical** In psychiatry, denoting an unusual or rare variant of a known disorder.

**atypical child** Child with distorted personality development; often used in connection with brain-damaged or autistic children.

**atypical depression** Diagnosis used to describe depression characterized by weight gain and hypersomnia rather than weight loss and insomnia.

**atypical psychosis** Disorder whose psychotic features are related to a specific culture, e.g., koro; a certain time or event, e.g., postpartum psychosis; or a unique symptomatology, e.g., Capgras' syndrome. Also called psychotic disorder not otherwise specified, in DSM-III-R.

**audit** *See* medical audit.

**auditory amnesia** NEUROLOGICAL AMNESIA (1).

**auditory hallucination** Hallucination primarily involving sound.

**aura** **1.** Warning sensations that a person usually experiences just before an epileptic seizure. **2.** Sensory prodrome that precedes a classic migraine headache.

**authority figure** Real or projected person in a position of power; transferentially, a projected parent.

**autism** *See* autistic thinking; infantile autism.

**autistic disorder** DSM-III-R term for infantile autism.

**autistic thinking** Thinking in which the thoughts are largely narcissistic and egocentric, with emphasis on subjectivity rather than objectivity, and without regard for reality; used interchangeably with autism and dereism. *See also* infantile autism.

**autoerotism** **1.** Sexual arousal of oneself without the participation of another person; term coined by Havelock Ellis, that is presently used interchangeably with masturbation. **2.** In psychoanalysis, a primitive phase in object relationship development preceding the narcissistic stage; in narcissism, there is a love object, but there is no love object in autoerotism.

**automatic judgment** Reflex performance of a way of acting based on a fixed set of beliefs or values.

**automatic obedience** Compliance to commands without exercising critical judgment; a feature of catatonia.

**automatism** Undirected behavior not controlled by conscious thought.

**automysophobia** Abnormal fear of smelling bad or of being unclean.

**autonomic nervous system** Part of the nervous system that functions outside of consciousness and that directs such visceral functions as respiration, heart rate, and digestion; subdivided into sympathetic (adrenergic) and parasympathetic (cholinergic) divisions.

**autonomic side effect** Disturbance of autonomic nervous function that may result from the use of antipsychotic or antidepressant drugs, particularly the phenothiazine and tricyclic derivatives. Common side effects of such agents include orthostatic hypotension, blurred vision, nasal congestion, dry mouth, and constipation; such anticholinergic effects are more prominent with tricyclic antidepressants than with phenothiazines.

**autonomous ego function** Operation present at birth, such as perception, intuition, thinking, speaking, language, and aspects of motor development; first described by Heinz Hartmann. *See also* ego psychology.

**autophobia** Abnormal fear of being alone or of self.

**autoplasty** Adaptation to stress by changing intrapsychic processes. *Compare* alloplasty.

**autoscopic psychosis** Rare disorder in which the patient sees a phantom or specter of his or her own body; usually psychogenic in origin, but may also be caused by lesions in the temporoparietal lobe of the brain.

**autotopagnosia**   Inability to recognize and identify the parts of one's own body. *See also* finger agnosia.

**auxiliary therapist**   Co-therapist. *See also* co-therapy.

**average**   Central value in a frequency distribution around which other values are distributed. Also called the mean.

**aversive conditioning**   AVERSIVE THERAPY.

**aversive therapy**   Behavior therapy that involves the repeated coupling of an unpleasant or painful stimulus, such as an electric shock, with an undesirable behavior pattern in an effort to eliminate the undesirable behavior. Also called aversive conditioning.

**avoidance and escape learning**   In escape learning, an animal learns a response to get out of a place where it does not want to be; e.g., it jumps off an electric grid whenever the grid is charged. Avoidance learning requires an additional response: the same animal on the grid will learn to avoid a shock if it quickly pushes a lever when a light signal goes on. Escape learning and avoidance learning are two forms of aversive control using negative reinforcement; behavior that terminates the source of aversive stimuli is strengthened and maintained.

**avoidant attachment**   According to Mary Ainsworth, a form of attachment in which children avoid returning to their mothers after being separated. Also called shyness disorder. *Compare* secure attachment. *See also* resistant attachment.

**avoidant disorder of childhood or adolescence**   In DSM-III-R, a disorder of childhood or adolescence characterized by a persistent withdrawal or excessive shrinking from strangers.

**avoidant personality disorder**   Personality disorder characterized by low self-esteem, hypersensitivity to rejection, and social withdrawal, but with a desire for affection and acceptance.

**axon**   Single structure in a nerve cell that conducts nervous impulses away from the cell body and its dendrites.

**aypnia**   Insomnia; inability to sleep.

# B

**barbiturate**  Any of a class of sedative-hypnotic drugs derived from barbituric acid that acts as a central nervous system depressant and readily produces psychic and physical dependence; e.g., phenobarbital, secobarbital, thiopental sodium.

**basal ganglia**  Collectively, the corpus striatum, substantia nigra, subthalamic nucleus, and substantia innominata, which are involved in disorders of movement, thought processes, affect, cognition, and symptoms of psychosis.

**basic anxiety**  As conceptualized by Karen Horney, the main-spring from which neurotic trends get their intensity and pervasiveness; characterized by vague feelings of loneliness, helplessness, and fear of a potentially hostile world. *See also* anxiety.

**basic benefits**  Insurance term that refers to minimum payments or coverage for medical or psychiatric care.

**bathophobia**  Abnormal fear of depths.

**battered child syndrome**  Physical damage to a child sustained as a result of repeated beatings, usually by a parent, parent surrogate, or relative.

**battery tests**  Individual tests used together make up a psychological battery; e.g., Halstead-Reitan Neuropsychological Battery. A test battery can give more information about different areas of function than an individual test and can increase the level of confidence if there is a positive correlation between them.

**BCA**  Blue Cross Association.

**BEAM**  Brain electrical activity mapping.

**Beard, George M.** (1839–1883)  American psychiatrist who in 1869 introduced the term "neurasthenia."

**Beers, Clifford** (1876–1943)  Author of *A Mind That Found Itself* (1909) and who is generally considered to have founded the mental hygiene movement.

**behavioral disorders of childhood**  *See* disruptive behavior disorders.

**behavioral medicine**  Application of principles of behavior therapy to the prevention, diagnosis, treatment, and rehabilitation of medical disorders; applies to such areas as stress prevention and reduction, pediatric and adult patient management and compliance, pain control, and life-style modification. Biofeedback, relaxation training, behavior therapy, and hypnosis are important treatment modalities.

**behavioral neurology** Field of study that attempts to combine psychiatry and neurology to explain abnormal behavior as a disorder of brain metabolism or as a result of structural alterations of the central nervous system.

**behavioral science** Scientific discipline concerned with any aspect of human behavior, including interpersonal relationships, development, values, experiences, and activities; the behavioral sciences include sociology, psychology, psychiatry, anthropology, and ethology.

**behavior contract** Therapeutic strategy that rewards a person for a desired behavior.

**behaviorism** School of psychological thought founded by John B. Watson that regards only measurable and observable behavior as the appropriate subject matter for human psychology; holds that human behavior can be described in terms of principles that do not require consideration of unobservable mental events, such as ideas and emotions. *See also* behavior therapy.

**behavior modification** *See* behavior therapy.

**behavior therapy** Psychiatric treatment modality that focuses on overt and objectively observable behavior and uses various conditioning techniques derived from learning theory to directly modify the patient's behavior; aims exclusively at symptomatic improvement, without addressing psychodynamic causation. Behavior therapy techniques include assertiveness training, aversive therapy, flooding, implosion, reciprocal inhibition and desensitization, shaping, and systematic desensitization. *See also* behaviorism; conditioning.

**Bender-Gestalt Test** Psychological test, designed by Lauretta Bender, that measures the subject's ability to reproduce a set of geometric designs; is useful for measuring visuomotor coordination as a means of detecting brain damage. Also called visual motor gestalt test.

**benzodiazepines** Any of a group of drugs used mainly to treat anxiety; also used as sedatives, muscle relaxants, anticonvulsants, anesthetics, and hypnotics. *See* Appendix 1.

**bereavement**   Feeling of grief or desolation, especially at the death or loss of a loved one. *See also* mourning.

**bestiality**   Sexual deviation in which a person engages in sexual relations with an animal. *See also* zoophilia.

**beta (β) error**   TYPE 2 ERROR.

**beta waves**   As measured by an electroencephalogram (EEG), brain waves that are between 14 and 30 Hz; altered in certain epileptic conditions.

**bias**   In statistics, an error in the construction of the assessment instrument that favors one outcome over another.

**binge eating, binge and purge**   *See* bulimia nervosa.

**biodynamics**   System of psychoanalytic psychiatry, introduced by Jules H. Masserman, which holds that all behavior results from the organism's genetic potentialities, from the various paths and speed of maturation, and from its unique experiences.

**biofeedback**   Provision of information to a person regarding one or more physiological processes in an effort to enable the person to gain some element of voluntary control over bodily functions that normally operate outside consciousness. *See also* learned autonomic control.

**biogenic amine**   Endogenous compound believed to play an important role in brain function as a central synaptic neurotransmitter substance; biogenic amines include the catecholamines (epinephrine, norepinephrine, dopamine) and serotonin, an indolamine.

**biogenic amine hypothesis**   Theory of mood disorders which proposes that depression is associated with an absolute or relative deficiency of catecholamines, particularly norepinephrine, at functionally important receptor sites in the brain; conversely, elation may be associated with an excess of such amines.

**biological psychiatry**   School of psychiatric thought emphasizing biochemical, neurological, and pharmacological factors in the causation and treatment of psychiatric disorders.

**biological rhythm**   Periodic variation in physiological and psychological functions. For example, a circadian rhythm shows a periodicity of about 24 hours; an ultradian rhythm has a cycle shorter than 1 day; an infradian rhythm is longer than 1 day.

**bipolar I**   Bipolar disorder in which a patient meets the criteria for a full manic episode, usually sufficiently severe to require hospitalization.

**bipolar II** Bipolar disorder in which a patient has at least one depressive episode and at least one hypomanic episode.

**bipolar disorder** A mood disorder in which the patient exhibits both manic and depressive episodes. Previously called manic-depressive illness, circular type. *See also* manic-depressive illness.

**birth trauma** Otto Rank's term to describe the birth process, which he considered the basic source of anxiety in human beings.

**bisexual** Denoting or characterized by sexual attraction to and sexual contact with members of both sexes.

**bisexuality** Existence of the qualities of both sexes in the same person. Freud postulated that the sexes differentiated both biologically and psychologically from a common core; that differentiation between the two sexes was relative, rather than absolute; and that regression to the common core occurs to varying degrees in both normal and abnormal conditions. *Compare* bisexual; heterosexuality; homosexuality. *See also* androgyny.

**bizarre delusion** False belief that is patently absurd or fantastic.

**blackout** *See* alcoholic blackout.

**black-patch syndrome** Psychosis induced by sensory deprivation as a result of eye patches used after cataract surgery.

**blank screen** Neutral backdrop on which the patient projects a gamut of transferential irrationalities; passivity of analysts allows them to act as blank screens.

**Bleuler, Eugen** (1857–1939) Swiss psychiatrist known for his important studies in schizophrenia, a term he coined and preferred over the earlier term "dementia praecox."

**blind spot** In psychiatry, an area of a person's personality of which he or she is totally unaware; unperceived areas are repressed, since their recognition would arouse painful or unpleasant emotions. In the course of group or individual psychotherapy, such blind spots often appear obliquely as projected ideas, intentions, and emotions. *See also* projection; scotoma.

**blocking** Involuntary cessation or interruption of thought processes or speech because of unconscious emotional factors. Also called thought deprivation.

**blood-brain barrier** Series of biologically active membranes that regulate the passage of substances into and out of the central nervous system; maintains a chemical homeostasis between the cerebrospinal fluid and the venous and arterial systems.

**blood level**   In psychiatry, the measurement of the concentration of drugs in plasma or serum to determine their therapeutic effect.

**Blue Cross Association (BCA)**   State-regulated association of over 80 independent insurance plans that pays primarily for inpatient hospital service; Blue Shield pays for physicians' services during the patient's hospital stay. In contrast to commercial insurance carriers, BCA is a nonprofit organization whose premiums cover administrative expenses and benefits and provide a reserve to cover financial losses. Benefits for psychiatric services are limited compared with those for other medical illnesses, although inpatient psychiatric care is less limited than outpatient care.

**blunted affect**   Disturbance of affect manifested by a severe reduction in the intensity of externalized feeling tone; one of the fundamental symptoms of schizophrenia, as outlined by Eugen Bleuler.

**board certified psychiatrist**   Psychiatrist who has passed the examinations of the American Board of Psychiatry and Neurology.

**board eligible psychiatrist**   Psychiatrist who has finished an approved 4-year residency program and is eligible to take the examinations of the American Board of Psychiatry and Neurology.

**body dysmorphic disorder**   Disorder characterized by an unrealistic concern that part of the body is deformed. Also called dysmorphobia.

**body image**   Conscious and unconscious perception of one's body at any particular time.

**body language**   Expression of thoughts and feelings by body posture and movement.

**bonding**   Nonsexual feelings of love, respect, and communality among individuals of the same sex. Specifically, a mother's feelings for her infant, but often used to refer to the general mother-infant relationship; fathers often bond to infants. *See also* attachment.

**borderline personality disorder**   Personality disorder marked by instability in various areas, impulsiveness, suicidal acts, self-mutilations, identity problems, and feelings of emptiness or boredom.

**borderline psychosis**   BORDERLINE STATE.

**borderline state**   State in which the symptoms are so unclear or transient that it is difficult to classify the patient as psychotic or nonpsychotic. Also called borderline psychosis.

**Bowlby, John** (1907–1990)  British psychoanalyst who formulated the theory of attachment to describe the mother-infant relationship. *See also* attachment; bonding.

**bradykinesia**  Slowness of motor activity, with a decrease in normal spontaneous movement.

**bradylalia**  Abnormally slow speech, common in depression.

**bradylexia**  Inability to read at normal speed.

**brain**  That part of the central nervous system contained within the cranium; includes the cerebrum, midbrain, cerebellum, pons, and medulla.

**brain abscess**  Localized, suppurative, infectious process involving a part of the brain; may produce an organic mental disorder as well as focal neurologic signs.

**brain electrical activity mapping (BEAM)**  Response of brain electrical activity to sensory stimuli which is recorded by computer averaging techniques that produce a topographic color map of brain activity.

**brain imaging**  Radiological techniques that allow assessment in vivo of structural and functional neuroanatomy; include computed tomography (CT), magnetic resonance imaging (MRI), regional cerebral blood flow (rCBF), positron emission tomography (PET), and brain electrical activity mapping (BEAM).

**brain metabolism**  Chemical changes in the brain that convert small molecules into large ones (anabolism) and large molecules into small ones (catabolism), and that account for cellular function and repair.

**brain stem**  Area of the brain comprising the mesencephalon, pons, and medulla oblongata, whose basic functions concern respiration, cardiovascular activity, sleep, and consciousness; also the site of the ascending biogenic amine (dopamine, noradrenalin, serotonin) pathways to higher brain areas.

**brain syndrome**  *See* organic mental disorder.

**brainwashing**  Any technique designed to manipulate human thought or action against the desire, will, or knowledge of the person involved; usually refers to systematic efforts to indoctrinate nonbelievers. Also called coercive persuasion.

**brain wave**  Rhythmic wave-like electrical pattern in an encephalogram.

**Brawner decision**  *See* Model Penal Code.

**Breuer, Josef** (1842–1925) Viennese physician who collaborated with Freud in studies of cathartic therapy, as reported in *Studies on Hysteria* (1895); he withdrew as Freud proceeded to introduce psychoanalysis, but left important imprints on that discipline, such as the concepts of the primary and secondary processes.

**brief psychotherapy** Psychotherapy in which the sessions are limited to 10 to 15 in number and during which time attempts to modify behavior occur; used in both individual and group settings.

**brief reactive psychosis** DSM-III-R category for a psychosis of less than 4 weeks' duration, with sudden onset after a major stress.

**Brigham, Amariah** (1798–1849) One of the founders of the American Psychiatric Association and the first editor of its journal.

**Brill, A. A.** (1874–1948) First American analyst (1908) who translated several of Freud's more important works, was active in the formation of the New York Psychoanalytic Society (1911), and remained a foremost propagator of psychoanalysis as a lecturer and writer.

**Briquet's syndrome** SOMATIZATION DISORDER.

**broad affect** Normal range (varies both within and among cultures) of the expression of a subjectively experienced feeling state (e.g., euphoria, anger, sadness); normal expression of affect involves variability in facial expression, pitch of voice, and hand and body movements.

**Broca's aphasia** MOTOR APHASIA.

**brooding compulsion** INTELLECTUALIZATION.

**bruxism** Grinding or gnashing of the teeth, typically occurring during sleep.

**bulimia nervosa** Episodic, uncontrolled, compulsive, and rapid ingestion of large amounts of food over a short period of time (binge eating) followed by self-induced vomiting, use of laxatives or diuretics, fasting, or vigorous exercise in order to prevent weight gain (binge and purge).

**burned-out schizophrenic** Chronic schizophrenic person who is apathetic and withdrawn, with minimal florid psychotic symptoms but with persistent and often severe schizophrenic thought processes. Also called anergic schizophrenic.

**burnout** Syndrome of physical or emotional exhaustion considered to be a stress reaction to unrelenting performance and emotional demands stemming from one's occupation; symptoms include impaired work performance, fatigue, insomnia, increased susceptibility to physical illness, and reliance on alcohol (or other substances) with a tendency to escalation into physiologic dependency or possibly suicide.

**butyrophenone**  Any of a class of antipsychotic drugs of which haloperidol (Haldol) is a representative example.

# C

**C.A.** Chronological age.

**cacodemonomania** Condition in which patients think they are possessed by a devil or other evil spirit.

**caffeine** Alkaloid found in coffee, tea, and cola drinks which acts as a psychomotor stimulant; caffeine intoxication results from the excessive ingestion of caffeine.

**Canadian Psychiatric Association (CPA)** National organization of Canadian psychiatrists whose purpose is to further the development of psychiatric education, research, and practice in Canada.

**cannabis** *See* marijuana.

**canonical correlation** Multivariate technique for simultaneously finding the relationship of linear combinations of two or more predictors and two or more outcomes.

**Capgras' syndrome** Delusional disorder in which the patient believes that persons in the environment are not their real selves but are doubles imitating the patient or impostors imitating someone else.

**capitation** Prepayment fee based on a fixed number of persons that covers all health care services.

**care and protection proceedings** Intervention by a court on behalf of a child when the parents or caretakers provide inadequately for the child's welfare.

**carebaria** Sensation of discomfort or pressure in the head.

**caregiver** **1.** Any person involved in the identification, prevention, or treatment of illness or disability. **2.** In child psychiatry, a person who tends to the needs of an infant or child. Also called caretaker.

**case control study** Study in which the illness is the dependent variable, already being present for the subject to be identified; such studies are therefore retrospective.

**case history study** Retrospective study that samples persons with a given disorder.

**case register** Medical records in central data banks.

**castration anxiety** Anxiety concerning a fantasied loss of or injury to the genitalia.

**castration complex** In psychoanalytic theory, a group of unconscious thoughts and motives that are referable to the fear of losing the genitalia, usually as punishment for forbidden sexual desires.

**catalepsy** Condition in which persons maintain the body position into which they are placed; observed in severe cases of catatonic schizophrenia. Also called waxy flexibility; cerea flexibilitas. *See also* command automatism.

**cataphasia** VERBIGERATION.

**cataplexy** Temporary sudden loss of muscle tone, causing weakness and immobilization; can be precipitated by a variety of emotional states, and it is often followed by sleep; commonly seen in narcolepsy.

**catastrophic anxiety** Anxiety associated with organic mental disorders when patients are aware of their defects in mentation; the anxiety may be overwhelming.

**catathymia** Situation in which elements in the unconscious are sufficiently affect-laden to produce changes in conscious functioning.

**catathymic crisis** Suddenly occurring, isolated, and nonrepetitive act that develops from a state of intolerable tension.

**catatonia** State of stupor; especially a type of schizophrenia characterized by muscular rigidity, stupor, and negativism.

**catatonic excitement** Excited, uncontrollable motor activity seen in catatonic schizophrenia.

**catatonic posturing** Voluntary assumption of an inappropriate or bizarre posture, generally maintained for long periods of time.

**catatonic rigidity** Fixed and sustained motoric position that is resistant to change.

**catatonic schizophrenia** *See* catatonia.

**catatonic state** State characterized by muscular rigidity and immobility (catatonia), usually associated with schizophrenia.

**catatonic stupor** Stupor in which patients ordinarily are well aware of their surroundings.

**catchment area** In psychiatry, a circumscribed geographic area served by a particular community mental health center.

**catecholamine** Biogenic monoamine containing a catechol group. Norepinephrine, epinephrine, and dopamine are catecholamines with important effects on peripheral and central nervous system activity.

**categorical attitude** ABSTRACT THINKING.

**categorical thought** Term introduced by Jean Piaget to refer to abstract thinking. *See also* secondary process.

**catharsis** Release of ideas, thoughts, and repressed materials from the unconscious, accompanied by an affective emotional response and relief; commonly observed in the course of both individual and group psychotherapy, but can also occur outside therapy. *See also* abreaction; conversational catharsis.

**cathexis** In psychoanalysis, a conscious or unconscious investment of psychic energy in an idea, a concept, an object, or a person. *Compare* acathexis.

**CAT scan** Incorrect but commonly used variant of "CT scan." *See also* computed tomography.

**Cattell Infant Intelligence Scale** Psychological test used to assess general motor and cognitive development in infants aged 3 months to 2 years.

**causalgia** Burning pain that may be either organic or psychic in origin.

**cause-effect relationship** Relationship in which one action causes a specific reaction.

**central nervous system (CNS)** The spinal cord and the brain.

**cephalalgia** Headache.

**cerea flexibilitas** CATALEPSY.

**cerebral arteriosclerosis** Arteriosclerotic involvement (hardening) of arteries of the brain; may lead to organic mental disorder.

**cerebral electrotherapy (CET)** Treatment employing low-intensity pulses of direct electrical current, used primarily in the treatment of depression, anxiety, and insomnia. *Compare* electroconvulsive therapy.

**cerebrovascular accident** Cerebral hemorrhage, thrombosis, or embolism. Also called stroke; apoplexy.

**CET** CEREBRAL ELECTROTHERAPY.

**character** Constellation of relatively fixed personality traits and attributes that govern a person's habitual modes of response.

**character analysis** Psychoanalytic treatment that concentrates on character defenses.

**character defense** Personality trait that serves an unconscious defensive purpose.

**character disorder**   Pattern of personality characterized by maladaptive, inflexible behavior.

**Charcot, Jean M.** (1825–1893)   French neurologist noted for describing hysteria and treating it by means of hypnosis; Freud based much of his early work on Charcot's pioneering studies in hysteria.

**chemical dependence**   *See* drug dependence.

**chemotherapy**   DRUG THERAPY.

**child abuse**   *See* battered child syndrome.

**child analysis**   Application of psychoanalytic principles to the treatment of the child.

**childhood schizophrenia**   DSM-III term for pervasive developmental disorder.

**chi square**   Statistical technique in which variables are categorized in order to determine whether a distribution of scores is due to chance or to experimental factors.

**chlorpromazine**   Aliphatic phenothiazine derivative used primarily as an antipsychotic agent and in the treatment of nausea and vomiting. *See* Appendix 1.

**cholinergic**   Relating to nerve fibers, tracts, or pathways in which synaptic transmission is mediated by acetylcholine; e.g., parasympathetic nerve fibers and somatic motoneurons; also refers to processes activated by acetylcholine.

**chorea**   Movement disorder characterized by random and involuntary quick, jerky, purposeless movements. *See also* extrapyramidal dyskinesia; Huntington's chorea.

**chronobiology**   Study of biological rhythms that objectively explores and quantifies mechanisms of time structure in biological systems.

**chronological age (C.A.)**   *See* intelligence quotient.

**chronophobia**   Fear of time characterized by panic, anxiety, and claustrophobia. Sometimes called prison neurosis, since almost all prisoners are affected by it in some fashion.

**circadian rhythm**   *See* biological rhythm.

**circumstantiality**   Disturbance in the associative thought and speech processes in which a patient digresses into unnecessary details and inappropriate thoughts before communicating the central idea; observed in schizophrenia, obsessional disturbances, and certain cases of dementia. *See also* tangentiality.

**civil commitment** In statutes governing hospitalization of the mentally ill, a legal term meaning a warrant for imprisonment; as recommended by the American Psychiatric Association and the American Bar Association, "commitment" has been replaced by "hospitalization."

**claims review** Method of peer review consisting of the examination of claims for the reimbursement of treatment after it has been rendered.

**clairvoyance** Extrasensory perception in which there is an alleged ability to perceive that which is out of sight or cannot be seen.

**clang association, clanging** Association or speech directed by the sound of a word rather than by its meaning; punning and rhyming may dominate the person's verbal behavior; seen most frequently in schizophrenia or mania.

**classical conditioning** *See* conditioning.

**classic migraine** *See* migraine.

**claustrophobia** Abnormal fear of closed or confining spaces.

**client-centered psychotherapy** Nondirective form of psychotherapy, originated by Carl Rogers, in which the therapeutic process focuses on the patient's own thinking and feeling which the therapist merely helps to clarify through understanding and empathy; developed as a reaction against the authoritativeness and interpretation of the more traditional psychotherapies.

**climacteric** Menopause and immediate postmenopausal period in women; sometimes used to refer to the same age period in men.

**clinical psychologist** Psychologist with additional training and experience in a clinical setting who specializes in evaluation and treatment of mental disorders.

**clinical psychology** Branch of psychology concerned with the application of psychological principles to the prevention, treatment, and understanding of psychopathology.

**clouding of consciousness** Any disturbance of consciousness in which the person is not fully awake, alert, and oriented.

**cluster suicides** Suicides that occur together in geographic groups or in temporal association. *See also* copy-cat suicides.

**cluttering** Disturbance of fluency involving an abnormally rapid rate and erratic rhythm of speech that impedes intelligibility; the affected individual is usually unaware of communicative impairment.

**CNS** Central nervous system.

**cocaine** Alkaloid, obtained from leaves of the coca plant, whose systemic effects include striking central nervous system stimulation manifested by garrulousness, restlessness, excitement, and feelings of increased muscular strength and mental capacity; also an effective topical local anesthetic.

**coefficient of correlation** Statistical term referring to the relation between two sets of paired measurements. Correlation coefficients are positive, negative, or curvilinear, depending on whether the variations are in the same direction, the opposite direction, or both directions. They can be computed in a variety of ways, the most common being the product-moment method (r); another method is rank correlation (p). Correlation coefficients are intended to show degree of relation, but they do not imply a causal relationship between variables.

**coercive persuasion** BRAINWASHING.

**coexistent culture** Alternative system of values, norms, and patterns for behavior; the group therapy experience often leads to an awareness of other systems as legitimate alternatives to one's own system.

**cognition** Mental process of knowing and becoming aware; an ego function closely associated with judgment.

**cognitive development** Progressive acquisition of conscious thought and problem-solving abilities that begins in infancy and follows an orderly sequence of more or less discrete stages.

**cognitive dissonance** Incongruity in a person's beliefs, thoughts, or actions that produces an uncomfortable tension state that the person is motivated to change.

**cognitive therapy** Structured and directive form of therapy developed by Aaron T. Beck that emphasizes how patients think about themselves and the future; consists of reversing the cognitive triad of negative expression of self, negative expression of future, and negative view of the world.

**cognitive triad** Belief system described by the psychiatrist Aaron Beck that is present in depressed persons who have a negative view of the self, a negative interpretation of present and past experience, and a negative expectation of the future.

**cohesion** *See* group cohesion.

**cohort** Group chosen from a well-defined population; cohort studies provide direct estimates of risk associated with a suspected causal factor.

**coitus interruptus** Sexual intercourse that is interrupted before the man ejaculates.

**cold turkey** Abrupt withdrawal from opiates, or any addictive central nervous stimulant, without the benefit of methadone or other drugs; a term originated by drug addicts to describe their chills and consequent goose-flesh. Abstinence-oriented therapeutic communities use this type of detoxification.

**collective experience** Term coined by S. R. Slavson for the common emotional experiences of a group of people, which, in the setting of group psychotherapy, accelerates the therapeutic process. Identification, mutual support, reduction of ego defenses, sibling transferences, and empathy help integrate the individual member into the group.

**collective unconscious** Psychic contents outside the realm of awareness that are common to mankind in general. Carl Jung, who introduced the term, believed that the collective unconscious is inherited and derived from the collective experience of the species, that it transcends cultural differences, and that it explains the analogy between ancient mythological ideas and the primitive projections observed in some patients who have never been exposed to those ideas. Also called objective psyche.

**coma** State of profound unconsciousness from which a person cannot be roused, with minimal or no detectable responsiveness to stimuli; seen in injury or disease of the brain, in such systemic conditions as diabetic ketoacidosis and uremia, and in intoxications with alcohol and other drugs. Coma may also be seen in severe catatonic states and in hysteria.

**coma vigil** Coma in which the eyes remain open; typically seen in acute organic mental syndromes associated with systemic infection.

**combat fatigue** Disabling physical and mental reaction to the stresses of military battle.

**combined therapy** Psychotherapy in which the patient is in both individual and group treatment with the same or two different therapists. In marriage therapy, it is the combination of married couples group therapy with either individual sessions with one spouse or conjoint sessions with the marital pair. *See also* co-therapy.

**command automatism**   Condition closely associated with catalepsy in which suggestions are followed automatically.

**command negativism**   *See* negativism.

**commitment**   Legal process by which a person is confined to a mental hospital, usually against his or her will.

**common migraine**   *See* migraine.

**communication disorder**   Form of speech or writing that impairs communication because of aberrancy of rate, content, or form but not because of failure to follow semantic or syntactic rules; e.g., pressure of speech, tangentiality, echolalia, perseveration.

**community**   *See* therapeutic community.

**community mental health center**   Community or neighborhood mental health facility or a group of affiliated agencies that serve as a locus for the delivery of various services of community psychiatry. *See also* community psychiatry.

**community psychiatry**   Psychiatry focusing on the detection, prevention, and early treatment of mental disorders and social deviance as they develop in the community, rather than as they are perceived and encountered at large centralized psychiatric facilities; particular emphasis is placed on the environmental factors that contribute to mental illness.

**compensation**   Conscious or, usually, unconscious defense mechanism by which a person tries to make up (compensate) for an imagined or real physical or psychological deficiency.

**compensation neurosis**   Neurosis induced by the desire for monetary compensation. It is believed that some persons, after sustaining an injury, develop neurotic symptoms in the hope of monetary gain.

**competence**   Ability to perform or accomplish an action or task that another person of similar background and training, or any human being, could reasonably be expected to perform; mental capacity.

**competency to stand trial**   Ability to be tried in a court of law. A person is competent to stand trial when, at the time of the trial, he or she (1) understands the nature of the charge and the potential consequences of conviction and (2) is able to assist his or her attorney in his or her defense.

**competition**   Literally, the struggle for the possession or use of limited goods, concrete or abstract. In psychiatry, a rivalry that may exist between persons in which gratification for one person largely precludes gratification for the other.

**complementarity of interaction**   Concept of bipersonal and multi-personal psychology in which behavior is viewed as a response to stimulation, and interaction replaces the concept of reaction; each person in an interactive situation plays both a provocative role and a responsive role.

**complementary role**   *See* role.

**complex**   Group of interrelated ideas, mainly unconscious, that have a common emotional tone and strongly influence the person's attitudes and behavior; introduced by Jung, who called it a feeling-toned idea.

**complex partial seizure**   Epilepsy characterized by recurrent behavioral disturbances. Complex hallucinations or illusions, frequently gustatory or olfactory, often herald the onset of the seizure, which typically involves a state of impaired consciousness resembling a dream (dreamy state) during which paramnestic phenomena, such as dèjá vu and jamais vu, are experienced and the patient exhibits repetitive, automatic, or semipurposeful behavior; in rare instances, violent behavior may be prominent. Electroencephalography reveals a localized seizure focus in the temporal lobe. Also called psychomotor epilepsy; temporal lobe epilepsy.

**compulsion**   Uncontrollable, repetitive, and unwanted urge to perform an act; serves as a defense against unacceptable ideas and desires, and failure to perform the act leads to overt anxiety. *See also* obsession.

**compulsive personality**   Personality characterized by rigidity, over-conscientiousness, extreme inhibition, inability to relax, and the performance of repetitive patterns of behavior. In DSM-III-R, described under obsessive-compulsive personality disorder.

**computed tomography (CT)**   Radiologic imaging technique for presenting anatomical features from a cross-sectional plane of the body, generated by computer synthesis of x-ray transmission data obtained from many different directions through the given plane; gray and white matter are indistinguishable on CT scans.

**conation**   That part of a person's mental life concerned with cravings, strivings, motivations, drives, and wishes as expressed through behavior or motor activity.

**concordance**   In studies of twins, the degree of similarity between the two members of each pair with respect to the presence or absence of a particular trait. *Compare* discordance.

**concrete operations**  *See* Piaget, Jean.

**concrete thinking**  Thinking characterized by actual things and events and immediate experience, rather than by abstractions; seen in young children, in those who have lost or never developed the ability to generalize (as in certain organic mental disorders), and in schizophrenic persons. *Compare* abstract thinking.

**concussion**  Immediate and transient impairment of brain function resulting from a head injury; usually, an alteration of consciousness is involved.

**condensation**  Mental process in which one symbol stands for a number of components.

**conditioned reinforcer**  *See* reinforcement.

**conditioned response**  *See* conditioning.

**conditioned stimulus**  *See* conditioning.

**conditioning**  Procedure resulting in the acquisition or learning of more or less permanent changes in behavior. There are two main types of conditioning: (1) Classical conditioning, in which a neutral stimulus is repeatedly paired with a stimulus (unconditioned stimulus) that naturally elicits a response (unconditioned response) until the neutral stimulus (conditioned stimulus) comes to elicit that response (now the conditioned response) by itself. Also called Pavlovian conditioning and respondent conditioning. (2) Operant conditioning, a procedure developed by B. F. Skinner in which a spontaneously emitted behavior (operant behavior) is either rewarded (reinforced) or punished and, as a result, then occurs with a frequency that is either increased (in the case of reinforcement) or decreased (in the case of punishment). Also called instrumental conditioning. *See also* behavior therapy.

**conditioning therapy**  *See* behavior therapy.

**conditions not attributable to a mental disorder**  DSM-III-R category given to a person who may or may not have a mental disorder but who has a problem which may require intervention by a psychiatrist. Included are marital problem, occupational problem, phase of life or other life circumstance problem, malingering, complicated bereavement, antisocial behavior, academic problem, other interpersonal problem, other specified family circumstance, and noncompliance with medical treatment.

**conduct disorder**  In DSM-III-R, a childhood disorder characterized by antisocial behavior. There are three types of conduct disorder depending on whether conduct problems are initiated as part of a group (group type), individually (solitary aggressive type), or both (undifferentiated type).

**confabulation** Unconscious filling of gaps in memory by imagining experiences or events that have no basis in fact, commonly seen in organic amnestic syndromes; should be differentiated from lying. *See also* paramnesia.

**confidence interval** Range of values with a specified probability of including the population mean with a specified level of confidence; typically associated with a certain probability level, e.g., the 95% confidence interval has a 95% chance of including the population mean.

**confidentiality** Ethical principle by which the physician is bound to hold secret all information given him or her by the patient. Certain states do not legally recognize confidentiality and can require the physician to divulge such information if needed in a legal proceeding. *See also* privilege.

**conflict** Mental struggle arising from the clash of opposing impulses, drives, or demands. *See also* extrapsychic conflict; intrapsychic conflict.

**conflict-free area** Part of one's personality or ego that is well integrated and does not cause any conflicts, symptoms, or displeasures.

**confrontation** Act of letting a person know where one stands in relationship to that person, what one is experiencing, and how one is perceived. Used in a spirit of deep involvement, this technique is a powerful tool for changing relationships; used as an attempt to destroy another person, it can be harmful. In group and individual therapies, the value of confrontation is likely to be determined by the therapist.

**confusion** Disturbance of consciousness manifested by a disordered orientation in relation to time, place, or person.

**congenital** Referring to conditions present at birth, including hereditary conditions and those resulting from prenatal development or the process of birth itself.

**conjoint therapy** Type of marriage therapy in which a therapist sees the partners together in joint sessions. Also called triadic or triangular therapy (since two patients and one therapist work together). *See also* quadrangular therapy.

**conjugal paranoia** Paranoia characterized by delusions of jealousy; with no evidence or little evidence, a spouse or lover becomes convinced that his or her partner is being unfaithful.

**conscience** The part of the self that judges one's own values and performance; often used synonymously with superego.

**conscious** **1.** One of three divisions of Freud's topographic theory of the mind (the others being the preconscious and the unconscious), referring to that portion of mental functioning within the realm of awareness at all times. **2.** More generally, the state of having present knowledge of oneself, one's acts, and one's surroundings and thus a functioning sensorium. **3.** Denoting a state of awareness, with response to external stimuli.

**consciousness** State of being conscious. *See also* sensorium.

**consensual validation** Continuous comparison of the thoughts and feelings of group members toward one another that tends to modify and correct interpersonal distortions; introduced by Harry Stack Sullivan to refer to the dyadic therapeutic process between doctor and patient.

**conservation** According to Piaget, the crucial difference between preoperational and concrete operational thought, in which a child discovers which values remain invariant in the course of any kind of change or transformation.

**conservator** Legal guardian designated to take over and protect the interests of an individual.

**constitution** One's intrinsic psychological or physical endowment. Broadly, it includes an aggregate of characteristics that have developed from the interaction of hereditary and environmental influences; more narrowly, it indicates characteristics that are purely hereditary or genetically determined.

**constitutional types** Categories of a person's traits based on physical and psychological characteristics (e.g., ectomorphic, endomorphic, mesomorphic).

**constricted affect** Reduction in intensity of feeling tone less severe than that of blunted affect but clearly reduced.

**constructional apraxia** Inability to copy a drawing, such as a cube, clock, or pentagon, as a result of a brain lesion.

**consultation-liaison psychiatry** Clinical psychiatry carried out in the medical or surgical wards of a general hospital; the psychiatrist collaborates closely with nonpsychiatric physicians in the total care of the patient.

**contagion** Force that operates in large groups or masses. When the level of psychological functioning has been lowered, some sudden upsurge of anxiety can spread through a group, accelerated by a high degree of suggestibility, gradually mounting to panic, and the whole group may be simultaneously affected by a primitive emotional upheaval.

**content thought disorder**  Disturbance in thinking in which a person exhibits delusions that may be multiple, fragmented, and bizarre.

**continuous reinforcement**  A schedule of reinforcement in which a reward is administered every time a response is emitted.

**contract**  Explicit, bilateral commitment to a well-defined course of action; in group or individual therapy, the therapist-patient contract is to attain the treatment goal.

**control group**  In an experimental design, the group in which a condition or factor being tested is deliberately omitted; for example, in a study measuring the effects of a new drug, the control group may be given a placebo instead of the drug. *Compare* experimental group.

**controlled substance**  Drug that has the potential to be abused and is classified by the Drug Enforcement Administration (DEA) into one of five levels of control: I, high abuse potential and no accepted medical use (e.g., heroin); II, high abuse potential with medical use (e.g., amphetamine); III, moderate abuse potential (e.g., codeine); IV, low abuse potenial, i.e., preparations containing limited amounts of narcotic and non-narcotic ingredients (e.g., cough medicines).

**controlling**  Excessive attempt to manage or regulate events or objects in the environment to minimize anxiety and to resolve inner conflicts.

**conversational catharsis**  Release of repressed or suppressed thoughts and feelings in group and individual psychotherapy as a result of verbal interchange.

**conversion**  Unconscious defense mechanism by which the anxiety that stems from an intrapsychic conflict is converted and expressed in a symbolic somatic symptom; the hallmark of conversion disorder, but also seen in a variety of mental disorders.

**conversion disorder**  Somatoform disorder in which the patient experiences an involuntary limitation or alteration of physical function that is an expression of a psychological conflict or need, not of a physical disorder. *See also* hysterical neurosis.

**convulsive disorder**  *See* epilepsy.

**convulsive therapy**  Psychiatric treatment involving administration of chemical substances or electric current to induce loss of consciousness or a convulsive reaction, to alter favorably the course of a mental disorder; e.g., electroconvulsive therapy, insulin coma therapy.

**cooperative therapy**   CO-THERAPY.

**coping mechanism**   Unconscious or conscious way of dealing with stress.

**coprolalia**   Involuntary use of vulgar or obscene language; observed in some cases of schizophrenia and in Tourette's disorder.

**coprophagia**   Eating of filth or feces.

**coprophilia**   Excessive interest in filth or feces. Sexual pleasure associated with feces is a perversion associated with fixations at the anal stage of psychosexual development.

**coprophobia**   Abnormal fear of excreta.

**copy-cat suicides**   Suicides that occur in persons who are geographically related; usually occurs among adolescents within a limited time period. *See also* cluster suicides.

**correctional psychiatry**   Practice of psychiatry on persons incarcerated in jail or prison; presents special problems in relation to confidentiality and countertransference.

**corrective emotional experience**   Re-exposure under favorable circumstances to an emotional situation that the patient could not handle in the past; as advocated by Franz Alexander, the therapist temporarily assumes a particular role to generate the experience and facilitate reality testing.

**correlation**   Statistical index of the relationship among variables. The most common correlation coefficient is the Pearson Product Moment Correlation, an index of bivariate association that varies between $-1.0$ and $1.0$. *See also* coefficient of correlation.

**Cotard's syndrome**   DELUSION OF NIHILISM.

**co-therapy**   Psychotherapy in which more than one therapist treat the individual patient or the group. Also called cooperative, dual, multiple, or three-cornered therapy. *See also* combined therapy.

**counseling**   Form of guidance in which a trained person offers advice or education about specific problems in living, e.g., marriage, child rearing, mourning.

**counterphobia**   State in which a phobic person shows a preference for the very situation that is feared.

**countertransference**   Conscious or unconscious emotional response of the therapist to the patient; determined by the therapist's inner needs, rather than by the patient's needs, and may reinforce the patient's earlier traumatic history if not checked by the therapist. *See also* transference.

**couples therapy** *See* family therapy; marriage therapy.

**covert sensitization** Method of reducing the frequency of behavior by associating it with the imagination of an unpleasant consequence.

**CPA** Canadian Psychiatric Association.

**crack** Freebase form of cocaine prepared by heating a mixture of cocaine hydrochloride, water, and baking soda, which is then dried into a solid and broken into small pieces (rocks); it is inexpensive, has a rapid onset of action, and is highly addictive.

**creativity** Ability to produce something new. Silvano Arieti described creativity as the tertiary process, a balanced combination of primary and secondary processes, in which materials from the id are used in the service of the ego.

**cretinism** Mental and physical retardation resulting from severe thyroid deficiency in infancy and childhood.

**Cri-du-chat** High-pitched catlike cry characteristic of the syndrome of mental and physical retardation caused by partial deletion of chromosome 5.

**criminal responsibility** Legal term meaning the ability to formulate a criminal intent at the time of an alleged crime. A person cannot be convicted of a crime if it can be proved that he or she lacked criminal responsibility by reason of insanity.

**crisis** In psychiatry, a distressing sense of psychological disequilibrium that has an acute onset and that causes impaired functioning in a variety of interpersonal and vocational areas.

**crisis intervention** Brief therapeutic approach used in emergency rooms of general or psychiatric hospitals that is ameliorative, rather than curative, of acute psychiatric emergencies; treatment factors often focus on environmental modification, although interpersonal and intrapsychic factors are also considered. *See also* hot line.

**critical period** Specific period of early development during which an organism acquires certain patterns of behavior as a result of internal or external clues. *See also* imprinting.

**critical ratio** In a statistical study involving 30 or more subjects, a ratio constructed to determine whether differences found between two items are larger than could be expected from chance alone.

**cross-cultural psychiatry**   Comparative study of mental illness and health among various societies around the world.

**CT scan**   Computed tomography.

**cult**   System of beliefs and rituals, especially involving devoted attachment to or extravagant admiration of a person or principle, based on dogma or religious teachings; devoted adherents to such a system are called cultists.

**cultural anthropology**   *See* anthropology.

**cultural deprivation**   Restricted participation in the culture of the larger society.

**cultural psychiatry**   Branch of psychiatry concerned with mental illness in relation to the cultural environment; symptoms regarded as psychopathological in one cultural setting may be acceptable and normal in another.

**culture shock**   Psychological response of a person who is suddenly thrust into an alien culture or has divided loyalties to two different cultures.

**culture specific syndrome**   Disorder of behavior that occurs within or is limited to a specific culture; e.g., amok, koro, latah.

**cunnilingus**   Use of the mouth or tongue to stimulate the female genitalia.

**Cushing's syndrome**   Hyperadrenocorticism characterized by muscle wasting, obesity, osteoporosis, atrophy of the skin, and hypertension; emotional lability is common and frank psychoses are occasionally observed.

**custody**   Term used to describe a parent's legal rights over a child; in cases of disputed custody, the child is awarded to the party who will best serve the interests of the child.

**CVA**   Cerebral vascular accident.

**cybernetics**   Norbert Wiener's term for the comparative study of computers and the human nervous system.

**cyclazocine**   Narcotic antagonist that blocks the effects of morphine and heroin.

**cycloplegia**   Paralysis of the muscles of accommodation in the eye; observed at times as an autonomic side effect (anticholinergic effect) of antipsychotic or antidepressant medication.

**cyclothymia**  Mood disorder characterized by a nonpsychotic disturbance of at least 2 years length with numerous periods of both
depressive and manic syndromes not severe enough to be
classified as depressive or manic episodes.

**cynophobia**  Abnormal fear of dogs.

# D

**DaCosta's syndrome** Chest pain, palpitations, and lightheadedness occurring as a somatic manifestation of pathological anxiety. Also called neurocirculatory asthenia; soldier's heart.

**day hospital** Form of partial hospitalization in which a patient spends the day in the hospital and returns home at night. *Compare* night hospital; weekend hospital.

**day residue** In Sigmund Freud's dream theory, the content of the dream imagery that is derived from events of the previous day.

**DEA** Drug Enforcement Administration.

**death instinct** AGGRESSIVE DRIVE.

**decathexis** ACATHEXIS.

**decision tree** algorithm.

**decoding** Technical term for the process of understanding spoken language.

**decompensation** Deterioration of psychic functioning due to a breakdown of defense mechanisms.

**decomposition** In psychiatry, the division of a person into separate personalities or identities, as seen in the paranoid schizophrenic person who splits the persecutor into separate entities.

**defense mechanism** Unconscious process acting to relieve conflict and anxiety arising from one's impulses and drives.

**defensive emotion** Strong feeling that serves as a screen for a less acceptable feeling, one that would cause a person to experience anxiety if it appeared. For example, expressing the emotion of anger is often more acceptable to a patient than expressing the fear that the anger covers up; in that instance, anger is defensive.

**deficit** In psychiatry, the absence of a function or capability that would normally be present, e.g., judgment.

**deinstitutionalization** Discharge from the hospital to community, particularly of those chronically mentally ill patients who would otherwise be hospitalized for long periods of time.

**déjà entendu** Illusion that what one is hearing one has heard previously. *See also* paramnesia.

**déjà pensé** Condition in which a thought never entertained before is incorrectly regarded as a repetition of a previous thought.

**déjà vu** Illusion of visual recognition in which a new situation is incorrectly regarded as a repetition of a previous experience. *See also* paramnesia.

**delirium** Acute reversible organic mental disorder characterized by confusion and some impairment of consciousness; generally associated with emotional lability, hallucinations or illusions, and inappropriate, impulsive, irrational, or violent behavior.

**delirium tremens (DTs)** Acute and sometimes fatal reaction to withdrawal from alcohol, usually occurring 72–96 hours after the cessation of heavy drinking; distinctive characteristics are marked autonomic hyperactivity (tachycardia, fever, hyperhidrosis, dilated pupils), usually accompanied by tremulousness, hallucinations, illusions, and delusions. Called alcohol withdrawal delirium in DSM-III-R. *See also* formication.

**delta sleep** SLOW WAVE SLEEP.

**delta waves** As measured by an electroencephalogram (EEG), brain waves that are less than 4 Hz, indicative of deep sleep.

**delusion** False belief that is firmly held, despite objective and obvious contradictory proof or evidence and despite the fact that other members of the culture do not share the belief. Types of delusion include: **bizarre delusion,** one that is patently absurd or fantastic; **delusion of control,** that a person's thoughts, feelings, or actions are not one's own but are being imposed by some external force; **delusion of grandeur (grandiose delusion),** exaggerated concept of one's importance, power, knowledge, or identity; **delusion of jealousy (delusion of infidelity),** that one's lover is unfaithful; **delusion of persecution,** that one is being attacked, harassed, cheated, or conspired against; **delusion of poverty,** that one is or will be without material possessions; **delusion of reference,** that events, objects, or the behavior of others have a particular and unusual meaning specifically for oneself; **encapsulated delusion,** one without significant effect on behavior; **fragmentary delusion,** poorly elaborated delusion, often one of many with no apparent interconnection; **nihilistic delusion, delusion of negation** (Cotard's syndrome), that the world and everything related to it have ceased to exist; **paranoid delusion,** combined delusion of grandeur and persecution; **religious delusion,** one involving the Deity or theological themes; **sexual delusion,** one centering on sexual identity, appearances, practices, or ideas; **somatic delusion,** pertaining to the functioning of one's body; **systematized delusion,** a group of elaborate delusions related to a single event or theme.

**delusional depression** Depressive disorder characterized by false, fixed ideas, i.e., delusions; listed in DSM-III-R as major depression, severe, with psychotic features.

**delusional (paranoid) disorder** Psychotic disorder in which there are persistent delusions, e.g., erotomanic, grandiose, jealous, persecutory, somatic, and unspecified; symptoms of a major mood disorder are absent and the delusions lack the bizarre quality often seen in schizophrenia.

**dementia** Organic mental disorder characterized by general impairment in intellectual functioning, frequently characterized by failing memory, difficulty with calculations, distractibility, alterations in mood and affect, impairment in judgment and abstraction, reduced facility with language, and disturbance of orientation. Although generally irreversible because of underlying progressive degenerative brain disease, dementia may be reversible if the cause can be treated. *Compare* amentia.

**dementia associated with alcoholism** DSM-III-R term for alcoholic deterioration.

**dementia praecox (precox)** Obsolete term for schizophrenia.

**demography** Statistical study of populations, including births, marriages, mortality, health, geographic distribution, and population shifts.

**demophobia** Abnormal fear of crowds.

**dendrite** Projection from the nerve cell body, usually profusely branched and studded with small spikes (dendritic spines) that are the sites of synaptic connection; most dendrites receive neurotransmissions from an axon.

**denial** Defense mechanism in which the existence of unpleasant realities is disavowed; refers to a keeping out of conscious awareness any aspects of either internal or external reality that, if acknowledged, would produce anxiety.

**dependence on therapy** Pathological need of a patient for therapy, created out of the belief that one cannot survive without it.

**dependency** State of reliance on another, as for security, love, protection, or mothering.

**dependent personality disorder** Personality disorder characterized by lack of self-confidence, a tendency to have others assume responsibility for significant areas of one's life, and a subordination of one's own needs and wishes to those of the others on whom one is dependent; solitude is extremely discomforting.

**dependent variable** In research methodology, those qualities that measure the influence of the independent variable or the outcome of the experiment; e.g., measurement of a person's specific physiologic reactions to a drug. Also called outcome variable.

**depersonalization.** Sensation of unreality concerning oneself, parts of oneself, or one's environment that occurs under extreme stress or fatigue; seen in schizophrenia, depersonalization disorder, and schizotypal personality disorder.

**depersonalization disorder** In DSM-III-R, a dissociative disorder characterized by a feeling that one's reality is temporarily lost. Also called depersonalization neurosis.

**depersonalization neurosis** DEPERSONALIZATION DISORDER.

**depression** Mental state characterized by feelings of sadness, loneliness, despair, low self-esteem, and self-reproach; accompanying signs include psychomotor retardation or at times agitation, withdrawal from interpersonal contact, and vegetative symptoms such as insomnia and anorexia. The term refers either to a mood that is so characterized or to a mood disorder.

**depressive neurosis** DYSTHYMIA.

**depth psychology** Psychology that focuses on unconscious processes, rather than conscious processes.

**derailment** Gradual or sudden deviation in train of thought without blocking; sometimes used synonymously with loosening of association.

**derealization** Sensation of changed reality or that one's surroundings have altered; usually seen in schizophrenic persons.

**dereism** Mental activity that follows a totally subjective and idiosyncratic system of logic and fails to take the facts of reality or experience into consideration. *See also* autistic thinking.

**dereistic thinking** Mental activity not concordant with logic or experience.

**descriptive psychiatry** System of psychiatry focusing primarily on the study of observable symptoms and behavioral phenomena, rather than underlying psychodynamic processes; Emil Kraepelin's systematic description of mental illness was an early example. *See also* dynamic psychiatry.

**descriptive statistics** Methods used to summarize, organize, and describe observations; e.g., the mean, standard deviation, and variance.

**desensitization** *See* systematic desensitization.

**designer drug** Any version of a regulated drug whose chemical structure has been modified so that it falls outside the restrictions placed on the regulated drug it imitates; usually a drug of abuse used to alter states of consciousness or to produce pleasurable feelings.

**detachment** Separation; divorce from emotional involvement, characterized by distant interpersonal relationships.

**determinism** Concept that nothing occurs by chance alone; instead, things result from specific causes or forces. This school of thought denies the notion of free will.

**detoxification** Any treatment aimed at the restoration of normal physiological function after a disturbance by the use of some drug or chemical substance. Also called detoxication. *See also* cold turkey.

**detumescence** Subsiding of a penile erection; also used to describe the subsiding of genital engorgement in both sexes.

**devaluation** Defense mechanism in which a person attributes excessively negative qualities to self or others.

**developmental arithmetic disorder** Academic skills disorder characterized by marked impairment in the development of arithmetic skills that interferes with academic achievement or other activities of daily living. Also called acalculalia; Gerstmann's syndrome; congenital arithmetic disability; dyscalculia; arithmetic disorder.

**developmental articulation disorder** Language or speech disorder in which there is a consistent failure to correctly articulate a speech sound at the developmentally appropriate age. Also called functional speech disorder, infantile perseveration, and infantile articulation.

**developmental coordination disorder** Motor skills disorder in which there is a marked impairment in the development of motor coordination which interferes with academic achievement or with activities of daily living.

**developmental disorders** Disorders originating before adulthood that continue to constitute a handicap. In DSM-III-R, the developmental disorders include mental retardation, pervasive developmental disorders, and specific developmental disorders.

**developmental expressive language disorder** Language and speech disorder in which there is marked impairment in the development of expressive language; interferes with academic achievement or with activities of daily living that require the expression of verbal (or sign) language.

**developmental expressive writing disorder** Academic skills disorder characterized by marked impairment in the development of expressive writing skills; significantly interferes with academic achievement or with activities of daily living that require expressive writing skills.

**developmental reading disorder** Academic skills disorder characterized by omissions, distortions, and substitutions of words and by slow, halting reading; there is marked impairment in the development of word recognition skills and reading comprehension. Also called specific reading disability and developmental word blindness.

**developmental receptive language disorder** Language and speech disorder in which there is marked impairment in the development of language comprehension which significantly interferes with academic achievement or with activities of daily living that require comprehension of verbal (or sign) language.

**developmental word blindness** DEVELOPMENTAL READING DISORDER.

**deviation** Departure from the average or norm.

**Dexamethasone Suppression Test (DST)** Test used to confirm a diagnostic impression of major depression. The patient is given 1 mg of dexamethasone (a long-acting synthetic glucocorticoid) by mouth at 11 p.m., and plasma cortisol is measured at 8 a.m., 4 p.m., and 11 p.m. Plasma cortisol above 5 $\mu$g/dL (nonsuppression) is considered abnormal, i.e., positive; suppression of cortisol indicates that the hypothalamic-adrenal-pituitary axis is functioning properly.

**Diagnostic and Statistical Manual of Mental Disorders (DSM)** Handbook for the classification of mental illnesses that is primarily descriptive and does not describe the theories or causes of disorders; first issued by the American Psychiatric Association in 1952 (DSM-I). The present revised third edition (DSM-III-R) was issued in 1987; the fourth edition (DSM-IV) is scheduled for publication in 1993 and will closely adhere to the 10th revision of the World Health Organization's *International Classification of Diseases.*

**Diagnostic Related Groups (DRGs)** Classification system consisting of 470 disease categories, developed in the 1970s as a way to help health care personnel determine the appropriate length of hospitalization for any given patient; assignment to a DRG category is based on principal diagnosis, treatment procedures, personal attributes (e.g., age, sex), complications, and discharge status.

**diathesis-stress paradigm** In psychopathology, a view that abnormal behavior is a function of a series of stresses in predisposed individuals (due to hereditary, temperamental, and sociocultural factors).

**differential diagnosis** Determination of which of two or more diseases with similar symptoms is the one that afflicts the patient.

**differential reinforcement** Procedure in which desirable behavior is reinforced and problematic or less desirable behavior is extinguished or punished.

**differentiation** First of Margaret Mahler's four subphases of the separation-individuation process, occurring from ages 5 to 10 months, when the child is able to distinguish between self and other objects.

**2,5-dimethoxy-4-methylamphetamine (DOM)** Synthetic (derivative) drug with hallucinogenic properties. Also colloquially called STP.

**dimethyltryptamine (DMT)** Tryptamine congener that acts as a psychedelic capable of producing hallucinations, other disorders of perception, and altered moods and states of consciousness.

**DIMS** Disorders of initiating and maintaining sleep.

**dipsomania** Compulsion to drink alcoholic beverages.

**disability** Defined by the federal government as: "Inability to engage in any substantial gainful activity by reason of any medically determinable physical or mental impairment which can be expected to last or has lasted for a continuous period of not less than 12 full months."

**disco drugs** Slang term for nitrates (as substances of abuse).

**disconnection syndrome** Group of neurological disorders produced after interruption of connection fibers from the cerebrum to other centers of the nervous system.

**discordance** In studies of twins, the degree of dissimilarity between the two members of each pair with respect to the presence or absence of a particular trait. *Compare* concordance.

**discriminant analysis**   Multivariate method for finding the relationship between a single discrete outcome and a linear combination of two or more predictors.

**discrimination**   Process of distinguishing between different but often similar stimuli and reacting appropriately; more specifically, the occurrence of operant behavior in environments in which the behavior has been reinforced but not in those in which it has not been reinforced. *See also* discriminative stimulus.

**discriminative stimulus**   Environmental event correlating with the operation of a certain reinforcement matrix, such that behavior that has been reinforced in the presence of the stimulus but not in its absence tends to occur only when the stimulus is present.

**disinhibition**   **1.** Removal of an inhibitory effect, as in the reduction of the inhibitory function of the cerebral cortex by alcohol. **2.** In psychiatry, a greater freedom to act in accordance with inner drives or feelings and with less regard for restraints dictated by cultural norms or one's superego.

**disintegration**   Psychic disorganization in which a person is unable to recognize reality and may develop delusions, hallucinations, or overwhelming anxiety and panic.

**disorders of excessive somnolence (DOES)**   Disorders characterized by excessive amounts of sleep or excessive daytime sleepiness. *See also* somnolence.

**disorders of initiating and maintaining sleep (DIMS)**   Disorders characterized by inability to fall asleep or repeated awakening after falling asleep. *See also* insomnia disorder; dyssomnias.

**disorganized schizophrenia**   DSM-III-R term replacing hebephrenic schizophrenia. *See also* hebephrenia.

**disorientation**   Confusion; impairment of awareness of time, place, and person (the position of the self in relation to other persons); characteristic of organic mental disorders.

**displacement**   Unconscious defense mechanism by which the emotional component of an unacceptable idea or object is transferred to a more acceptable one.

**disposition**   Sum total of a person's inclinations as determined by his or her mood.

**disruptive behavior disorders**   Disorders characterized by inattention, overaggressiveness, delinquency, destructiveness, hostility, feelings of rejection, negativism, or impulsiveness. In DSM-III-

R, they include attention-deficit hyperactivity disorder, conduct disorder, and oppositional defiant disorder.

**dissociation** Unconscious defense mechanism involving the segregation of any group of mental or behavioral processes from the rest of the person's psychic activity; may entail the separation of an idea from its accompanying emotional tone, as seen in dissociative and conversion disorders.

**dissociation syndrome** Functional inability of the brain to process information from one area to another; first described by neurologist Norman Geschwind. *See also* disconnection syndrome.

**dissociative disorders** Mental disorders characterized by a sudden temporary alteration in consciousness, identity, or motor behavior. In DSM-III-R, they include psychogenic amnesia, psychogenic fugue, multiple personality disorder, and depersonalization disorder. *See also* hysterical neurosis.

**distortion** 1. Misrepresentation of reality. 2. In psychoanalysis, the process of modifying unacceptable unconscious mental elements so that they are allowed to enter consciousness in a more acceptable but disguised form.

**distractibility** Inability to focus one's attention; the patient does not respond to the task at hand but attends to irrelevant phenomena in the environment.

**distractible speech** Pattern of speech in which a person repeatedly changes subjects in response to nearby stimuli.

**distributive analysis and synthesis** Therapeutic application of Adolf Meyer's psychobiological school of psychiatry; systematic investigations of patients' entire past experiences yield constructive syntheses of their assets and liabilities and lead to an effort to enable them to adapt to their environment.

**disulfiram** Drug used in the treatment of alcoholics. By altering the metabolism of alcohol, it produces unpleasant physical sensations that discourage the patient from further consumption of alcohol (trade name, Antabuse).

**Dix, Dorothea Lynde** (1802–1887) Former schoolteacher who devoted her life to improving institutional care for the mentally ill.

**dizygotic twins** Twins (fraternal) who develop from two separately fertilized ova; in contrast, monozygotic (identical) twins develop from a single fertilized ovum.

**DMT**   Dimethyltryptamine.

**doctor-patient relationship**   Human interchange that exists between the person who is sick and the person who is selected to heal because of training and experience.

**DOES**   Disorders of excessive somnolence.

**DOM**   2,5-Dimethoxy-4-methylamphetamine.

**dominance   1.** Disposition to play a commanding, controlling, or prevailing role over others. **2.** In neurology, the control of language function by one side of the cerebral cortex. **3.** In genetics, the ability of a gene (dominant gene) to be expressed in the phenotype of the bearer to the exclusion of another gene (recessive gene) with which it is paired.

**dopamine**   Biogenic amine (catecholamine) that inhibits prolactin; functional integrity of the dopaminergic system is impaired in depression and in Parkinson's disease.

**dopamine hypothesis**   Theory that there may be an excess of dopamine in the brains of schizophrenic persons.

**double bind**   As formulated by Gregory Bateson, a situation involving the simultaneous communication of conflicting messages from one person to another, in which the response to either message is met with disapproval or rejection; believed to be a characteristic mode of interaction in some families with a schizophrenic member.

**double-blind study**   Study in which, for example, one or more drugs and a placebo are compared in such a way that neither the patient nor the persons directly or indirectly involved in the study know which is being given to the patient; the drugs being investigated and the placebo are coded for identification.

**double personality**   *See* multiple personality disorder.

**Down's syndrome**   Syndrome of mental retardation associated with a variety of abnormalities caused by replication of chromosome 21 three times. Also called trisomy 21 syndrome. Formerly called mongolism.

**Draw-A-Person (DAP) Test**   Easily administered test used with both children and adults, usually with the instructions, "I'd like you to draw a picture of a person; draw the best person you can." A general assumption is that the drawing of a person represents the expression of the self or of the body in the environment.

**drawing test**   Any of a variety of psychological tests in which the subject is asked to draw certain familiar objects, such as people, trees, and houses; attitudes and feelings are often revealed in the way the subject depicts those objects.

**dread**  Massive or pervasive anxiety, usually related to a specific danger.

**dream**  Mental activity during sleep in which thoughts, emotions, and images are experienced as though real; associated with rapid eye movement (REM) sleep. Dreams were regarded by Freud as providing an outlet for the discharge in disguised form of unconscious and often unacceptable impulses and wishes.

**dream anxiety disorder**  Nightmare; a long frightening dream from which one awakens terror stricken.

**dreamy state**  Altered state of consciousness, likened to a dream situation, that develops suddenly and from which the patient usually recovers within a few minutes; accompanied by visual, auditory, and olfactory hallucinations and most commonly associated with temporal lobe lesions.

**DRGs**  Diagnostic Related Groups.

**drive**  Hypothetical construct used to explain motivated behavior: a basic urge that produces a state of psychic tension that motivates the person into action to alleviate the tension; currently preferred over Freud's term "instinct." *See also* aggressive drive; sexual drive.

**drug abuse**  Use of any drug, usually by self-administration, in a manner that deviates from approved social or medical patterns. Called psychoactive substance abuse in DSM-III-R.

**drug dependence**  Habituation or addiction to the use of a drug or chemical substance, with or without physical dependence; physical dependence indicates an altered physiological state due to repeated administrations of a drug, the cessation of which results in the appearance of a withdrawal or abstinence syndrome characteristic for the particular drug. Called psychoactive substance dependence in DSM-III-R.

**Drug Enforcement Administration (DEA)**  Agency of the federal government that regulates distribution of controlled substances such as opioids, barbiturates, and other drugs of potential abuse. *See also* Appendix 3.

**drug holiday**  Limited period of time during which the administration of a psychoactive drug is discontinued in order to control dosage and side effects or to evaluate baseline behavior.

**drug-induced parkinsonism**  PSEUDOPARKINSONISM.

**drug interaction** Effect that one drug has on the actions of one or more other drugs given at the same time; effects of either drug may be increased, diminished, or inactivated as a result of the interaction.

**drug levels** Blood serum or plasma level of psychotropic drugs. *See also* pharmacokinetics.

**drug therapy** Use of chemical substances in the treatment of a disease or disorder. Also called chemotherapy.

**drug tolerance** *See* tolerance.

**DSM** *Diagnostic and Statistical Manual of Mental Disorders.*

**DST** Dexamethasone Suppression Test.

**DTs** delirium tremens.

**dual-sex therapy** Specific form of psychotherapy developed by William Masters and Virginia Johnson in which treatment is focused on a particular sexual disorder. The crux of the program is the round-table session, in which both a male therapist and a female therapist are present with the patient couple; special exercises are prescribed for the couple, the overall goal being to diminish fears of sexual performance and to facilitate communication in sexual and nonsexual areas.

**dual therapy** CO-THERAPY.

**dummy** Uncommonly used term for placebo; e.g., dummy drug.

**Durham rule** Federal court ruling in 1954 holding that "an accused is not criminally responsible if his unlawful act was the product of mental disease or mental defect." It has since been replaced by the American Law Institute formulation of insanity, which states that "a person is not responsible for criminal conduct if at the time of such conduct as a result of mental disease or defect he lacks substantial capacity either to appreciate the wrongfulness of his conduct or to conform his conduct to the requirements of law." *See also* M'Naghten rule.

**dyad** Pair of persons in an interactional situation, such as husband and wife, mother and father, co-therapists, or patient and therapist.

**dyadic session** Psychotherapeutic session involving only two persons, the therapist and the patient.

**dynamic psychiatry** System of psychiatry concerned with the mental mechanisms and emotional processes that govern and motivate human behavior, in contradistinction to descriptive psychiatry, which focuses on observable behavioral phenomena.

**dynamic reasoning** Franz Alexander's term for the formation of all the clinical evidence gained from free-associative anamnesis into a psychological reconstruction of the patient's development.

**dynamics** *See* psychodynamics.

**dysarthria** Impairment of articulation, the motor activity of shaping phonated sounds into speech.

**dyscalculia** Difficulty in performing calculations.

**dysdiadochokinesis** *See* adiadochokinesis.

**dysgeusia** Impairment of the sense of taste.

**dysgraphia** Difficulty in writing.

**dyskinesia** Any disturbance of movement, as in extrapyramidal dyskinesia.

**dyslalia** Faulty articulation due to structural abnormalities of the articulatory organs or impaired hearing.

**dyslexia** A specific learning disability syndrome involving an impairment of the ability to read; unrelated to the person's intelligence. *Compare* alexia.

**dysmetria** Impaired ability to gauge distance relative to bodily movements.

**dysmnesia** Impaired memory.

**dysmorphobia** BODY DYSMORPHOBIC DISORDER.

**dyspareunia** Physical pain in sexual intercourse, usually emotionally caused and more commonly experienced by women; may also result from cystitis, urethritis, or other organic conditions.

**dysphagia** Difficulty in swallowing.

**dysphasia** Difficulty in comprehending oral language (receptive dysphasia) or in trying to express verbal language (expressive dysphasia).

**dysphonia** Difficulty or pain in speaking.

**dysphoria** Feeling of unpleasantness or discomfort; a mood of general dissatisfaction, restlessness, depression, and anxiety.

**dysphoric mood** *See* dysphoria.

**dysprody** Loss of normal speech melody (prosody).

**dyssocial behavior** Former term for antisocial behavior.

**dyssomnias** In DSM-III-R, one of the two major categories of sleep disorders, the other being parasomnias; disturbances in the amount, quality, or timing of sleep, including insomnia disorders, hypersomnia disorders, and sleep-wake schedule disorder.

**dysthymia**  Mood disorder characterized by depressed mood. Also called depressive neurosis. *See also* depression.

**dystonia**  Extrapyramidal motor disturbance consisting of slow, sustained contractions of the axial or appendicular musculature; one movement often predominates, leading to relatively sustained postural deviations; acute dystonic reactions (facial grimacing, torticollis) are occasionally seen with the initiation of antipsychotic drug therapy.

# E

**eating disorders**   Disorders characterized by a marked disturbance in eating behavior; in DSM-III-R, they include anorexia nervosa, bulimia nervosa, pica, and rumination disorder of infancy.

**echolalia**   Repetition of another person's words or phrases, as observed in certain cases of schizophrenia, particularly the catatonic types. The behavior is considered by some authors to be an attempt by the patient to maintain a continuity of thought processes.

**echopraxia**   Repetition of another person's movements, as observed in some cases of catatonic schizophrenia.

**ecology**   Study of the mutual relationships between living things and their environment; includes such studies as the differential incidence of mental disorders in various populations and the distribution of crime and delinquency within a specified geographical area.

**ecopsychiatry**   Study of genetic data and hypotheses about the role of social factors in mental disease.

**ecstasy**   **1.** State of rapturous delight. **2.** Slang term for methylenedioxymethamphetamine (MDMA). *See* Appendix 2.

**ECT**   Electroconvulsive therapy.

**ectomorphic**   Thin, characterized by a linear body build with slight musculature; one of Sheldon's constitutional types. *Compare* endomorphic; mesomorphic.

**educable**   Capable of achieving a fourth-grade or fifth-grade academic level; describes the mildly mentally retarded (I.Q. of 50–55 to 70). *Compare* trainable.

**educational psychology**   Area of psychology concerned with the application of psychological theories to teaching.

**EEG**   Electroencephalogram.

**ego**   One of the three components of the psychic apparatus in the freudian structural framework, the others being the id and the superego. It occupies a position between the primal instincts and the demands of the outer world, therefore mediating between the person and external reality. In so doing, it performs the important functions of perceiving the needs of the self, both physical and psychological, and the qualities and attitudes of the environment. It evaluates, coordinates, and integrates those perceptions so that internal demands can be adjusted to external requirements. It is also responsible for certain defensive functions to protect the person against the demands of the id and the superego. Although the ego has some conscious components, many of its operations are automatic; adaptation to reality is perhaps its most important function.

**ego-alien**  Denoting aspects of a person's personality that are viewed as repugnant, unacceptable, or inconsistent with the rest of the personality. Also called ego-dystonic. *Compare* ego-syntonic.

**ego analysis**  Psychoanalytic study of the manner in which the ego operates, especially in relation to intrapsychic conflicts. *See also* ego psychology.

**ego boundaries**  Concept introduced by Paul Federn that refers to the ability of the intact ego to differentiate the real from the unreal. Ego boundaries prevent repressed unconscious material from overwhelming the ego; when that happens, a person experiences depersonalization and derealization. Boundaries are said to be weakened in schizophrenia and dissociative states.

**egocentric**  Self-centered; selfishly preoccupied with one's own needs; lacking interest in others.

**ego-coping skill**  Adaptive method or capacity developed by a person to deal with or overcome a psychological or social problem.

**ego defense**  Defense mechanism to protect the person against the demands of the id and the superego.

**ego-dystonic**  EGO-ALIEN.

**ego-dystonic homosexuality**  State of a person who has unwanted and distressful homosexual arousal and wishes to acquire or increase heterosexual arousal.

**ego ideal**  Part of the personality representing a fusion of the ego and the superego; feelings of self-satisfaction are experienced when the person's thoughts, behavior, or impulses coincide with an internalized goal or ideal.

**egomania**  Morbid self-preoccupation or self-centeredness. *See also* narcissism.

**ego model**  Person after whom one patterns the ego.

**ego psychology**  Study of the operations of ego in regard to control and regulation of instinctual drives, the relation to reality, and the development of object relations. *See also* ego analysis.

**ego strength** Degree to which the ego's functions, e.g., perception, thinking, speaking, are maintained.

**ego-syntonic** Denoting aspects of a person's personality that are viewed as acceptable and consistent with his or her total personality. *Compare* ego-alien.

**eidetic image** Unusually vivid or exact mental image of objects previously seen or imagined.

**ejaculation** Expulsion of semen and seminal fluid from the urethra, as in male orgasm.

**ejaculatory incompetence** INHIBITED MALE ORGASM.

**elaboration** Unconscious process of embellishing the symbolic content of a dream.

**elation** Affect consisting of feelings of joy, euphoria, triumph, intense self-satisfaction, or optimism.

**elective mutism** Childhood mental disorder in which a child who is able and willing to speak to selected persons persistently refuses to speak in other social or school situations.

**Electra complex** Female analogue of the Oedipus complex in the male; infrequently used term to describe unresolved developmental conflicts influencing a woman's relationships with men.

**electroconvulsive therapy (ECT)** Convulsive therapy, usually for depression, that involves the application of electric current to the brain for a fraction of a second through scalp electrodes to induce a convulsive reaction and unconsciousness.

**electroencephalogram (EEG)** Recording of the brain's electrical potentials obtained by scalp electrodes.

**electromyogram (EMG)** Recording of the electrical activity of muscles at specific sites.

**electroshock therapy (EST)** *See* electroconvulsive therapy.

**electrostimulation** In aversion therapy, a negative conditioning technique consisting of (usually painful) electric shocks.

**elevated mood** Air of confidence and enjoyment; a mood more cheerful than normal but not necessarily pathologic.

**elimination disorders** Inability as a result of physiologic or psychologic immaturity to maintain bowel control (functional encopresis) or bladder control (functional enuresis).

**elopement**  Escape; absenting oneself from a mental hospital without permission.

**emancipated minor**  Legal term for a minor who exercises general control over his or her life and hence has the legal rights of an adult.

**EMG**  Electromyogram.

**emotion**  Complex feeling state with psychic, somatic, and behavioral components; external manifestation of emotion is affect.

**emotional deprivation**  Relative lack of environmental or interpersonal experiences during the early developmental years. *See also* sensory deprivation.

**emotional disorder**  Lay term for a mental illness or mental disorder; in common usage it does not specifically imply a mood disorder or schizophrenia.

**emotional disturbance**  Emotional disorder or illness. *See also* mental disorder.

**emotional illness**  General term for a behavioral or psychological syndrome or pattern associated with distress, disability, or increased risk of suffering.

**emotional insight**  Deeper level of understanding or awareness that is more likely to lead to positive changes in personality and behavior.

**emotional lability**  Excessive emotional responsiveness characterized by unstable and rapidly changing emotions.

**emotional support**  Encouragement, hope, and inspiration given to one person by another.

**empathy**  Intellectual and emotional awareness and understanding of another person's state of mind, involving the projection of oneself into another person's frame of reference; an important ability in a successful therapist or a helpful group member. *Compare* sympathy.

**empty nest syndrome**  Depression that can occur in men and women when their youngest child is about to leave or has left home.

**encapsulated delusion**  Delusion that has no significant effect on behavior.

**encephalitis**  Inflammation of the brain.

**encephalopathy**  Any disease of the brain.

**encopresis**  Involuntary passage of feces, usually occurring at night or during sleep. Also called functional encopresis in DSM-III-R.

**encounter group**  Form of sensitivity training, introduced and developed by Jacob Moreno in 1914, that emphasizes the experiencing of individual relationships within the group and that minimizes intellectual and didactic input; the group focuses on the present, rather than concerning itself with the past or outside problems of its members. *See also* sensitivity training group.

**endemic**  Belonging, native, restricted, or peculiar to a particular people, country, locality, or region.

**endocrine disorder**  Dysfunction of any of the endocrine glands, frequently with psychiatric manifestations.

**endogamy**  Marriage within a specific group. *Compare* exogamy.

**endogenous depression**  Type of depression that originates within the person and is not related to external events, with a cause that is biologic or somatic. Also called nonreactive depression.

**endomorphic**  Obese, with prominence of the abdomen; one of Sheldon's constitutional types. *Compare* ectomorphic; mesomorphic.

**endorphin**  Any of several endogenous opioid peptides (α-, β-, or γ-endorphin) found in highest concentrations in the pituitary gland and which has analgesic and behavioral effects in animals. *See also* enkephalin.

**engram**  Memory trace, the neurophysiological substrate of memory.

**enkephalin**  Endogenous opioid peptide released by β-endorphin that has analgesic properties and many of the actions of morphine.

**enuresis**  Incontinence of urine during sleep. Also called functional enuresis in DSM-III-R.

**epidemiology**  In psychiatry, the study of the incidence, prevalence, control, and distribution of mental disorders within a particular population.

**epigenesis**  Term introduced by Erik Erikson to refer to the stages of ego and social development.

**epilepsy**  Neurological disorder resulting from a sudden, excessive, disorderly discharge of neurons in either a structurally normal or a diseased cerebral cortex; characterized by paroxysmal recurrence of short-lived disturbances of consciousness, involuntary convulsive muscle movements, psychic or sensory disturbances, or some combination thereof. Termed idiopathic epilepsy when there is no identifiable organic cause. For types of epilepsy, see the specific term.

**epileptic dementia**  Epilepsy accompanied by progressive mental and intellectual impairment; some believe that the circulatory disturbances during epileptic attacks cause nerve cell degeneration and lead to dementia.

**epileptic equivalent**  Epileptic phenomenon that is neither grand mal nor petit mal. *See also* complex partial seizure.

**epileptic personality**  EXPLOSIVE PERSONALITY.

**epinephrine**  Sympathomimetic catecholamine formed from norepinephrine and the major hormone secreted by the adrenal medulla; its release during states of fear or anxiety produces many of the physiological changes associated with those emotions. Also called adrenaline.

**episodic**  Denoting an illness in which there are sustained disturbances clearly distinguished from previous functioning.

**epistemology**  Study or theory of the nature and grounds of knowledge, especially with reference to its limits and validity.

**erectile dysfunction**  MALE ERECTILE DISORDER.

**eremophobia**  Abnormal fear of being by oneself.

**ergasia**  Adolf Meyer's term for a person's total activity, as opposed to the functioning of parts of the whole.

**Erikson, Erik** (1902-1990)  Psychoanalyst noted for his theory of ego development and psychosocial development, which he conceptualized in terms of social adaptation as it relates to Sigmund Freud's formulations.

**erogenous zone**  Any area of the body, principally the genitals, anus, and mouth, capable of being stimulated sexually.

**Eros**  SEXUAL DRIVE.

**erotic**  Invested with sexual feeling.

**erotomania**  Pathological preoccupation with sexual activities or fantasies.

**erythrophobia**  Abnormal fear of blushing.

**escape learning**  *See* avoidance and escape learning.

**ESP**  Extrasensory perception.

**EST**  Electroshock therapy.

**estrogen**  Hormone produced mainly by the ovaries and responsible for the development of the female reproductive organs and secondary sex characteristics; e.g., estradiol, estriol, estrone. *Compare* androgen.

**ethnocentrism**   Conviction that one's own group is superior to other groups; impairs one's ability to evaluate members of another group realistically or to communicate with them on an open, equal, and person-to-person basis.

**ethnology**   Branch of anthropology dealing with the division of mankind into races and their origin, history, customs, and institutions.

**ethology**   Study of animal behavior; often applied to the understanding of human behavior.

**etiology**   Study of the causes of disease and their mode of operation.

**euergasia**   Word used by Adolf Meyer to mean normal mental functioning.

**euphoria**   Exaggerated feeling of well-being that is inappropriate to apparent events; may be induced by drugs such as opiates, amphetamines, and alcohol.

**euphoric mood**   *See* euphoria.

**euphorohallucinogen**   Substance capable of producing euphoric hallucinations.

**euthymic**   Denoting a normal mood.

**evasion**   Act of not facing up to or of strategically eluding something; consists of suppressing an idea that is next in a thought series and replacing it with another idea closely related to it. Also called paralogia; perverted logic.

**event-related euphoria**   Morbid or abnormal sense of well-being associated with a specific situation or event.

**evoked potential (EP)**   Following repetitive stimuli, the characteristic EEG waveform that remains after averaging out most of the brain electrical activity; clinically useful in evaluating the functional integrity of the somatosensory or special sensory pathways.

**exaltation**   Feeling of intense elation and grandeur.

**excited**   Agitated, purposeless motor activity uninfluenced by external stimuli.

**excitement phase**   Stage in the human sexual response after sexual stimulation, as described by Masters and Johnson, characterized by an objective sense of pleasure and accompanying physical changes (penile erection and vaginal lubrication).

**executive ego function**   That part of the ego that helps maintain or manage one's relationship to and sense of reality.

**exhaustion state** Final stage of the body's response to major stress, as in the general adaptation syndrome.

**exhibitionism** Paraphilia in which a man exposes his genitals to females in a socially inappropriate fashion; rarely occurs in women.

**existentialism** Philosophic theory that questions the purpose and nature of existence itself; a fundamental focus is on the meaning of life in face of death and the end of one's personal existence.

**existential psychotherapy** Type of therapy, based on existential philosophy, that puts the emphasis on here-and-now interaction and on feeling experiences, rather than on rational thinking; little attention is given to patient resistances, and the therapist is involved on the same level and to the same degree as the patient. *See also* phenomenology.

**exogamy** Marriage outside of a specific group; in a biological sense, the union of gametes of unrelated parents. *Compare* endogamy.

**exogenous** In psychiatry, denoting disordered behavior produced by forces outside of the body, as in adjustment disorder.

**exorcism** Magical practice in which mystical incantations are invoked to remove demons that are alleged to have entered the mind.

**expansive mood** Mood characterized by feelings of grandiosity.

**experiencing** Feeling emotions and sensations, as opposed to thinking; being involved in what is happening, rather than standing back at a distance and theorizing.

**experimental bias** Error in construction of an experiment or study that favors one outcome over another.

**experimental design** Manner in which an experiment is logically organized in order to maximize the probability of obtaining real effects.

**experimental group** In an experimental design, the group that is exposed to the experimental manipulation under study. *Compare* control group.

**experimental neurosis** Abnormal behavior produced in a laboratory setting; used by Ivan Pavlov to describe symptoms of extreme and persistent agitation that he produced in dogs.

**expert witness** Legal concept that refers to the physician in the courtroom who is deemed sufficiently knowledgeable in a field to draw informed conclusions from data, e.g., that a patient meets the required criteria for commitment or for an insanity defense.

**explosive personality** Personality type characterized by rigidity, egocentricity, selfishness, religiosity, seclusiveness, explosive outbursts of emotion, and extreme rage reactions when frustrated; enuresis is common. Also called epileptic personality, although, as usually described, it does not occur in more than 20% of known epileptic persons.

**expressive aphasia** MOTOR APHASIA.

**expressive dysphasia** Difficulty in expressing verbal language; the ability to understand language is intact.

**extended-family therapy** Type of family therapy that involves family members, beyond the nuclear family, who are closely associated with it and affect it. *See also* social network therapy.

**externalization** More general term than projection that refers to the tendency to perceive in the external world and in external objects elements of one's own personality, including instinctual impulses, conflicts, moods, attitudes, and styles of thinking.

**external validity** Statistical term that refers to how well a test measures what it purports to measure and identifies what it is supposed to identify.

**extinction** Process by which an operant behavior occurs less frequently when its performance is no longer reinforced.

**extrapsychic conflict** Conflict that arises between a person and his or her environment. Also called interpersonal conflict. *Compare* intrapsychic conflict.

**extrapyramidal dyskinesia** Movement disorder related to dysfunction of the extrapyramidal motor system; signs include a variety of involuntary movements and postures, muscular rigidity, tremor, and gait disturbance, as seen in Parkinson's disease, chorea, athetosis, and hemiballismus. Extrapyramidal dyskinetic syndromes may occur as a side effect of antipsychotic drugs; such drug-induced extrapyramidal effects include a parkinsonian syndrome, akathisia, acute dystonic reactions, and tardive dyskinesia.

**extrapyramidal effect** Bizarre, involuntary motor movement; a central nervous system side effect sometimes produced by antipsychotic drugs. *See also* extrapyramidal dyskinesia.

**extrapyramidal motor system** Polysynaptic neural pathways involving the basal ganglia and related subcortical nuclei that influence motor behavior.

**extrapyramidal syndrome**    Abnormalities of movement related to injury of motor pathways other than the pyramidal tract; e.g., parkinsonism, akathisia, dystonia, tardive dyskinesia.

**extrasensory perception (ESP)**    Experiencing of an external event by means other than the five senses, as by telepathy or clairvoyance.

**extroversion, extraversion**    State of one's energies being directed outside oneself. *Compare* introversion.

# F

**factitious disorder**   Mental disorder characterized by the voluntary production of false or unreal physical or psychological symptoms; unlike malingering, there is no apparent goal or obvious benefit. *Compare* somatoform disorders.

**factor analysis**   Data reduction technique used to reduce a large number of variables to a smaller number of linear combinations of variables.

**false negative**   Diagnosis of a disorder as being absent in a person (tested negative) when in fact it is present.

**false positive**   Diagnosis of a disorder as being present in a person (tested positive) when in fact it is not present.

**falsifiable hypothesis**   Testable hypothesis that can be confirmed or disconfirmed.

**family neurosis**   Mental disorder in which a person's psychopathology is unconsciously interrelated with that of other members of the family.

**family therapy**   Treatment of more than one member of a family in the same session; family relationships and processes are explored as potential causes of mental disorder in one or more of the family members. *See also* extended-family therapy.

**fantasy**   Daydream; fabricated mental picture of a situation or chain of events. A form of thinking dominated by unconscious material and primary processes that seeks wish fulfillment and immediate solutions to conflicts; may serve as the matrix for creativity or for neurotic distortions of reality.

**father surrogate, father substitute**   In psychoanalysis, a person onto whom the patient projects his or her father image and to whom he or she responds unconsciously in an inappropriate and unrealistic manner, with the feelings and attitudes held toward the real father.

**fausse reconnaissance**   False recognition, a feature of paramnesia.

**faux de mieux**   Literally, "for want of anything better," connoting in psychiatry a person's choosing a homosexual relationship when no partner of the opposite sex is available.

**FDA**   Food and Drug Administration.

**fear** Unpleasurable emotional state consisting of psychophysiological changes in response to a realistic threat or danger. *Compare* anxiety.

**feeble-mindedness** Obsolete term for mental retardation.

**feedback** **1.** In a given system, the return, as input, of some form of information regarding the output; used as a regulatory mechanism. **2.** In psychiatry, the verbally or otherwise expressed response to a person's behavior by another person or a group.

**fellatio** Use of the mouth or tongue to stimulate the male genitalia.

**femaleness** Anatomic and physiologic features relating to female procreative functions.

**female sexual arousal disorder** Sexual arousal disorder characterized by the persistent or recurrent partial or complete failure to attain or maintain the lubrication-swelling response of sexual excitement until the completion of the sexual act. Formerly called inhibited sexual excitement.

**feminine identity** Inner sense of gender affiliation with females. *Compare* masculine identity.

**Ferenczi, Sandor** (1873–1933) Hungarian psychoanalyst who was one of Sigmund Freud's early followers and a brilliant contributor to all aspects of psychoanalysis; he came to favor more active and personal techniques than Freud's, to the point that his adherence to psychoanalysis during his last years was questioned.

**fetishism** Paraphilia in which sexual excitement and gratification are achieved by substituting an inanimate object (such as a shoe, piece of underwear, or other article of clothing) for a human love object.

**field theory** Conceptual approach to the study of personality formulated by Kurt Lewin that focuses on an operational analysis of the causal determinants of human behavior; it is expressed in geometric and mathematical terms borrowed from physics in an attempt to provide a framework suitable to the scientific study of human behavior. The person and his or her environment together constitute the life space, a complex field of forces acting on the personality and determining behavior.

**finger agnosia** Agnosia characterized by inability to name fingers; suggests a lesion in the dominant parietal lobe.

**fixation** **1.** Arrest of psychosexual development at any stage before complete maturation. **2.** Close and paralyzing attachment to another person, such as one's mother or father.

**fixed-interval schedule**  *See* schedule of reinforcement.

**fixed-ratio schedule**  *See* schedule of reinforcement.

**flagellantism, flagellation**  Process by which sexual partners are aroused and gratified by whipping or being whipped.

**flashback hallucinosis**  Spontaneous recurrence, after a drug-free period, of hallucinations similar to those experienced during an acute toxic episode; often associated with repeated ingestions of LSD. Hallucinations are predominantly visual and may last for months after the last use of a drug.

**flat affect**  Absence or near absence of any signs of affective expression.

**flexibilitas cerea**  CATALEPSY.

**flight of ideas**  Rapid succession of fragmentary thoughts or speech in which content changes abruptly and speech may be incoherent, as seen in mania.

**floccillation**  Aimless plucking or picking, usually at bed-clothes or clothing, commonly seen in senile psychosis and delirium.

**flooding**  Behavior therapy designed to extinguish phobias or anxiety through the presentation of the aversive stimuli in intense forms until the emotional responses cease.

**fluent aphasia**  Aphasia characterized by inability to understand the spoken word; fluent but incoherent speech is present. Also called Wernicke's aphasia.

**folie à deux**  Mental illness shared by two persons, usually involving a common delusional system; if it involves three persons, it is referred to as folie à trois, etc. Called induced psychotic disorder in DSM-III-R.

**follow-up examination**  To the physician, the aftercare and monitoring of patients' responses to treatment and the state of their physical health or mental status.

**Food and Drug Administration (FDA)**  Federal agency that sets standards for the sale and use of drugs, food substances, and cosmetics.

**forensic psychiatry**  Branch of psychiatry concerned with the legal aspects of mental illness.

**foreplay**  Sexual play that precedes sexual intercourse. Also called forepleasure.

**forepleasure**  FOREPLAY.

**formal operations**   Jean Piaget's label for completely developed logical thinking capacities. *See also* Piaget, Jean.

**formication**   Tactile hallucination involving the sensation that tiny insects are crawling over the skin; most commonly encountered in cocaine addiction and delirium tremens.

**for-profit hospital**   Investor-owned or proprietary hospital; hospital owned and operated by physicians or corporations that earns a profit for its investors.

**fragmentary delusion**   Poorly elaborated delusion, often one of many with no apparent interconnection.

**fraternal twins**   DIZYGOTIC TWINS.

**free association**   Investigative psychoanalytic technique devised by Freud in which the patient seeks to verbalize without reservation or censorship the passing contents of his or her mind.

**freebase**   Cocaine hydrochloride mixed with ammonia and an alkali solution, and then extracted with a solvent into a crystalline form. *See also* crack.

**free-floating anxiety**   Severe, pervasive, generalized anxiety that is not attached to any particular idea, object, or event; observed particularly in anxiety disorders, although it may be seen in some cases of schizophrenia.

**frequency**   Number of cases having a certain score or characteristic; relative frequency measures the number of persons in a specific group (e.g., sex or age) who have a disorder.

**frequency distribution**   Statistical description of raw data in terms of the number of cases that fall into each interval within a set of data; often presented graphically in the form of a frequency histogram or frequency polygram.

**Freud, Anna** (1895–1982)   Daughter of Sigmund Freud noted for her contributions to the developmental theory of psychoanalysis and the mechanisms of defense.

**Freud, Sigmund** (1856–1939)   Austrian psychiatrist and the founder of psychoanalysis. With Josef Breuer, he explored the potentialities of cathartic therapy and then went on to develop the analytic technique and such fundamental concepts as mental sublimation, as well as superego, ego, and id formation and their applications throughout all spheres of human behavior. Among his publications are *The Interpretation of Dreams* (1899), *Studies on Hysteria* (1895, with Breuer), and *Three Essays on the Theory of Sexuality* (1905).

**frigidity**   Colloquial term referring, in the female, to lack of sexual response or feeling, ranging from complete lack of arousal to incomplete climax.

**frontal lobe syndrome**   Organic mental disorder characterized by a marked change in personality, with development of certain relatively characteristic patterns of relating to the environment that have been associated with lesions of the frontal lobes; such patterns include emotional lability, impairment in impulse control and social judgment, and marked apathy and indifference. Called organic personality syndrome in DSM-III-R.

**frottage, frotteurism**   Sexual aberration in which arousal results from rubbing up against someone, usually without specific genital contact, as in a crowd; a person so afflicted is a frotteur.

**frustration**   Result of the thwarting of any goal-directed behavior; the ability to tolerate frustration and delay gratification is considered a sign of maturity and good ego strength.

**fugue**   Dissociative disorder characterized by a period of almost complete amnesia, during which a person actually flees from an immediate life situation and begins a different life pattern; apart from the amnesia, mental faculties and skills are usually unimpaired. *See also* psychogenic amnesia.

**fulfillment**   Satisfaction of a need or wish.

**functional**   Denoting changes in functioning not attributable to known organic alterations.

**functional disorder**   Disorder that is not caused by an anatomical defect or any other identifiable or demonstrable cause. *Compare* organic disorder.

**functional encopresis**   DSM-III-R term for encopresis.

**functional enuresis**   DSM-III-R term for enuresis.

**functional speech disorder**   DEVELOPMENTAL ARTICULATION DISORDER.

**fusion**   In psychoanalysis, the joining together of instincts.

# G

**GABA**  γ-(gamma) aminobutyric acid.

**GAF Scale**  GLOBAL ASSESSMENT OF FUNCTIONING SCALE.

**galactorrhea**  Abnormal discharge of milk from the breast; may be a result of the endocrine influence of phenothiazine drugs.

**galvanic skin response (GSR)**  Measurable change in the electrical resistance of the skin, used as an index of emotional response.

**γ-(gamma) aminobutyric acid (GABA)**  Inhibitory amino acid neurotransmitter synthesized by the actions of glutamic acid decarboxylase; GABA receptors are located at postsynaptic sites.

**gamophobia**  Abnormal fear of marriage.

**Ganser's syndrome**  Rare atypical dissociative disorder, seen in prisoners, characterized by a giving of approximate answers to questions and of talking past the point; to be distinguished from factitious disorder and malingering.

**gargoylism**  Old name for the gargoyle-like facies and dwarfism seen in Hunter's and Hurler's syndromes: metabolic disorders of mucopolysaccharide metabolism characterized by severe developmental skeletal deformities and mental retardation.

**GAS**  General adaptation syndrome.

**gatekeeper**  In community psychiatry, a person who evaluates the degree of psychological or environmental stress sufficient to enable a patient to gain access to the mental health care system.

**gateway drugs**  Substances of abuse, such as alcohol and marijuana, that provide major portals of entry into abuse of other drugs; considered particularly dangerous because they are believed by so many to be relatively harmless.

**Gault decision**  U.S. Supreme Court 1967 decision mandating fair and accurate fact-finding procedures for juveniles when serious punishment could be inflicted should they be found guilty; rights guaranteed the juvenile include the right to notification of the specific charges, the right to counsel, the right against self-incrimination, and the right to confront and cross-examine the accusers.

**gay**  **1.** Popular term for a homosexual, especially male. **2.** Denoting a homosexual or the lifestyle thereof.

**gegenhalten**   Neurological term for involuntary active resistance to passive movement of the extremities, as may occur in cerebral cortical disorders.

**gender identity**   Culturally determined sets of attitudes, behavior patterns, and physical attributes usually associated with masculinity and femininity. *Compare* sexual identity.

**gender identity disorder**   Psychosexual disorder in which a person feels discomfort with and inappropriateness of his or her biological sex, with a marked preference for the clothing and activities of the opposite sex and/or repudiation of the sex organs. *See also* transsexualism.

**Gender role**   Public declaration of gender; the image of maleness or femaleness that is communicated to others which may or may not coincide with gender identity.

**general adaptational syndrome (GAS)**   Hans Selye's term for the responses of the body to major stress, passing through the alarm reaction, resistance and, finally, exhaustion.

**generalization**   Process by which a behavior occurs in a setting in which it had not previously been reinforced.

**generalized anxiety**   *See* free-floating anxiety.

**generalized anxiety disorder**   DSM-III-R classification of anxiety disorder characterized by chronic generalized anxiety not attached to any particular idea, object, or event. *See* free-floating anxiety.

**general paralysis, general paresis**   Organic mental disorder caused by chronic (tertiary) neurosyphilis.

**general systems theory**   Theoretical framework asserting that the universe is composed of interacting components that are interrelated; in psychiatry, it emphasizes an integrated, holistic approach to understanding behavior.

**genetic counseling**   Presentation and discussion, generally with a prospective parental couple, of factors involved in the inheritance of pathological conditions as they relate to the couple's genetic endowment.

**genetic endowment**   Characteristics that are inherited, usually regarding potential capacities of intelligence, temperament, and general adaptability.

**genetic marker**   Detectable sign of the presence of or vulnerability to inherited disease, such as a measurable biochemical abnormality.

**genetic material**  In psychiatry, data from a patient's personal past history that are useful in developing an understanding of the psychodynamics of his or her present adaptation.

**genital phase**  Final stage of psychosexual development, occurring during puberty, in which sexual gratification is achieved from genital-to-genital contact and the capacity exists for a mature, affectionate relationship with someone of the opposite sex.

**genotype**  Genetic endowment of a person, consisting of a set of genes received from each parent at the time of conception. *Compare* phenotype.

**geriatric psychiatry**  Branch of psychiatry concerned with the mental disorders that accompany old age. Also called geropsychiatry.

**geriatrics**  Branch of medicine concerned with the aged and the problems of aging. *See also* gerontology.

**gerontology**  Scientific study of aging.

**gerontophilia**  Sexual attraction for the old and the aged by a young person.

**geropsychiatry**  GERIATRIC PSYCHIATRY.

**Gerstmann's syndrome**  DEVELOPMENTAL ARITHMETIC DISORDER.

**Gesell Developmental Schedules**  Developmental landmarks in infants and children that cover ages 8 weeks to 3.5 years. Data are obtained by direct observation of the child's responses to standard toys and other controlled stimulus objects and are supplemented by developmental information provided by the mother or primary caretaker; the schedules yield scores indicating the child's level of development in four separate areas: motor, adaptive, language, and personal and social.

**gestalt psychology**  School of psychology primarily concerned with perceptual processes; a major tenet is that the whole is greater than the sum of its parts. Its development is associated particularly with Max Wertheimer, Wolfgang Koehler, and Kurt Koffka.

**gestalt therapy**  Psychotherapy developed by Frederick S. Perls that emphasizes the treatment of the person as a whole: one's biological component parts and their organic functioning, one's perceptual configuration, and one's interrelationships with the outside world. It can be used in either an individual or a group therapy setting; focuses on the sensory awareness of the person's here-and-now experiences, rather than on past recollections or

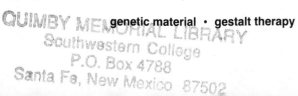
QUIMBY MEMORIAL LIBRARY
Southwestern College
P.O. Box 4788
Santa Fe, New Mexico 87502

future expectations; and uses role playing and other techniques to promote the patient's growth process and development to full potential.

**Gilles de la Tourette syndrome**   *See* Tourette's disorder.

**global aphasia**   Combination of grossly nonfluent aphasia and severe fluent aphasia.

**Global Assessment of Functioning Scale (GAF Scale)**   Scale used in DSM-III-R to describe the highest social, occupational, or educational level of functioning of a person in the 12 months preceding the current evaluation.

**globus hystericus**   Hysterical symptom in which a person is disturbed by the sensation of a lump in the throat.

**glossolalia**   Unintelligible jargon that has meaning to the speaker but not to the listener.

**glossophobia**   LALOPHOBIA.

**go-around**   Technique used in group therapy in which the therapist requires each member of the group to respond to another member, a theme, or an association to encourage the participation of all members in the group.

**gonadal dysgenesis**   TURNER'S SYNDROME.

**grandiose delusion**   DELUSION OF GRANDEUR. *See* delusion.

**grandiosity**   Exaggerated feeling of one's importance, power, knowledge, or identity. *See also* delusion of grandeur.

**grand mal epilepsy**   Major form of epilepsy in which gross tonic-clonic convulsive seizures are accompanied by loss of consciousness and, often, incontinence of stool or urine; frequently preceded by an aura.

**gray-out syndrome**   Psychosis that occurs in pilots flying at high altitudes, out of sight of the horizon.

**grief**   Alteration in mood and affect consisting of sadness appropriate to a real loss; normally, it is self limited. *See also* depression; mourning.

**group**   *See* therapeutic group.

**group analytic psychotherapy**   Term applied by S. H. Foulkes to his pioneering group therapy procedure in which interventions dealt primarily with group, rather than individual, forces and processes, and the group was used as the principal therapeutic agent.

**group cohesion**   Mutual bonds formed between members of a group as a result of their concerted effort for a common interest and purpose; until cohesiveness is achieved, the group cannot concentrate its full energy on a common task.

**group dynamics** Phenomena that occur in groups from their inception to their termination. Interactions and interrelations among members and between the members and the therapist create tension, which maintains a constantly changing group equilibrium; interactions and the tension created are highly influenced by individual members' psychological makeup, unconscious instinctual drives, motives, wishes, and fantasies. Understanding and effectively using group dynamics are essential in group treatment. Also called group process.

**group mind** Autonomous and unified mental life in an assemblage of people bound together by mutual interests; a concept used by group therapists who focus on the group as a unit rather than on the individual members.

**group practice** Delivery of medical services by three or more physicians formally organized to provide care, consultation, diagnosis, and treatment; they share the use of equipment and personnel, and income from the medical practice is distributed among the members of the group.

**group pressure** Demand by group members that individual members submit and conform to group standards, values, and behavior.

**group process** GROUP DYNAMICS.

**group psychotherapy** Application of psychotherapeutic techniques to a group of patients, using interpatient interactions to effect changes in the maladaptive behavior of the individual members.

**group relations theory** *See* Allport's group relations theory.

**GSR** Galvanic skin response.

**guardianship** Person appointed by the courts for the care and management of a person or the property of another, as of a minor or a person incapable of managing his or her affairs.

**guilt** Emotional state associated with self-reproach and the need for punishment. In psychoanalysis, refers to a neurotic feeling of culpability that stems from a conflict between the ego and the superego that begins developmentally with parental disapproval and becomes internalized as conscience in the course of superego formation. Guilt has normal psychological and social functions, but special intensity or absence of guilt characterizes many mental disorders, such as depression and antisocial personality disorder, respectively. Some psychiatrists distinguish shame as a less internalized form of guilt that relates more to others than to the self.

**gustatory hallucination**   Hallucination primarily involving taste.

**gynecomastia**   Female-like development of the male breasts; may occur as a side effect of antipsychotic drugs due to increased prolactin levels.

**gynephobia**   Abnormal fear of women.

**gyrectomy**   Psychosurgery involving excision of a cerebral gyrus.

# H

**habeas corpus**   Legal term for the right to petition a court to decide whether confinement has been undertaken with due process of law.

**habit**   Behavior pattern acquired by frequent repetition that leads to regularity or increased facility of performance.

**habituation**   **1.** Simple form of learning in which the response to a repeated stimulus lessens over time. **2.** Psychological dependence on the continued use of a drug or chemical substance to maintain a sense of well being, which can result in addiction.

**halfway house**   Facility for mental patients who no longer need the full facilities of a hospital but are not yet ready to return to their communities.

**hallucination**   False sensory perception occurring in the absence of any relevant external stimulation of the sensory modality involved. For types of hallucinations, see the specific term.

**hallucinogenic drug, hallucinogen**   Chemical agent that produces hallucinations, such as LSD and mescaline. *See also* euphorohallucinogen; psychotomimetic drug.

**hallucinosis**   State in which a person experiences hallucinations without any impairment of consciousness.

**haloperidol**   Butyrophenone antipsychotic drug (trade name, Haldol). *See* Appendix 1.

**Halstead-Reitan Scale**   Battery of neuropsychological tests used to determine the location and effects of specific brain lesions. A great variety of functions are tested: concept function, abstraction, and visual acuity; dexterity; spatial memory; auditory perception, attention, and concentration; finger-oscillation; speech-sounds perception; visual perception; time sense; and sensory stimulation, stereognosis, and tactile perception.

**Hamilton Depression Scale**   Scale of depression based upon a clinical interview with the patient in which the examiner asks about guilt, suicide, sleep habits, weight change, and other symptoms of depression.

**haphephobia**   Abnormal fear of being touched.

**haplology**   Rapid speech in which syllables are omitted; seen in certain manias and in schizophrenic conditions.

**haptic hallucination**   TACTILE HALLUCINATION.

**hashish**   Dried resinous tops of the marijuana plant (*Cannabis sativa*); the active ingredient is tetrahydrocannabinol, which is a potent psychedelic drug.

**Health and Human Services**   Federal organization composed of the following: Office of Human Development Services, Public Health Service (includes Centers for Disease Control; Food and Drug Administration; Health Resources and Services Administration; National Institutes of Health; Alcohol, Drug Abuse, and Mental Health Administration; Agency for Toxic Substances and Disease Registry; and Indian Health Service), Social Security Administration, Health Care Financing Administration, and Family Support Administration. Formerly called Department of Health, Education, and Welfare (HEW).

**health insurance**   Insurance that reimburses one for the costs of medical care or lost income arising from medical disability; may include coverage for the care of mental conditions.

**health maintenance organization (HMO)**   Form of group practice by physicians, often including psychiatrists, and allied health professionals to provide comprehensive health services to subscribers who pay a fixed premium.

**Health Systems Agency (HSA)**   Nonprofit, federally mandated, statewide organizations that promote or limit the development of health services and faculties depending on the needs of the particular state or locale. HSAs develop long- and short-term goals and plans, approve health care proposals requesting federal funding, review existing facilities and services, and suggest future consideration and renovation projects based on their findings.

**healthy identification**   Modeling of oneself, consciously or unconsciously, on another person who has a sound psychic makeup; such identification has constructive results. *See also* imitation.

**hearsay**   Out-of-court statement offered to prove the truth of the matter asserted; usually inadmissible as testimony.

**hebephrenia**   Complex of symptoms, considered a form of schizophrenia, characterized by wild or silly behavior or mannerisms, inappropriate affect, frequent hypochondriacal complaints, and delusions and hallucinations that are transient and unsystematized. Hebephrenic schizophrenia is listed in DSM-III-R as disorganized schizophrenia. *See also* schizophrenia.

**hedonism**   Pleasure-seeking behavior. *Compare* anhedonia.

**helplessness** **1.** Learned: State of apathy that occurs as a type of experimental neurosis in animals who cannot escape an aversive stimulus; proposed as the animal model of human depression in which a patient feels helpless to control events. **2.** Psychic: State that occasions the first expressions of anxiety in humans, e.g., the experience of birth.

**hematophobia** Abnormal fear of the sight of blood.

**herd instinct** Desire to belong to a group and to participate in social activities; used by Wilfred Trotter to indicate the presence of a hypothetical social instinct in humans. In psychoanalysis, herd instinct is viewed as a social phenomenon, rather than as an instinct.

**hermaphrodite** Person who has both female and male gonadal tissue, usually with one sex dominating.

**heroin** Diacetylmorphine; an illicit, addictive alkaloid opioid that requires subsequent larger and larger amounts to achieve the same narcotic and analgesic effects. Injected intravenously, it produces a more rapid onset of euphoria than does morphine.

**heterogeneity** Dissimilarity in the genotypal structure of individuals originating through sexual reproduction.

**heterosexuality** Sexual attraction or contact between opposite-sex persons. The capacity for heterosexual arousal is probably innate, biologically programmed, and triggered in very early life, perhaps in part by olfactory modalities as seen in lower animals. *Compare* bisexuality; homosexuality.

**heterozygous** Possessing different allelic forms of a gene at a given locus in homologous chromosomes.

**heuristic** **1.** Involving or serving as an aid to learning, discovery, or problem-solving by experimental and especially trial-and-error methods. **2.** Of or relating to exploratory problem-solving techniques that utilize self-educating techniques.

**5-HIAA** 5-Hydroxyindoleacetic acid.

**histrionic personality disorder** Condition in which the patient, usually an immature and dependent person, exhibits unstable, overreactive, and excitable self-dramatizing behavior that is aimed at gaining attention and is at times seductive, although the person may not be aware of that aim.

**HMO** Health maintenance organization.

**holism** In psychiatry, the study of the total person as a distinctive entity, rather than as a collection of various characteristics.

**holophrastic** Using a single word to express a combination of ideas; schizophrenic persons may use holophrastic language.

**homeless** Persons who have no permanent place of residence, often sleeping in the street, many of whom require psychiatric treatment or hospitalization.

**homeostasis** Tendency to maintain a constancy and stability of bodily processes to ensure optimal functioning; the state of bodily equilibrium and the processes whereby such equilibrium is maintained.

**homosexuality** Sexual attraction or contact between same-sex persons. Some authors distinguish two types: overt and latent. *Compare* bisexuality; heterosexuality.

**homosexual panic** Sudden, acute onset of severe anxiety precipitated by the unconscious fear or conflict that one may be a homosexual or act out homosexual impulses.

**homovanillic acid (HVA)** Phenol found in human urine; as the major metabolite of dopamine, it is most often measured in psychiatric research.

**Horney, Karen** (1885–1952) Psychiatrist and psychoanalyst whose theories of the genesis of neurosis emphasized environmental and cultural factors and thus departed from the biological-instinctual framework of orthodox freudian thought.

**hostile transference** *See* transference.

**hostility** Conflict, opposition, or resistance in thought or principle.

**hot line** Telephone assistance service for crisis intervention.

**HSA** Health Systems Agency.

**5-HT** 5-Hydroxytryptamine.

**humanistic theory** Group of diverse theories that share a holistic conceptualization that emphasizes the uniqueness, value, dignity, and worth of each human being as an individual. Human behavior is considered understandable only in terms of the meaning of experiences for the individual person; it represents a complex interplay of numerous physical, psychological, and sociocultural factors.

**humiliation** Sense of disgrace, dishonor, and shame; often experienced by depressed patients.

**humor** Defense mechanism that allows the overt expression of feelings and thoughts without personal discomfort or immobilization and does not produce an unpleasant effect on others; allows the individual to tolerate and yet focus on what is too terrible to be borne. Differs from wit, a form of displacement that involves distraction from the affective issue.

**Huntington's chorea**  Hereditary and progressive central nervous system disease characterized by jerking motions and progressive mental deterioration; inherited as an autosomal dominant, with onset in adult life.

**HVA**  Homovanillic acid.

**hydrocephalus**  Excessive accumulation of cerebrospinal fluid which dilates the cerebral ventricles.

**hydrophobia**  In psychiatry and psychology, an abnormal fear of water.

**hydrotherapy**  Use of water by external application in the treatment of disease.

**5-hydroxyindoleacetic acid (5-HIAA)**  Metabolite of serotonin, the concentration of which can be measured in cerebrospinal fluid and serum; determination of 5-HIAA concentrations is used in psychiatric research and may help guide clinical practice.

**5-hydroxytryptamine (5-HT)**  SEROTONIN.

**hyperactivity**  Increased muscular activity. The term is commonly used to describe a disturbance found in children that is manifested by constant restlessness, overactivity, distractibility, and difficulties in learning. Also called hyperkinesis. *See also* attention-deficit hyperactivity disorder; minimal brain dysfunction.

**hyperalgesia**  Excessive sensitivity to pain.

**hyperesthesia**  Increased sensitivity to tactile stimulation.

**hyperkinesis**  HYPERACTIVITY.

**hyperkinetic reaction of childhood**  DSM-II diagnosis replaced by "attention deficit disorder with hyperactivity" in DSM-III, and "attention-deficit hyperactivity disorder" in DSM-III-R. *See also* minimal brain dysfunction.

**hyperkinetic syndrome**  Disorder characterized by excessive muscular activity (hyperactivity) such as restlessness, aggressiveness, and destructive activity. *See also* attention-deficit hyperactivity disorder; minimal brain dysfunction.

**hypermnesia**  Exaggerated degree of retention and recall. It can be elicited by hypnosis and may be seen in certain prodigies; also may be a feature of obsessive-compulsive disorder, some cases of schizophrenia, and manic episodes of bipolar disorder.

**hyperorexia** Extreme appetite. *See also* bulimia nervosa.

**hyperpragia** Excessive thinking and mental 'activity, generally associated with the manic phase of bipolar disorder.

**hypersomnia** Excessive time spent asleep which may be nonorganic, organic, narcoleptic, idiopathic, part of the Klein-Levin syndrome, or primary in nature.

**hypertensive crisis** HYPERTENSIVE ENCEPHALOPATHY.

**hypertensive encephalopathy** Acute syndrome in which severe hypertension is associated with headache, nausea, vomiting, visual disturbances, convulsions, and alterations in consciousness characterized by confusion, somnolence, stupor, and coma. Prompt lowering of the blood pressure by pharmacological means may reverse the picture in 24–48 hours; if the blood pressure is not controlled, intracerebral hemorrhage and a fatal outcome may result. Usually, the patient has entered the malignant phase of essential or secondary hypertension, with marked blood pressure elevation (generally in the range of 250/150 mm Hg) and evidence of cardiac decompensation, declining renal function, and advanced hypertensive retinopathy; also seen as a side effect of monoamine oxidase inhibitors when tyramine-containing foods are consumed. Also called hypertensive crisis.

**hyperventilation** Excessive breathing, generally associated with anxiety, which can cause a reduction in blood carbon dioxide that produces symptoms of lightheadedness, palpitations, numbness and tingling periorally and in the extremities, and occasionally syncope.

**hypervigilance** Continual scanning of the environment for signs of threat.

**hypesthesia** Diminished sensitivity to tactile stimulation.

**hypnagogic hallucination** Hallucination occurring while falling asleep, not ordinarily considered pathological.

**hypnoanalysis** Use of hypnosis in psychoanalysis to gain access to unconscious processes that the patient cannot reveal by means of ordinary therapeutic maneuvers.

**hypnodrama** Psychodrama under hypnotic trance; the patient is put into a hypnotic trance and encouraged to act out various past experiences.

**hypnoid state** Freud's term describing an alteration of consciousness that occurs characteristically in hysteria during periods of emotional stress; characterized by heightened suggestibility and provides a basis for hysterical somatic symptom formation.

**hypnophobia**   Abnormal fear of sleep.

**hypnopompic hallucination**   Hallucination occurring while awakening from sleep, ordinarily not considered pathological.

**hypnosis**   Artificially induced alteration of consciousness characterized by increased suggestibility and receptivity to direction.

**hypnotherapy**   Therapy that makes use of hypnosis.

**hypnotic**   Drug used for the express purpose of producing sleep. *Compare* sedative.

**hypoactive sexual desire disorder**   Sexual desire disorder characterized by deficiency or absence of sexual fantasies and desire for sexual activity.

**hypochondriacal neurosis**   HYPOCHONDRIASIS.

**hypochondriasis**   Somatoform disorder characterized by excessive, morbid anxiety about one's health; hypochondriacal patients exhibit a predominant disturbance in which the physical symptoms or complaints are not explainable on the basis of demonstrable organic findings and are apparently linked to psychological factors. Also called hypochondriacal neurosis.

**hypoglycemia**   Abnormally small concentration of glucose in the circulating blood; associated with anxiety and depression.

**hypomania**   Mood abnormality with the qualitative characteristics of mania but somewhat less intense.

**hypothalamus**   Principal center in the forebrain for integration of visceral functions involving the autonomic nervous system. Functions include regulation of sexual activity, water, fat, and carbohydrate metabolism, and temperature; also appears to play a role in the nervous mechanisms underlying moods and motivational states.

**hysteria**   *See* hysterical neurosis.

**hysterical anesthesia**   Functional disorder characterized by the absence of tactile sensation in an area of the body; observed in certain cases of conversion disorder.

**hysterical neurosis**   Diagnostic category (also called hysteria) for a neurosis involving a sudden impairment of function in response to emotional stress. In the conversion type, there is functional impairment in one of the special senses or in the voluntary nervous system; the dissociative type is manifested by an alteration in state of consciousness or by such symptoms as amnesia, disorientation, fugue, somnambulism, or multiple personality. Also called conversion disorder and dissociative disorder, respectively, in DSM-III-R.

**hysterical personality** *See* histrionic personality disorder.

**hysterics** Expression of emotion often accompanied by crying, laughing, and screaming; a term generally used by laypersons rather than by psychiatrists.

# I

**iatrogenic**  Denoting an unfavorable response to a mode of treatment induced by the treatment itself. *Compare* idiopathic.

**ICD**  International Classification of Diseases.

**ice**  Pure form of methamphetamine that can be either inhaled or injected intravenously by abusers; its psychological effects last for hours and are particularly potent. Unlike the cocaine of crack, which has to be imported, ice is a synthetic drug that can be manufactured in domestic illicit laboratories.

**ICT**  Insulin coma therapy.

**Id**  One of the three components of the psychic apparatus in the freudian structural framework, the others being the ego and superego. It operates unconsciously; harbors the innate, biological, instinctual drives; is the source of psychic energy (libido); follows the pleasure principle; seeks immediate reduction of drive tension without regard for external reality; and is under the influence of the primary-process mental activity that characterizes the unconscious.

**idealization**  Mental mechanism whereby a person consciously or unconsciously overestimates an admired attribute or aspect of another person.

**idea of reference**  Misinterpretation of incidents and events in the outside world as having a direct personal reference to oneself; occasionally observed in normal persons, but frequently seen in paranoid patients. If present with sufficient frequency or intensity or if organized and systematized, they constitute delusions of reference.

**ideas of unreality**  Thought that events are artificial, illusory, unpredictable, or do not exist.

**ideational shield**  Intellectual, rational defense against the anxiety that persons would feel if they became vulnerable to the criticisms and rejection of others; as a result of their fear of being rejected, they may feel threatened if they criticize another person, an act that is unacceptable to them. In both group and individual therapy, conditions are set up that allow the participants to lower the ideational shield.

**idée fixe**  Fixed idea that is recurrent and most often associated with obsessional states.

**identical twins**  MONOZYGOTIC TWINS.

**identification**  Unconscious defense mechanism by which a person patterns himself or herself after another person; in the process, the self is more or less permanently altered. *See also* healthy identification; imitation.

**identification with the aggressor**  Unconscious process by which a person incorporates within himself or herself the mental image of a person who represents a source of frustration from the outside world; a primitive defense that operates in the interest and service of the developing ego. A classic example of this defense occurs toward the end of the oedipal stage, when a boy, whose main source of love and gratification is his mother, identifies with his father who represents the source of frustration, being the powerful rival for the mother; the child cannot master or run away from his father, so he is obliged to identify with him.

**identity**  One's global role in life and the perception of the sense of self; problems with identity are common during adolescence, in schizophrenia, and in the borderline and schizotypal personalities.

**identity crisis**  Social role conflict as perceived by a person; loss of the sense of personal sameness and historical continuity, and/or inability to accept or adopt the role the person believes is expected by society. Identity crises are frequent in adolescence.

**identity disorder**  In DSM-III-R, a disorder characterized by a chaotic sense of self; a loss of the sense of personal sameness, usually involving a social role conflict as perceived by the individual. It is common in adolescence, when adolescents feel unwilling or unable to accept or adopt the roles they believe are expected of them by society; often manifested by isolation, withdrawal, rebelliousness, negativity, and extremism.

**idiopathic**  Without known or identifiable cause. *Compare* iatrogenic.

**idiot**  Obsolete and pejorative term for a classification of mental retardation in which individuals have a mental age of less than 3 years.

**idiotropic**  Egocentric or introspective.

**idiot-savant**  Mentally retarded person who is able to perform unusual mental feats in sharply circumscribed intellectual areas, such as complicated calculations or puzzle solving.

**I-It** Philosopher Martin Buber's description of damaging interpersonal relationships. If a person treats himself or herself or another person exclusively as an object, he or she prevents mutuality, trust, and growth. When pervasive in a group, I-It relationships prevent human warmth, destroy cohesiveness, and retard group process. *Compare* I-Thou.

**illogicality** Pattern of speech or thinking in which conclusions that are reached do not follow logically; may take the form of unwarranted or faulty inferences.

**illuminism** State of hallucination in which a patient converses with imaginary supernatural creatures.

**illusion** Perceptual misinterpretation of a real external stimulus. *Compare* hallucination.

**imago** Jungian term referring to an idealized unconscious mental image of a key person in someone's early life.

**imbecile** Obsolete and pejorative term for a classification of mental retardation in which individuals have a mental age of 3–7 years.

**imitation** Duplication or mimicking of behaviors or portions of behaviors observed in a model. *See also* identification.

**immediate memory** Reproduction, recognition, or recall of perceived material within seconds after presentation. *Compare* long-term memory; short-term memory.

**impaired insight** Diminished ability to understand the objective reality of a situation.

**impaired judgment** *See* judgment.

**implosion** Behavior therapy technique in which anxiety-arousing stimuli are vividly presented in imagination; the patient repeatedly experiences intense anxiety in the absence of objective danger until the anxiety response is extinguished.

**impotence** Inability to achieve penile erection. The official DSM-III-R diagnosis is male erectile disorder.

**imprinting** Particular kind of learning that occurs during an early critical developmental stage in animals, characterized by rapid acquisition and great resistance to extinction. It seems to represent a biologically predetermined proclivity to learn certain persistent species-specific behavior patterns, given exposure to the proper stimulus during the critical stage, but its precise role in human behavioral development has not been established.

**improvisation** In psychodrama, the acting out of situations without prior preparation.

**impulse**  Psychic striving or urge to perform an action. *See also* drive; instinct.

**impulse control**  Ability to resist an impulse, drive, or temptation to perform some action.

**impulse control disorders**  Mental disorders in which there is weak impulse control with impulsive behavior that is usually irresistible, pleasurable, and aimed at obtaining immediate gratification, without regard for the consequences of the behavior, e.g., pathological gambling, kleptomania, pyromania, intermittent explosive disorder, trichotillomania.

**impulsion**  Blind following of internal drives without regard for social acceptance or pressure from the superego, normally seen in young children. In adults, it is common in those with weak defensive organizations; in such cases it tends to be a symbolic phenomenon.

**inappropriate affect**  Emotional tone out of harmony with the idea, thought, or speech accompanying it.

**incest**  Sexual activity between close blood relatives. Common patterns are father-daughter, mother-son, and between siblings; may also be homosexually oriented.

**incidence**  Research term for the number of cases of a disease whose onset occurs during a specific period of time. *See also* prevalence.

**incidence rate**  Rate at which new cases of a disease or a condition are occurring. The incidence rate per 1,000 persons in the population is the number of new cases that occur within a defined unit of time, divided by the persons exposed or at risk during the same time unit, multiplied by 1,000.

**incoherence**  Communication that is disconnected, disorganized, or incomprehensible. *See also* word salad.

**incompetence**  Legal term indicating that thought processes are inadequate for sound judgment and may lead to maladaptive or abnormal behavior; legally, incompetent persons cannot be held responsible for their actions.

**incorporation**  Primitive unconscious defense mechanism in which the psychic representation of another person or aspects of another person are assimilated into oneself through a figurative process of symbolic oral ingestion; represents a special form of introjection and is the earliest mechanism of identification.

**independent variable**  In research methodology, those qualities that the experimenter systematically varies, e.g., time, dosage.

**individual psychology** System of psychiatric theory developed by Alfred Adler that stresses compensation and overcompensation for feelings of inferiority in a person's strivings to adapt to the social milieu, and emphasizes the interpersonal nature of a person's problems; applied by some practitioners to group psychotherapy and counseling.

**individual therapy** Traditional dyadic therapeutic technique in which a psychotherapist treats only one patient during a given therapeutic session.

**individuation** Jungian term denoting a process whereby the person molds and develops a healthy integrated individual personality through maximum differentiation and development of each system of the personality. *See also* actualization.

**Indoklon therapy** Type of biologic therapy in which a convulsive seizure is induced by the inhalation of the drug Indoklon (hexafluorodiethyl ethcr).

**indolamine** Class of biogenic amines that contain an indole ring and are derived from the essential amino acid tryptophan; includes lysergic acid diethylamide (LSD) and serotonin. Monoamine oxidase inhibitors elevate the levels of indolamines by delaying their breakdown.

**induced psychotic disorder** Rare disorder in which the delusional system of the patient has developed out of a close relationship with another person who had a previously established, similar delusional system. Called shared paranoid disorder in DSM-III; in the past, also called folie à deux.

**industrial psychiatry** Branch of psychiatry concerned with workers' adjustments to their jobs and with the effects of a business organization on its members.

**ineffability** Ecstatic state in which a person insists that his or her experience is inexpressible and indescribable, that it is impossible to convey what it is like to one who never experienced it.

**infancy** Childhood period of helplessness and marked dependency, generally the first year of life.

**infantile articulation** DEVELOPMENTAL ARTICULATION DISORDER.

**infantile autism** Syndrome beginning in infancy and characterized by withdrawal and self-absorption, failure to develop attachment to a parental figure, ineffective communication and mutism, preoccupation with inanimate objects, and an obsessive demand for sameness in the environment. Also called Kanner's syndrome; autistic disorder in DSM-III-R. *See also* autistic thinking.

**infantile dynamics**   Psychodynamic integrations, such as the Oedipus complex, that are organized during childhood and continue to exert an unconscious influence on adult personality.

**infantile perseveration**   DEVELOPMENTAL ARTICULATION DISORDER.

**infantile sexuality**   Freudian concept regarding the erotic life of infants and children, that, from birth, infants are capable of erotic activities; encompasses the overlapping phases of psychosexual development during the first 5 years of life and includes the oral phase (birth to 18 months), the anal phase (ages 1 to 3), and the phallic phase (ages 2 to 6).

**infant psychiatry**   That aspect of child psychiatry concerned with the diagnosis, treatment, and prevention of maladaptive psychological functioning in infants.

**inferential statistics**   Methods used for drawing general conclusions about probabilities on the basis of a sample. *See also* statistical inference.

**inferiority complex**   Concept, originated by Alfred Adler, that everyone is born with a feeling of inferiority or inadequacy secondary to real or fantasied organic or psychological deficits; how the inferiority or feeling of inferiority is handled determines a person's behavior in life. *See also* masculine protest.

**informal admission**   As a general hospital model, a patient admitted to a psychiatric unit is free to enter and to leave, even against medical advice.

**information theory**   System dealing with the transmission, reception, and distortion of communicated messages.

**informed consent**   Consent given by a patient to a physician to perform a procedure legally requires that the patient be informed of the nature of the proposed procedure, its risks, its proposed benefits, and the available alternatives; the major problem in giving informed consent, legally and psychologically, is the extent or depth of disclosure.

**infradian rhythm**   *See* biological rhythm.

**infusion**   Introduction of fluid other than blood, e.g., medicines, into a vein.

**inhalant**   Substance taken in by breathing. Production of psychoactive effects by the ingestion of such volatile substances as gasoline, airplane glue, aerosols (especially spray paints), or rubber cement, warrants the DSM-III-R diagnosis of inhalant dependence or inhalant abuse.

**inhibited female orgasm** Recurrent and persistent inhibition (absence) of the female orgasm, referring to the inability of a female to achieve orgasm by masturbation or coitus. Also called anorgasmia.

**inhibited male orgasm** Difficulty or inability of a male in achieving ejaculation during coitus. Also called ejaculatory incompetence; retarded ejaculation. *See also* primary retarded ejaculation; secondary retarded ejaculation.

**inhibited sexual excitement** Former term for female sexual arousal disorder.

**inhibition** Limitation or renunciation of ego functions occurring consciously, alone or in combinations, to evade anxiety arising out of conflict with instinctual impulses, the superego, or environmental forces or figures.

**initial insomnia** Falling asleep with difficulty; usually seen in anxiety disorder. *Compare* middle insomnia; terminal insomnia.

**insane** Of or pertaining to one who is of unsound mind. A legal rather than a psychiatric term.

**insanity** Legal concept denoting a mental disturbance, due to which a person lacks criminal responsibility for an alleged crime and hence cannot be convicted of the crime. *See also* American Law Institute formulation of insanity; Durham rule; M'Naghten rule.

**insanity defense** Criminal law defense plea that a person lacks criminal responsibility by reason of insanity.

**insecurity** Feelings of helplessness, unprotectedness, and inadequacy in the face of manifold anxieties arising from uncertainty regarding one's goals, ideals, abilities, and relations to others.

**insight** Conscious recognition of one's own condition. In psychiatry, it more specifically refers to the conscious awareness and understanding of one's own psychodynamics and symptoms of maladaptive behavior; highly important in effecting changes in the personality and behavior of a person.

**insight-oriented psychotherapy** Psychotherapy based on the principles of psychoanalysis in which persons develop a conscious awareness and understanding of their own psychodynamics and symptoms of maladaptive behavior. There is greater emphasis on day-to-day reality issues and a lesser emphasis on the development of transference issues than in psychoanalysis.

**insight therapy**   *See* insight-oriented psychotherapy.

**insomnia disorder**   Difficulty in falling asleep or difficulty in staying asleep. It can be related to another mental disorder (nonorganic), can be related to a known organic factor (such as a physical disorder or a medication), or can be primary (not related to a known organic factor or to another mental disorder). *See also* initial insomnia; middle insomnia; terminal insomnia.

**instinct**   Basic inborn urge or drive. Freud postulated the existence of two opposing primal instincts: a life instinct (eros) and a death instinct (thanatos). An extensive array of human instincts has been proposed, including possessive instinct, mastery instinct, and herd or social instinct. Because of its implication of a fixed, essentially unalterable, largely hereditary response or psychic tendency that does not involve learning or reason, the term has become ambiguous and controversial when applied to human behavior. Many modern psychoanalysts prefer the term "drive" for what Freud termed "instinct." *See also* drive.

**institutionalization**   Process of placing a patient in a facility for extended care, e.g., a mental hospital or nursing home.

**instrumental conditioning**   OPERANT CONDITIONING. *See* conditioning.

**insulin coma therapy (ICT)**   Type of biologic therapy in which large amounts of insulin are given to a psychotic patient, usually a schizophrenic, producing profound hypoglycemia and resulting in a coma; introduced by Manfred Sakel in 1933, it declined in use drastically after the introduction of antipsychotic drugs. An occasionally used early stage of this treatment is called subcoma therapy.

**intake**   Initial interview between a patient and a member of a psychiatric team, a term usually used in connection with admission to a mental health facility.

**integration**   Constructive organizing, absorbing, and incorporating into the personality of data and experience; also refers to an amalgamation of separate parts into a functioning integral whole.

**intellectual insight**   Knowledge of the reality of a situation without the ability to successfully use that knowledge to effect an adaptive change in behavior. *Compare* true insight.

**intellectualization**   Unconscious defense mechanism in which reasoning or logic is used in an attempt to avoid confrontation with an objectionable impulse and thus defend against anxiety. Also called brooding compulsion; thinking compulsion.

**intellectual subaverage functioning**   I.Q. of more than two standard deviations below the test mean obtained on an intelligence test.

**intelligence**   Capacity for learning and ability to recall, integrate constructively, and apply what one has learned; the capacity to understand and to think rationally.

**intelligence quotient (I.Q.)**   Numerical measure of mental capability determined by dividing a mental age (M.A.) score achieved on a specific test, such as the Stanford-Binet Test, by the patient's chronological age (C.A.) and multiplying by 100.

**intermission**   In psychiatry, the interval between attacks of a particular syndrome; when it is not certain that the symptoms will return, the interval is called a remission.

**intermittent explosive disorder**   Condition in which a person has discrete episodes of losing control of aggressive impulses resulting in serious assault or destruction of property; often caused by a disorder of brain physiology, particularly in the limbic system.

**intermittent reinforcement**   Any schedule of reinforcement in which the response is not always reinforced.

**International Classification of Diseases (ICD)**   World Health Organization's official list of disease categories subscribed to by all WHO member nations. ICD-CM is ICD's clinical modification, first published in 1979.

**internship**   First year of clinical training following medical school, now called postgraduate year I (PGY-I), which progresses onto residency training in a specialty area.

**interobserver reliability**   Degree of concurrence or disagreement among observers of a single event.

**interpersonal conflict**   EXTRAPSYCHIC CONFLICT.

**Interpersonal psychiatry**   Dynamic-cultural system of psychiatry based on Harry Stack Sullivan's interpersonal theory, which proposes that each person must be viewed as an entity interacting with the sociocultural and interpersonal environment; emphasis is on interactive experiences.

**interpersonal skill**   Effectiveness of adaptive behavior in relation to other persons; ability to express feelings appropriately, to be socially responsible and responsive, and to work in harmony with others.

**interpretation**  The formulation or description by the therapist to the patient of the therapist's understanding of the symbolic significance or meaning of any aspect of the patient's intrapsychic processes, behavior, or verbal productions; an attempt is made to construct into a more meaningful form the patient's resistances, defenses, transferences, and other symbolic activities, e.g., dreams, fantasies.

*Interpretation of Dreams, The*  Sigmund Freud's major presentation (1899) not only of his theories about the meaning of dreams, a subject hitherto regarded as outside scientific interest, but also of his concept of a mental apparatus topographically divided into unconscious, preconscious, and conscious areas.

**interview**  Person-to-person interaction in which information about a subject is collected. *See also* structured interview; unstructured interview.

**intoxication**  Organic mental disorder due to the recent ingestion or presence in the body of an exogenous substance producing maladaptive behavior by virtue of its effects on the central nervous system. The most common psychiatric changes involve disturbances of perception, wakefulness, attention, thinking, judgment, emotional control, and psychomotor behavior; the specific clinical picture depends on the nature of the substance ingested. For types of intoxication, see the specific term.

**intrapersonal conflict**  INTRAPSYCHIC CONFLICT.

**intrapsychic**  Referring to what originates, takes place, or is situated within the psyche or mind.

**intrapsychic ataxia**  *See* ataxia.

**intrapsychic conflict**  State of tension arising from the clash of two or more incompatible or opposing forces; e.g., wishes, needs, motives, thoughts operating within oneself. Also called intrapersonal conflict. *Compare* extrapsychic conflict.

**intravenous**  Denoting introduction of a substance into a vein or veins. *See also* infusion.

**introjection**  Unconscious, symbolic internalization of a psychic representation of a hated or loved external object with the goal of establishing closeness to and constant presence of the object; considered an immature defense mechanism. In the case of a loved object, anxiety consequent to separation or tension arising out of ambivalence toward the object is diminished; in the case of a feared or hated object, internalization of its malicious or aggressive characteristics serves to avoid anxiety by symbolically putting those characteristics under one's own control. *See also* incorporation.

**intropunitive**   Turning anger inward toward oneself; commonly observed in depressed patients.

**introspection**   Contemplating one's own mental processes so as to achieve insight.

**introversion**   State in which a person's energies are directed inward toward the self, with little or no interest in the external world. *Compare* extroversion.

**introverted personality disorder**   SCHIZOID PERSONALITY DISORDER.

**inversion**   Sigmund Freud's term for homosexuality, in which he distinguished three types: absolute, amphigenous, and occasional.

**involuntary admission**   Hospitalization of a person against his or her will. Following an application by a friend or relative for the admittance of a person who does not recognize the need for hospital care, certification by two physicians is required, which allows the patient to be hospitalized for 60 days. Patients have access to legal counsel and, if brought to court, a judge can order the patient's release. After 60 days, the case must be reviewed by a board (of psychiatrists, physicians, lawyers, and citizens not affiliated with the hospital). *See also* parens patriae.

**involuntary discharge**   Termination of hospitalization against a patient's will.

**involuntary treatment**   Care of a person, who has a mental disorder that constitutes a danger to self or others, against that person's will.

**involutional melancholia**   Depression occurring in late middle age in persons who generally have no history of previous mental illness. Characteristic manifestations include delusions of sin, guilt, or poverty; an obsession with death; preoccupation with somatic, particularly gastrointestinal, function; despair, dejection, agitation, anxiety, and insomnia; and, in some cases, paranoid ideation. The term is not used in DSM-III-R, but is replaced by the diagnosis of major depressive episode, melancholic type. Also called involutional psychosis.

**involutional psychosis**   INVOLUTIONAL MELANCHOLIA.

**I.Q.**   Intelligence quotient.

**irrelevant answer**   Answer that is not responsive to the question.

**irresistible impulse**   Concept that a person charged with a criminal offense is not responsible for his or her act if the act was committed under an impulse that the person was unable to resist because of mental disease. The courts have chosen to interpret this law in such a way that it has been called the "policeman-at-the-elbow" law; in other words, the court will grant the impulse to be irresistible only if it determines that the accused would have gone ahead with the act even if he or she had had a policeman at his or her elbow.

**irritability**   Abnormal or excessive excitability, with easily triggered anger, annoyance, or impatience.

**irritable mood**   State in which one is easily annoyed and provoked to anger. *See also* irritability.

**isolated explosive disorder**   Disorder of impulse control in which a person has a single episode characterized by a failure to resist a violent impulse against others.

**isolation**   In psychoanalysis, a defense mechanism involving the separation of an idea or memory from its attached feeling tone; unacceptable ideational content is thereby rendered free of its disturbing or unpleasant emotional charge. *Compare* relatedness. *See also* alienation.

**isophilic**   Term used by Harry Stack Sullivan to mean liking or feeling affectionate toward people of the same sex, without the sexual or erotic aspects of homosexuality.

**I-Thou**   Philosopher Martin Buber's conception that a person's identity develops from the true sharing by persons; basic trust can occur in a living partnership in which each member identifies the particular real personality of the other in his or her wholeness, unity, and uniqueness. In groups, I-Thou relationships promote warmth, cohesiveness, and constructive group process. *Compare* I-It.

# J

**jacksonian epilepsy**  Epilepsy characterized by recurrent episodes of focal motor seizures that usually begin with a highly localized tonic contraction or clonic movement which increases in severity and spreads progressively, often involving the entire body and terminating in a characteristic generalized convulsion with loss of consciousness; implies organic cerebral disease.

**jamais vu**  Paramnestic phenomenon characterized by a false feeling of unfamiliarity with a real situation that one has experienced.

**James-Lange theory of emotion**  Theory that the experience of emotion is preceded by a visceral or motor response, e.g., first the person runs and then feels fear.

**Janet, Pierre** (1859–1947)  Last great representative of the French school of psychiatry, known for his concept of psychological automatism and for his interest in cases of multiple personalities; first used the term "la belle indifférence."

**jargon aphasia**  Aphasia in which the words produced are neologistic, i.e., nonsense words created by the patient.

**JCAHO**  Joint Commission on Accreditation of Healthcare Organizations. Formerly JCAH, Joint Commission on Accreditation of Hospitals.

**JCMHC**  Joint Commission on Mental Health of Children.

**Joint Commission on Accreditation of Healthcare Organizations (JCAHO)**  Group of agencies that influence the standards and performance of hospitals and health organizations; they inspect hospitals every 2 years and determine requirements for hospital accreditation (on which hospital reimbursements from Medicare and Medicaid are contingent).

**Joint Commission on Mental Health of Children (JCMHC)**  Multidisciplinary agency authorized by U.S. Congress in 1965 to monitor the treatment of children with emotional illness.

**Joint Commission on Mental Illness and Health**  Multidisciplinary study group established in 1955 whose "Action for Mental Health" (1961) was instrumental in the legislation and federal funding for community mental health centers; with the passage of the Community Mental Health Centers Act in 1963, deinstitutionalization became a reality.

**Jones, Ernest** (1879–1958)  Welsh psychoanalyst, and one of Freud's early followers, who was an organizer of the American Psychoanalytic Association (1911) and of the British Psychoanalytical Society (1919) and a founder and long-time editor of the journal of the International Psychoanalytical Association; a prolific author most noted for his three-volume biography of Sigmund Freud.

**judgment**  Mental act of comparing or evaluating choices within the framework of a given set of values for the purpose of electing a course of action. If the course of action chosen is consonant with reality or with mature adult standards of behavior, judgment is said to be intact or normal; judgment is said to be impaired if the chosen course of action is frankly maladaptive, results from impulsive decisions based on the need for immediate gratification, or is otherwise not consistent with reality as measured by mature adult standards.

**Jung, Carl Gustav** (1875–1961)  Swiss psychiatrist and psychoanalyst, originally associated with Sigmund Freud, who later founded the school of analytic psychology.

**justice**  In the context of mental health, a fair distribution and application of psychiatric procedures.

# K

**Kanner's syndrome** INFANTILE AUTISM.

**kindling effect** Electrophysiologic process in which repeated subthreshold stimulation of a neuron eventually generates an action potential; at the organ level, repeated subthreshold stimulation of an area of the brain results in the generation of a seizure.

**kinesiology** Study of body movement, especially in the context of its communicative function.

**kinesthetic hallucination** Hallucination primarily involving bodily movement.

**kinesthetic sense** Sense by which muscular motion, tension, position, and posture are perceived. Also called proprioception.

**Kirkbride, Thomas S.** (1809–1883) American psychiatrist, one of the 13 original founders of the American Psychiatric Association, noted for his 1854 manual advocating reform in the design of institutions for the mentally ill.

**Klein, Melanie** (1882–1960) British psychoanalyst and child analyst whose theories of early development departed from orthodox freudian thought.

**Kleine-Levin syndrome** Condition characterized by periodic episodes of hypersomnia and bulimia; most often seen in adolescent boys and eventually disappears spontaneously.

**kleptomania** Pathological compulsion to steal.

**Klinefelter's syndrome** Chromosomal anomaly in which there is an extra X chromosome (karyotype 47-XXY). Affected persons are male in development, with small firm testes, eunuchoid habitus, variable gynecomastia and other signs of androgen deficiency, and elevated gonadotropin levels; there is an increased frequency of mental retardation (about 25%) and other forms of psychopathology, particularly antisocial behavior and delinquency. *See also* Turner's syndrome.

**Klüver-Bucy syndrome** Behavioral syndrome, first described in monkeys after bilateral temporal lobe ablation, characterized by increased oral, sexual, and aggressive behavior; loss of visual recognition; memory defect; and hyperreactivity to visual stimuli.

**Kohut, Heinz** (1913–1981)   Important innovator in psychoanalysis, who originated the psychoanalytic school of self-psychology, which requires that patients become aware of their excessive needs for approval and self-gratification.

**koro**   Acute delusional syndrome, seen in Southeast Asia and southern China, in which the patient suddenly becomes acutely anxious that his penis is shrinking and may disappear into his abdomen, in which case he will die.

**Korsakoff's psychosis**   Organic mental disorder seen in long-term alcoholics. Its major characteristic feature is a profound memory impairment, particularly for recent events, for which the individual attempts to compensate by confabulation. Called alcohol amnestic disorder in DSM-III-R. *See also* Wernicke's fluent encephalopathy.

**Kraepelin, Emil** (1865–1926)   German psychiatrist noted for his pioneering work in psychiatric nosology and classification systems, and who differentiated between manic-depressive psychoses and dementia precox (schizophrenia). One of the last representatives of the predynamic school of psychiatry, he is often considered the father of descriptive psychiatry.

**Kretschmer, Ernest** (1888–1964)   German psychiatrist noted for his theories of the relation of physique to character and personality.

# L

**la belle indifférence**  Inappropriate attitude of calm or lack of concern about one's disability; seen in patients with conversion disorder.

**labile**  Unstable; characterized by rapidly changing emotions.

**labile affect**  Affective expression characterized by repetitious and abrupt shifts.

**lability**  *See* emotional lability.

**laconic speech**  Condition characterized by a reduction in the quantity of spontaneous speech; replies to questions are brief and unelaborated, and little or no unprompted additional information is provided. Occurs in major depression, schizophrenia, and organic mental disorders. Also called poverty of speech.

**lacunar amnesia**  LOCALIZED AMNESIA.

**lalophobia**  Abnormal fear of speaking. Also called glossophobia.

**language disorder**  Disturbance of speech or writing characterized by failure to follow semantic and syntactic rules; e.g., incoherence, clang association, word approximation, neologism. *See also* communication disorder.

**lanugo**  Neonatal-like body hair; may be noted in anorexia nervosa.

**lapsus linguae**  Slip of the tongue.

**latah**  Culture-specific disorder found among Malaysians and characterized by either a sudden onset of unusual and inappropriate motor and verbal manifestations or by an echo reaction, in which the victim is compelled to imitate any words or actions to which he or she is exposed; in both forms affected persons cannot control or inhibit their behavior.

**late luteal phase dysphoric disorder (LLPDD)**  Pattern of emotional and behavioral symptoms that occur in women during the last week of the luteal phase of the menstrual cycle and remit within a few days after the onset of the follicular phase. Among the most commonly experienced symptoms are marked affective lability (e.g., sudden episodes of fearfulness, sadness, or irritability); persistent feelings of irritability, anger, or tension (feeling "on edge"); and feelings of depression and self-deprecating thoughts. In DSM-III-R, a proposed diagnostic category needing further study.

**latency phase**  Period of psychosexual development after the phallic phase and succeeded by the genital phase, extending from about age 5 to the beginning of adolescence at age 12; during this phase there is an apparent cessation of sexual preoccupation and a blockade of libidinal impulses, and boys and girls are inclined to choose friends and join groups of their own sex.

**latent content**  Hidden or unconscious meaning of symbolic representations, especially in fantasies and dreams. *See also* manifest content.

**latent homosexuality**  Unexpressed conscious or unconscious homoerotic wishes that are held in check. Sigmund Freud's theory of bisexuality postulated the existence of a constitutionally determined, although experientially influenced, instinctual masculine-feminine duality; normally, the opposite-sex component is dormant, but a breakdown in the defenses of repression and sublimation may activate latent instincts and result in overt homoeroticism.

**latent schizophrenia**  Condition characterized by clear schizophrenic symptoms without a history of prior overtly psychotic schizophrenic episodes. In DSM-III-R the condition is subsumed under the category of schizotypal personality disorder.

**learned autonomic control**  Learned regulation by a person of physiological responses that are under autonomic nervous system control. *See also* biofeedback.

**learned helplessness**  *See* helplessness (1).

**learning disability**  Disorder manifested in school-age children and characterized by specific difficulties in learning that are unrelated to intelligence, e.g., dyslexia.

**learning theory**  Approach to the understanding of human behavior that emphasizes the way in which learning comes about. Learning itself represents a change in behavior resulting from practice; through the application of certain laws of learning, learning theory attempts to explain the basic processes that are necessary for learning to occur.

**lesbianism**  Female homosexuality. Also called sapphism.

**lethologica**  Momentary forgetting of a name.

**leukotomy**  LOBOTOMY.

**Lewin, Kurt**  (1890–1947)  German psychologist who emigrated to the United States in 1933. Two of his chief theoretical contributions are the field approach (field theory) and group dynamics, each of which has been useful in the experimental study of human behavior in a social situation.

**Liaison Committee on Medical Education (LCME)**  Group sponsored by the American Medical Association and the Association of American Medical Colleges that is principally involved in accrediting activities in undergraduate medical education.

**liaison nursing**  Communication among nurses from various disciplines concerning the treatment of medical, surgical, and neuropsychiatric patients.

**liaison psychiatry**  *See* consultation-liaison psychiatry.

**libido**  In psychoanalysis, the psychic energy associated with the sexual drive (life instinct).

**life instinct**  SEXUAL DRIVE.

**lifetime expectancy**  Total probability of a person developing a disorder during a lifetime.

**lifetime prevalence**  Measure at a point in time of the number of persons who had a given disorder at some time during their lives.

**lilliputian hallucination**  Visual sensation that persons or objects are reduced in size, more properly regarded as an illusion. *See also* micropsia.

**limbic system**  James Papez' proposal (1939) that a reverberating circuit or system, consisting of the hippocampus, hypothalamus, anterior thalamus, and cingulate gyrus, was the central nervous system localization for emotions; current models also include the amygdala and septal area, as well as other neuroanatomic areas. Various parts of the limbic system have been associated with emotions, sex drive, eating behavior, rage, violence, memory, and motivation.

**lithium carbonate**  Lithium salt effective in the treatment of the manic phase of bipolar disorder and as a mood-stabilizing drug for chronic manic-depressive patients; may also be an effective antidepressant in some patients.

**Little Albert**  Eleven month old boy who was conditioned to fear furry objects in experiments conducted by American psychologist John B. Watson (1920) to demonstrate that phobias are learned responses based on classical conditioning.

**Little Hans**  Sigmund Freud's famous case history of a 5-year-old boy with a phobia. The boy's fear of horses, instead of his father, helped him to avoid hating his father, by whom he was threatened and whom he also loved.

**living will**   Legal document in which patients give instructions to their physicians about withholding life support measures, e.g., Do Not Resuscitate (DNR) if in extremis.

**LCME**   Liaison Committee on Medical Education.

**LLPDD**   Late luteal phase dysphoric disorder.

**LNNB**   Luria-Nebraska Neuropsychological Battery.

**lobotomy**   Neurosurgical procedure, introduced by Egas Moniz, in which one or more nerve tracts in a lobe of the cerebrum are severed. Prefrontal lobotomy is the ablation of one or more nerve tracts in the prefrontal area of the brain and has been used in the treatment of certain severe mental disorders that do not respond to other treatments. Also called leukotomy.

**localized amnesia**   Partial loss of memory; amnesia restricted to specific or isolated experiences. Also called lacunar amnesia; patch amnesia.

**locus ceruleus**   Nucleus (a collection of neuronal cell bodies) that is located in the pons (a region of the brain stem) and contains the largest population of noradrenergic neurons in a single identified brain region; these neurons project their axons to virtually every region of the brain and are thought to be involved in the regulation of mood, anxiety, and attention.

**logorrhea**   Copious, pressured, coherent speech; uncontrollable, excessive talking; observed in manic episodes of bipolar disorder. Also called tachylogia; verbomania; volubility.

**logotherapy**   Existential analysis based on spiritual values, rather than psychobiological laws.

**long-term memory**   Reproduction, recognition, or recall of experiences or information that were experienced in the distant past. Also called remote memory. *Compare* immediate memory; short-term memory.

**longitudinal study**   Examination or analysis carried out over a long period of time.

**loosening of associations**   Characteristic schizophrenic thinking or speech disturbance involving a disorder in the logical progression of thoughts, manifested as a failure to adequately verbally communicate; unrelated and unconnected ideas shift from one subject to another. *See also* tangentiality.

**Lou Gehrig's disease**   AMYOTROPHIC LATERAL SCLEROSIS.

**LP**   Lumbar puncture.

**LSD**   Lysergic acid diethylamide.

**lumbar puncture (LP)**   Use of a needle inserted into the lumbar spine intervertebral space to obtain cerebrospinal fluid for diagnostic purposes or to introduce local anesthetics or other drugs.

**Luria-Nebraska Neuropsychological Battery (LNNB)**   Based on the work of the Russian psychologist A. R. Luria, the test assesses a wide range of cognitive functions: memory; motor functions; rhythm; tactile, auditory, and visual functions; receptive and expressive speech; writing; spelling; reading; and arithmetic. It is extremely sensitive for identifying specific types of problems (e.g., dyslexia, dyscalculia) rather than being limited to more global impressions of brain dysfunction; it also helps localize the various cortical zones that are involved in a particular function and is useful in establishing left or right cerebral dominance. The test is designed for persons at least 15 years of age; a children's version for use with 8- to 12-year-olds is being developed.

**lust dynamism**   Harry Stack Sullivan's term to describe clearly stated sexual desires and abilities.

**lying**   Making statements that one knows consciously are false with intent to deceive; differentiated from confabulation, in which one is not conscious of lying.

**lysergic acid diethylamide (LSD)**   A potent psychotogenic drug discovered in 1942 that produces psychotic-like symptoms and behavior changes, including hallucinations, delusions, and time-space distortions. Commonly called acid.

# M

**macropsia**   False perception that objects are larger than they really are. *Compare* micropsia.

**magical thinking**   Notion that thinking something is the same thing as doing it or that it might cause it to happen; common in dreams, in certain mental disorders, and in children.

**magnetic resonance imaging (MRI)**   Diagnostic modality in which a patient's body is placed in a magnetic field and its hydrogen nuclei are excited by radio-frequency pulses at angles to the field's axis; resulting signals from the body's hydrogen ions are processed through a computer to produce an image; an excellent method for differentiating gray and white matter, visualizing cerebrospinal fluid, and estimating the size of ventricles.

**Mahler, Margaret** (1897–1985)   Hungarian-born psychiatrist and child analyst who described the separation-individuation process in children.

**maintenance drug therapy**   Stage in the course of chemotherapy at which, after the drug has reached its maximal efficacy, the dosage is reduced and sustained at the minimal therapeutic level that will prevent a relapse or exacerbation.

**major affective disorder**   *See* major depression.

**major depression**   Severe mood disorder characterized by one or more depressive episodes but no history of a manic episode; a DSM-III-R diagnosis. *See also* mood disorder.

**major depressive episode, melancholic type**   DSM-III-R diagnosis replacing involutional melancholia.

**major epilepsy**   *See* grand mal epilepsy.

**major motor seizure**   *See* grand mal epilepsy.

**major tranquilizer**   ANTIPSYCHOTIC.

**maladaptive**   Referring to any mental activity or behavior that is dysfunctional or counterproductive with regard to a person's ability to cope effectively with the problems and stresses of life.

**maladjustment**   Maladaptive reaction; poor, faulty, or inadequate coping ability.

**male erectile disorder**   DSM-III-R sexual arousal disorder characterized by the recurrent and persistent partial or complete failure to obtain or maintain penile erection until the completion of the sex act. Also called erectile dysfunction. *See also* impotence.

**maleness** Anatomic and physiologic features relating to the male's procreative functions.

**malingering** Feigning disease in order to achieve a specific goal, for example, to avoid an unpleasant responsibility. *Compare* factitious disorder.

**malpractice** Professional negligence including intentional or willful invasion of another's legally protected interests, such as battery or treatment without consent; must be demonstrated by the presence of *d*ereliction of a *d*uty *d*irectly causing *d*amages (the four D's of malpractice).

**mania** Mood disorder characterized by elation, agitation, hyperactivity and hyperexcitability, and accelerated thinking and speaking (flight of ideas); characterizes the manic phase of bipolar disorder. *See also* hypomania.

**manic** Denoting or characterized by mania. Sometimes used as a general description for a mentally disturbed person, often someone exhibiting violent or grossly irrational behavior.

**manic-depressive illness** Mood disorder characterized by severe alterations in mood that are usually episodic and recurrent. The unipolar type is characterized by either periodic episodes of mania (manic disorder) or periodic episodes of depression (depressive disorder). In the bipolar or circular type, the patient has at least one episode of each mood extreme and may alternate periodically between the two. Manic depressive illness has been replaced by bipolar disorder in DSM-III-R.

**manifest content** That part of a dream or fantasy that a person remembers and reports; in a dream, it represents a disguised and symbolic expression of the latent content of the dream.

**manipulation** Exploitativeness; the maneuvering by patients to get their own way, characteristic of antisocial personalities.

**mannerism** Stereotyped gesture or expression that is peculiar to a given person.

**mantra** In transcendental meditation, a Sanskrit syllable or word that is repeated over and over in an effort to produce total relaxation and control over one's state of consciousness.

**MAO** Monoamine oxidase.

**marasmus** Progressive emaciation, especially in malnourished infants and children, in which weight is often below the third percentile and markedly below appropriate weight for height.

**marathon** Technique developed by George Bach and Frederick

Stoller that incorporates a group meeting that usually lasts 8–72 hours (although some may last for a week), in which the session is interrupted only for eating and sleeping; the leader works for the development of intimacy and the open expression of feelings. The time-extended group experience culminates in intense feelings of excitement and elation.

**marijuana**  Dried leaves and flowers of *Cannabis sativa* (Indian hemp), which induce somatic and psychic changes in a person when smoked or ingested in sufficient quantity. Somatic changes include increased heart rate, rise in blood pressure, dryness of the mouth, and increased appetite; psychic changes include a dreamy-state level of consciousness, a sense of enhanced vividness of visual and auditory sensations, disturbances of time perception and memory-dependent, goal-directed behavior, disruptions of sequential thought processes, and euphoria and other alterations of mood. The compound believed to be responsible for most of its psychological effects is tetrahydrocannabinol (THC). In strong doses, marijuana can produce hallucinations and, at times, paranoid ideation. Also called pot; grass; weed; dope; Mary Jane.

**marital counseling**  Process whereby a trained counselor helps married couples resolve problems that arise and trouble them in their relationship; the husband and the wife are seen by the same worker in separate and joint counseling sessions that focus on immediate family problems. The theory and techniques of this approach were first developed in social agencies as part of family case work.

**marital problems**  Maladaptive behavior between spouses in various areas, e.g., attitudes toward sex, contraception, child rearing, money handling.

**marital therapy**  *See* marriage therapy.

**marriage therapy**  Type of family therapy that involves the husband and the wife and focuses on the marital relationship as it affects the individual psychopathology of the partners. The rationale for the method is the assumption that psychopathological processes within the family structure and in the social matrix of the marriage perpetuate individual pathological personality struc-tures, which find expression in the disturbed marriage and are aggravated by the feedback between partners.

**masculine identity**  Inner sense of gender affiliation with males. *Compare* feminine identity.

**masculine protest**  Adlerian doctrine that depicts a universal human tendency to move from a passive and feminine role to a masculine and active role; an extension of Alfred Adler's ideas about organic inferiority that became the prime motivational force in normal and neurotic behavior in his system.

**masculinity-femininity scale**  Any scale on a psychological test that assesses the relative masculinity or femininity of the testee. Scales vary and may focus, for example, on basic identification with either sex or preference for a particular sex role and are strongly influenced by cultural definitions of masculinity and femininity.

**masochism**  Paraphilia in which sexual gratification is derived from being physically or psychologically maltreated by a partner or oneself; first described by an Austrian novelist, Leopold von Sacher-Masoch (1836–1895). *See also* sadism; sadomasochistic relationship.

**masturbation**  Self-stimulation of the genitals for sexual pleasure. *See* autoerotism.

**maternal deprivation**  Result of the premature loss or absence of the mother. In a broader sense, the lack of proper mothering may constitute a form of maternal deprivation which may lead to severe emotional disorders in infants and children.

**maturational crises**  Normative stages of the life cycle that require adaptive coping or defense mechanisms.

**maximum security unit**  That part of an institution for the mentally ill reserved or those who have committed crimes or who are considered dangerous to others.

**MCE**  Medical care evaluation.

**MDMA**  3,4,-Methylenedioxymethamphetamine.

**mean**  Statistical measurement derived from adding a set of scores and then dividing by the number of scores. *See also* average.

**mean deviation**  Statistical measure of the variability in a set of values defined as the sum of the absolute differences between the values and the mean divided by the number of values.

**median**  Value in a set of values above and below which there are an equal number of values; e.g., in the series 1,3,5,9,13 the value 5 is the median. *See also* average.

**Medicaid**  Assistance program for certain needy and low-income persons, mandated by the federal government and financed by both federal and state governments; certain benefits, such as in-and outpatient hospital care, physicians' services, and laboratory tests, are required covered expenses, while other services may be provided at the state's option.

**medical audit**  Retrospective assessment of the quality and utilization of care, including investigation of suspected problems, analysis of the problems identified, and a plan for corrective action. Also called medical care evaluation (MCE).

**medical care evaluation (MCE)**  MEDICAL AUDIT.

**medical ethics**  Moral set of principles that determine what is right or wrong and good or bad, as they pertain to professional responsibilities and opinions relating to the values of patients, patients' families, and society at large. For related issues, see the specific term.

**medical record**  Written exposition describing a patient's diagnosis and treatment.

**medical review**  Evaluation of the quality of care and assessment of medical care or services judged in terms of cost effectiveness.

**Medicare**  Hospital and medical insurance system for the aged created in 1965 by amendments of the Social Security Act. Hospitalization in general hospitals for psychiatric conditions is covered in the same way as other conditions; benefits in psychiatric hospitals are limited to a total of 190 days during a lifetime.

**megalomania**  Morbid preoccupation with expansive delusions of power, importance, or wealth.

**megavitamin therapy**  *See* orthomolecular treatment.

**melancholia**  Severe depressive state. Used in the term "involutional melancholia" as a descriptive term and also in reference to a distinct diagnostic entity. *See also* involutional melancholia.

**memory**  Process whereby what is experienced or learned is established as a record in the central nervous system (registration), where it persists with a variable degree of permanence (retention) and can be recollected or retrieved from storage at will (recall). For types of memory, see the specific term.

**menarche**  Onset of menstrual function.

**mendacity**  Pathological lying.

**mens rea**  Legal term meaning an intent to do harm.

**mental aberration**  Pathological deviation from normal thinking; unrelated to a person's intelligence.

**mental age**  Measure of mental ability as determined by standard psychological tests.

**mental deficiency**   Term often used interchangeably with mental retardation, applied to individuals with an I.Q. of less than 70.

**mental disorder, mental disease**   Psychiatric illness or disease whose manifestations are primarily characterized by behavioral or psychological impairment of function, measured in terms of deviation from some normative concept.

**mental health**   State of emotional well-being in which persons are able to function comfortably within their society and in which their personal achievements and characteristics are satisfactory to them.

**mental hygiene**   **1.** Conditions and practices conducive to the establishment and maintenance of mental health. **2.** Field dealing with the prevention and early treatment of mental illness. *See also* orthopsychiatry.

**mental illness**   Mental disorder; any serious impairment of adjustment; any psychiatric disorder listed in the American Psychiatric Association's *Diagnostic and Statistical Manual of Mental Disorders* or in the World Health Organization's *International Classification of Diseases.*

**mental retardation**   Subaverage general intellectual functioning that originates in the developmental period and is associated with impaired maturation and learning, and social maladjustment. Degrees of retardation are commonly measured in terms of I.Q.: mild (50–55 to 70), moderate (35–40 to 50–55), severe (20–25 to 35–40), and profound (below 20–25).

**mental status**   General functional condition of mental and behavioral processes as determined by psychiatric assessment of a variety of areas of functioning, such as state of consciousness, mood and affect, thinking and speech, motor behavior, general knowledge, memory, calculation, judgment, abstraction, and insight.

**mental status examination (MSE)**   Clinical evaluation, and the sum total of the examiner's observations and impressions, of a person's psychological and behavioral experiences. MSE includes specific references to such areas as attitude and general behavior during interview and to sensorium, mental capacity, and other areas of function.

**merycism**   RUMINATION DISORDER OF INFANCY.

**mescaline**   Hallucinogenic drug obtained from buttons of the peyote cactus that has psychotomimetic effects similar to those of LSD.

**mesmerism**   Early term for hypnosis.

**mesomorphic**   Muscular, with a well proportioned physique; one of

Sheldon's constitutional types. *Compare* ectomorphic; endomorphic.

**meta-analysis**   General consensus of many studies that results in one common data base that helps to eliminate bias.

**metapsychiatry**   Branch of psychiatry concerned with altered states of consciousness, holistic health, and parapsychology.

**metapsychology**   Branch of theoretical or speculative psychology concerned with theories, hypotheses, or phenomena that are largely beyond the realm of empirical verification. *See also* parapsychology.

**methadone**   Orally active synthetic narcotic agent that is an effective analgesic with pharmacological actions qualitatively very similar to those of morphine. Its use in the maintenance treatment of heroin addicts is based on its extended duration of action in suppressing withdrawal symptoms in persons physically dependent on opiates.

**methadone maintenance treatment**   *See* methadone.

**3-methoxy-4-hydroxyphenylglycol (MHPG)**   Most significant metabolic product from central nervous system norepinephrine; excreted in urine.

**3,4-methylenedioxymethamphetamine (MDMA)**   Hallucinogen more commonly known as ecstasy.

**methyl-4-phenyl-1,2,3,6-tetrahydropyridine (MPTP)**   Contaminant of an illicitly made synthetic heroin that induces irreversible parkinsonism.

**metonymy**   Speech disturbance common in schizophrenia in which the affected person uses a word or phrase that is related to the proper one but is not the precise one that would ordinarily be used; for example, the patient speaks of consuming a "menu," rather than a "meal," or refers to losing the "piece of string" of the conversation, rather than the "thread" of the conversation. *See also* paraphasia; word approximation.

**Metrazol treatment**   Rarely used form of convulsive therapy in which a convulsive seizure is induced by injection of the drug Metrazol (pentylenetetrazol).

**Meyer, Adolf** (1866–1950)   American psychiatrist known for his concept of psychobiology and "commonsense" psychiatry.

**MHPG**   3-Methoxy-4-hydroxyphenylglycol.

**microcephaly**   Condition in which the head is unusually small as a result of defective brain development and premature ossification of the skull.

**micropsia** False perception that objects are smaller than they really are. Sometimes called lilliputian hallucination. *Compare* macropsia.

**MID** Multi-infarct dementia.

**middle age, middle adulthood** That period considered to be the prime of life, between the ages of approximately 40 to 65 years, following the termination of early adulthood.

**middle insomnia** Waking up after falling asleep without difficulty and then having difficulty in falling asleep again. *Compare* initial insomnia; terminal insomnia.

**midlife crisis** Syndrome that occurs in both sexes as they enter their early 40s or 50s, consisting of depression, substance abuse, concern about growing old, and fear of death; more common in adults with prior psychiatric illness than in normal adults.

**migraine** Severe unilateral, throbbing headache that appears periodically, usually beginning during the teenage years and continuing to recur with diminishing frequency during advancing years. Classic migraine is a syndrome ushered in by a transient derangement of neurological function, often a visual disturbance, followed by hemicranial headache, nausea, and vomiting, all of which last for anywhere from several hours to 1 or 2 days. Common migraine has the same character and time course but develops without any prodrome. Patients with migraine are typically described as tense, meticulous, hard-driving persons who appear to have a high frequency of associated emotional conflicts.

**mild mental retardation** *See* mental retardation.

**milieu therapy** Treatment that emphasizes appropriate socioenvironmental manipulation for the benefit of the patient; the setting is usually the psychiatric hospital. *See also* moral treatment; therapeutic community.

**mimicry** Simple, imitative motion activity of childhood.

**minimal brain dysfunction** Behavioral syndrome of childhood, now called attention-deficit hyperactivity disorder, characterized by learning difficulties, decreased attention span, distractibility, hyperactivity, impulsiveness, emotional lability, and, often, disturbances in perceptuomotor and language development; its psychopathological mechanisms have not been defined. The term implies neurological causation, but in most cases there are no major unequivocal neurological signs and there has been a tendency to apply the term as a convenient explanatory label to any child presenting with a specific learning difficulty or behavioral dysfunction. Although the syndrome has been diagnosed with increasing frequency over the past 20 years, its validity as a diagnostic entity has been questioned, and it is not listed as such in DSM-III-R.

**Minnesota Multiphasic Personality Inventory (MMPI)** Questionnaire type of psychological test for persons age 16 and over consisting of true-false statements that are coded in various scales that assess different dimensions of the person's personality structure and measure the closeness of fit with various psychiatric diagnostic categories.

**minor epilepsy**   PETIT MAL EPILEPSY.

**minor tranquilizer**   ANXIOLYTIC.

**Mitchell, S. Weir** (1830–1914)   American neurologist known for his concept of rest treatment to cure emotional disorders.

**mixoscopia**   Sexual perversion in which a person attains orgasm by watching his or her love object make love with another person.

**MMPI** Minnesota Multiphasic Personality Inventory.

**M'Naghten rule**   Set of rules established in 1843 in England to determine criminal responsibility, based on the person's ability to distinguish right from wrong. *See also* Durham rule; American Law Institute formulation of insanity.

**mode**   In a set of measurements, the value that appears most frequently. *See also* average.

**modeling**   Learning of a new skill or behavior by observation and imitation of another person.

**Model Penal Code**   American Law Institute's test of criminal responsibility: "A person is not responsible for criminal conduct if at the time of such conduct, as a result of mental disease or defect, he lacked substantial capacity to either appreciate the criminality (wrongfulness) of his conduct or to conform his conduct to the requirement of the law."

**moderate mental retardation**   *See* mental retardation.

**molecular psychiatry**   Etiological view of psychiatry based on neurotransmitter chemicals as measured in molecular quantities.

**mongolism**   Obsolete term for Down's syndrome.

**monoamine**   Biogenic amine or class of neurotransmitters that consists of three catecholamines (dopamine, norepinephrine, and epinephrine), an indolamine (serotonin), a quaternary amine (acetylcholine), and an ethylamine (histamine).

**monoamine oxidase (MAO)** Enzyme that deaminates monoamines and that functions. in the nervous system by breaking down monoamine neurotransmitters (e.g., norepinephrine, epinephrine, dopamine, and serotonin); has been subdivided into Type A and Type B.

**monoamine oxidase inhibitor** Agent that inhibits the enzyme monoamine oxidase (MAO). MAO inhibitors are highly effective as antidepressants and are also used in the treatment of panic disorders and some eating disorders.

**monomania** Morbid mental state characterized by preoccupation with one subject. Also called partial insanity.

**monozygotic twins** Twins who develop from a single fertilized ovum. In contrast, dizygotic or fraternal twins develop from two separately fertilized ova. Also called identical twins.

**mood** Pervasive and sustained feeling tone that is experienced internally and that, in the extreme, can markedly influence virtually all aspects of a person's behavior and his or her perception of the world. Distinguished from affect, the external expression of the internal feeling tone. For types of mood, see the specific term.

**mood-congruent delusion** Delusion with content that is mood appropriate, e.g., a depressed patient who believes he or she is responsible for the destruction of the world.

**mood-congruent hallucination** Hallucination with content that is consistent with either a depressed or a manic mood, e.g., a depressed patient hearing voices telling the patient he or she is a bad person; a manic patient hearing voices telling the patient he or she has inflated worth, power, or knowledge.

**mood-congruent psychotic features** DSM-III-R term that refers to hallucinatory or delusional phenomena with contents that consistently reflect the mood of a manic or depressed patient.

**mood disorders** Any of a group of clinical conditions characterized by a disturbance of mood (the internal emotional state of an individual), a loss of a sense of control, and a subjective experience of great distress; comprised of depression and mania. Called affective disorder in DSM-III. *See also* major depression.

**mood-incongruent delusion** Delusion based on incorrect reference about external reality, with content that has no association to mood or is mood-inappropriate, e.g., a depressed patient who believes he or she is the new Messiah.

**mood-incongruent hallucination** Hallucination not associated with real external stimuli, with content that is not consistent with either depressed or manic mood, e.g., in depression, hallucinations not involving such themes as guilt, deserved punishment, or inadequacy; in mania, not involving such themes as inflated worth or power.

**mood-incongruent psychotic features**  DSM-III-R term that refers to hallucinatory or delusional phenomena with contents that do not consistently reflect the mood of a manic or depressed patient.

**mood swing**  Oscillation of a person's emotional feeling tone between periods of elation and periods of depression.

**moral treatment**  Philosophy and technique of treating mental patients, developed in the 18th century, that involved the establishment of a humane therapeutic environment designed to maximize the chances for recovery; considered the forerunner of current milieu therapy.

**morbid perplexity**  Condition seen in schizophrenia in association with loss of ego boundaries; the patient exhibits profound confusion about his own identity and the meaning of existence.

**moron**  Obsolete and pejorative term for a classification of mental retardation in which an individual has a mental age of approximately 8 years.

**morphine**  Major phenanthrene alkaloid opium derivative that produces a combination of central nervous system excitation and depression; repeated administration can lead to tolerance, physical dependence, and psychological dependence; used as an analgesic, sedative, and anxiolytic. *See also* Appendix 2.

***Moses and Monotheism***  Title of a book by Sigmund Freud (1939) in which he undertook a historical but frankly speculative reconstruction of the personality of Moses and examined the concept of monotheism and the abiding effect of the patriarch on the character of the Jews; one of Freud's last works, it bears the imprint of his latter-day outlook and problems.

**mother surrogate**  In psychoanalysis, a mother substitute onto whom a patient projects his or her mother image and responds to unconsciously, in an inappropriate and unrealistic manner, with the feelings and attitudes that he or she had toward the real mother.

**motivation**  Force or energy associated with an internal state that propels a person to engage in behavior to satisfy a need or desire.

**motor aphasia**  Aphasia in which understanding is intact but the ability to speak is lost. Also called Broca's, expressive, or nonfluent aphasia.

**mourning** Syndrome following loss of a loved one, consisting of preoccupation with the lost individual, weeping, sadness, and repeated reliving of memories. *See also* bereavement; grief.

**MPD** Multiple personality disorder.

**MPTP** Methyl-4-phenyl-1,2,3,6-tetrahydropyridine.

**MRI** Magnetic resonance imaging.

**multi-infarct dementia** DSM-III-R category for an organic mental disorder in which a succession of strokes has led to a stepwise deterioration of intellectual function with associated focal neurological signs and symptoms.

**multiple delusions** Concurrent delusions in which the delusions need not be interconnected.

**multiple personality disorder** Dissociative reaction in which a person has two or more distinctive personalities, most of them knowing nothing of the others. In DSM-III-R, one of the dissociative disorders.

**multiple regression** Multivariate analysis in which a scaled variable is correlated with a linear combination of independent or predictor variables.

**multiple therapy** CO-THERAPY.

**multivariate analysis** Methods for considering the relationship of three or more variables, including multiple regression, multivariate analysis of variance, discriminant analysis, canonical correlation, and factor analysis.

**Munchausen syndrome** Condition characterized by the recurrent fabrication of clinically convincing simulations of disease. Called chronic factitious disorder with physical symptoms in DSM-III-R.

**muscarine** Naturally occurring alkaloid found in certain species of poisonous mushrooms; symptoms of mushroom poisoning develop within 30 minutes of ingestion and consist of vomiting, diarrhea, bronchospasm, hypertension, delirium, and shock.

**mutism** Organic or functional absence of the faculty of speech. *See also* stupor (2).

**mydriasis** Dilation of the pupil; sometimes occurs as an autonomic (anticholinergic) side effect of some phenothiazines and tricyclic antidepressant drugs.

**mysophobia** Abnormal fear of dirt or contamination.

# N

**naloxone**  Opiate antagonist that, unlike nalorphine which it has largely replaced as a narcotic antagonist, is essentially devoid of agonist effects. In opioid-dependent persons, small doses of naloxone precipitate moderate to severe withdrawal symptoms, an effect that can be used to diagnose physical dependence on narcotic drugs; however, the most important use of naloxone is in the treatment of narcotic overdosage. (Trade name, Narcan.)

**NAMI**  National Alliance for the Mentally Ill.

**narcissism**  Self-love linked to autoerotism but devoid of genitality. In psychoanalytic theory, it is divided into primary and secondary types: primary narcissism, the early infantile phase of object relationship development, when the child has not differentiated the self from the outside world and all sources of pleasure are unrealistically recognized as coming from within the self, giving the child a false sense of omnipotence; secondary narcissism, when the libido, once attached to external love objects, is redirected back to the self. *See also* autistic thinking.

**narcissistic personality disorder**  Personality disorder characterized by a grandiose sense of self-importance, preoccupation with fantasies of unlimited success, exhibitionistic need for attention and admiration, exaggerated responses to criticism or other perceived threats to self-esteem, and disturbance in interpersonal relationships.

**narcoanalysis**  NARCOTHERAPY.

**narcolepsy**  Sleep disorder characterized by recurrent, brief, uncontrollable episodes of sleep. *See also* hypersomnia.

**narcosis**  Drug-induced stupor.

**narcosynthesis**  NARCOTHERAPY.

**narcotherapy**  Psychotherapy conducted with the patient in a drug-induced stupor or semiconscious state, as by the administration of barbiturates; originally used in the treatment of acute disorders arising in the setting of military combat; also called narcoanalysis; narcosynthesis.

**narcotic**  Any natural or synthetic drug producing morphine-like analgesia, drowsiness, mental clouding, and, with prolonged use, physical dependence. *See also* opioid.

**narcotic blockade** Inhibition of the euphoric effects of even high doses of intravenous opioids, such as heroin, by the use of other drugs, such as methadone.

**National Alliance for the Mentally Ill (NAMI)** Self-help group and influential national advocacy network comprised of and supported by the family members and parents of schizophrenic patients.

**National Board of Medical Examiners (NBME)** National board, founded in 1915, for testing medical students by three examinations given during different stages of their medical education to qualify for licensure to practice medicine in the U.S.; the diploma is accepted in 50 states for obtaining licensure without further examination by the state.

**National Institute of Alcohol Abuse and Alcoholism (NIAAA)** *See* Alcohol, Drug Abuse, and Mental Health Administration.

**National Institute of Drug Abuse (NIDA)** *See* Alcohol, Drug Abuse, and Mental Health Administration.

**National Institute of Mental Health (NIMH)** *See* Alcohol, Drug Abuse, and Mental Health Administration.

**National Mental Health Association** Voluntary citizens' organization, founded in 1909 as the National Committee on Mental Hygiene, to promote mental health.

**National Training Laboratories (NTL)** Organization started in 1947 at Bethel, Maine, to train professionals who work with groups; interest in personal development eventually led to sensitivity training and encounter groups.

**natural group** Any group that tends to evolve spontaneously in human civilization, such as a kinship, tribal, or religious group in contrast to various contrived groups or aggregates of people who meet for a relatively brief time to achieve some goal.

**NBME** National Board of Medical Examiners.

**necromania** Pathological preoccupation with dead bodies.

**necrophilia** Sexual attraction to or sexual contact with dead bodies.

**necrophobia** Abnormal fear of dead bodies.

**need** Ambiguous term referring to an internal state of unsatisfaction or tension related to a wish, urge, desire, or other endogenous behavioral stimulus; classically, it implied an innate or instinctual internal stimulus. *See also* drive; instinct; motivation.

**negative reinforcement**   *See* reinforcement.

**negative transference**   *See* transference.

**negativism**   Verbal or nonverbal opposition or resistance to outside suggestions and advice; commonly seen in catatonic schizophrenia in which the patient resists any effort to be moved or does the opposite of what is asked.

**neologism**   New word or phrase whose derivation cannot be understood; often seen in schizophrenia. It has also been used to mean a word that has been incorrectly constructed but whose origins are nonetheless understandable (e.g., "headshoe" to mean "hat"), but such constructions are more properly referred to as word approximations.

**nervous breakdown**   Nonspecific lay term for mental disorder, often implying an acute decompensation.

**neurasthenia**   Condition characterized by vague functional physical and mental fatigue; not used in DSM-III-R.

**neurochemistry**   Branch of chemistry concerned with nervous system components, metabolism, and function.

**neurocirculatory asthenia**   DACOSTA'S SYNDROME.

**neuroendocrinology**   Subspecialty area concerned with the anatomical and functional relationships between the nervous system and the endocrine apparatus. *See also* psychoendocrinology.

**neurohormone**   Chemical messengers formed by neurosecretory cells and released into the bloodstream.

**neuroleptic drug**   ANTIPSYCHOTIC.

**neuroleptic malignant syndrome (NMS)**   Life-threatening complication of antipsychotic treatment, including such symptoms as muscle rigidity and dystonia, akinesia, mutism, obtundation, and agitation.

**neurological amnesia**   **1.** Auditory amnesia: loss of ability to comprehend sounds or speech. *See also* Wernicke's aphasia. **2.** Tactile amnesia: loss of ability to judge the shape of objects by touch. *See also* astereognosis. **3.** Verbal amnesia: loss of ability to remember words. **4.** Visual amnesia: loss of ability to recall or recognize familiar objects or printed words.

**neurologic disorders**   Disorders involving the organization and function of nervous tissue, including diseases of the peripheral nerves, the spinal cord, and the brain, which are based on organic pathology.

**neurologist**  Physician who specializes in diseases of the nervous system.

**neurology**  Medical specialty concerned with organic diseases of the nervous system.

**neuron**  Nerve cell, consisting of cell body, dendrites, and neuroaxon, which is the basic functional unit of the nervous system.

**neuronal plasticity**  Ability of the central nervous system to alter its functional organization; a capacity for change that serves as a mechanism to shape neuronal circuitry during development, to change the way information is processed, and to compensate for injury.

**neurophysiology**  Physiology of the nervous system.

**neuropsychiatry**  Medical specialty that combines psychiatry and neurology.

**neuroreceptors**  Neuronal and other nervous tissue sites that are stimulated or inhibited by neurotransmitters and/or psychotropic drugs.

**neuroscience**  Branch of the life sciences concerned with the anatomy, physiology, biochemistry, or molecular biology of nerves and nervous tissue and, especially, with their relation to behavior and learning.

**neurosis**  Mental or psychiatric disorder characterized primarily by anxiety, which may either be directly experienced and dominate the clinical picture or be unconsciously controlled and modified by various psychological mechanisms to produce other subjectively distressing and ego-alien symptoms. Although neuroses are not accompanied by gross distortion of reality or severe personality disorganization, normal functioning is impaired by the person's symptoms; they have no organic basis, are relatively persistent, and are treatable. Also called psychoneurosis.

**neurotic disorder**  *See* neurosis.

**neurotic process**  Process in which unconscious conflict is expressed by neurotic symptoms or personality disturbance.

**neurotoxin**  Agent, such as an antibody, causing destruction to nervous tissue.

**neurotransmitter**  Any specific chemical agent released by a presynaptic cell that, upon excitation, crosses the synapse to stimulate or inhibit the postsynaptic cell.

**NIAAA**  National Institute of Alcohol Abuse and Alcoholism.

**nicotine dependence**   Inability to control the use of and dependence on tobacco. Nicotine dependence and withdrawal are classified as disorders in DSM-III-R.

**NIDA**   National Institute of Drug Abuse.

**night hospital**   Part-time hospital facility in which patients function in the outside world during the day but return to the hospital at night. *Compare* day hospital; weekend hospital.

**nightmare**   Anxiety attack experienced while dreaming; character-ized by mild anxiety, good recall of the dream, and mild autonomic reactions. *Compare* dream anxiety disorder; sleep terror disorder.

**night-terror**   SLEEP TERROR DISORDER.

**nihilism**   Delusion of the nonexistence of the self or part of the self; also refers to an attitude of total rejection of established values or extreme skepticism regarding moral and value judgments.

**nihilistic delusion**   Depressive delusion that the world and every-thing related to it have ceased to exist.

**NIMH**   National Institute of Mental Health.

**nitrogen narcosis**   RAPTURE-OF-THE-DEEP SYNDROME.

**NMS**   Neuroleptic malignant syndrome.

**noesis**   Revelation in which immense illumination occurs in associa-tion with a sense that one has been chosen to lead and command.

**nominal aphasia**   Aphasia characterized by difficulty in giving the correct name of an object.

**nonaffective hallucination**   Hallucination whose content is appar-ently unrelated to either depression or elation. *Compare* illusion.

**noncomplementary role**   *See* role.

**noncompliance with medical treatment**   DSM-III-R category used when a patient does not cooperate with the physician in his or her medical care; motivated by denial of illness, by religious beliefs, or by decisions based on personal value judgments about the advantages and disadvantages of the proposed treatment.

**nondirective approach**   Technique in which the therapist follows the lead of the patient in the interview, rather than introducing his or her own theories and directing the course of the interview; applied in both individual and group therapy.

**nonfluent aphasia**   MOTOR APHASIA.

**nonparametric**   Denoting statistical methods that do not require restrictive assumptions about population distributions.

**nonreactive depression**  ENDOGENOUS DEPRESSION.

**noradrenaline**  NOREPINEPHRINE.

**norepinephrine**  Catecholamine neurotransmitter substance liberated by adrenergic postganglionic neurons of the sympathetic nervous system; the precursor of epinephrine present in the adrenal medulla and also found in many areas of the brain. A disturbance in its metabolism at important brain sites has been proposed as an important factor in the causation of mood disorders. Also called noradrenaline.

**normality**  In psychiatry, the absence of mental illness; that state of mental health about which there exists a scientific and professional consensus. The normal person has a sense of his or her own worth and maintains a confident and purposeful self-image.

**nosology**  Science of the classification of diseases.

**nosophobia**  PATHOPHOBIA.

**not-for-profit hospital**  Any hospital not maintained for the purpose of monetary gain. *Compare* for-profit hospital.

**not otherwise specified (NOS)**  Term used throughout DSM-III-R to describe unusual or uncharacteristic variations of different mental disorders; e.g., eating disorder NOS, tic disorder NOS, pervasive developmental disorder NOS.

**NREM sleep**  Non-REM sleep consisting of 4 stages, based on EEG findings: stage 1: low amplitude, first frequency immediately after sleep begins; stage 2: cycles of 12-16 Hz called sleep spindles; stages 3 and 4: increased amplitude and slow frequency EEG changes. *Compare* REM sleep.

**NTL**  National Training Laboratories.

**nuclear family**  Immediate members of a family, including the parents and the children.

**nuclear magnetic resonance (NMR)**  *See* magnetic resonance imaging.

**null hypothesis**  Research term for the hypothetical assumption that any difference observed between two groups or conditions or between a particular group and the general population is purely accidental and due to chance alone. *See also* Type 1 error; Type 2 error.

**nyctophobia**  Abnormal fear of darkness or of the night.

**nymphomania**  Abnormal, excessive, insatiable desire in a female for sexual intercourse. *Compare* satyriasis.

# O

**objective tests**  Typically, pencil-and-paper tests based on specific items and questions and that yield numerical scores and profiles easily subjected to mathematical or statistical analysis; e.g., Minnesota Multiphasic Personality Inventory (MMPI).

**object permanence**  As described by Jean Piaget, the child's (birth to 2 years) ability to understand that objects have an existence independent of his or her involvement with the object; the child is able to maintain a mental image of a person or object even though it is not present and not visible.

**object relation**  Emotional attachment formed between one person and another, as opposed to interest in and love for oneself.

**OBS**  Organic brain syndrome.

**obsession**  Persistent and recurrent idea, thought, or impulse that cannot be eliminated from consciousness by logic or reasoning; obsessions are involuntary and ego-dystonic. *See also* compulsion.

**obsessive-compulsive disorder**  Neurotic disorder characterized by the persistent recurrence of obsessions and compulsions.

**obsessive-compulsive personality**  Personality disorder characterized by perfectionism, overconscientiousness, and excessive inhibition with regard to self-expression and relaxation. Also called anancastic personality.

**occupational problem**  Maladaptive patterns related to work, e.g., job dissatisfaction and uncertainties about career choices.

**occupational psychiatry**  Area of psychiatry concerned with mental illness in industry, including the psychiatric aspects of absenteeism, vocational adjustment, operational fatigue, and accident proneness.

**occupational therapy**  Form of therapy in which the patient engages in useful, purposeful activities in a therapeutic social setting involving interaction with other patients and hospital personnel.

**oedipal phase**  PHALLIC PHASE. *See also* Oedipus complex.

**Oedipus complex**  Constellation of feelings, impulses, and conflicts in the developing child that concern sexual impulses and attraction toward the opposite-sex parent and aggressive, hostile, or envious feelings toward the same-sex parent; real or fantasied threats from the same-sex parent result in the repression of those feelings. Development of the Oedipus complex coincides with the phallic phase of psychosexual development; as one of Freud's most important concepts, the term was originally applied only to the male. *Compare* Electra complex.

**olfactory hallucination**  Hallucination primarily involving smell or odors.

**oligophrenia**  Old term for mental retardation.

**OMD**  Organic mental disorder.

**OMS**  Organic mental syndrome.

**onanism**  Coitus interruptus. Sometimes used interchangeably with masturbation.

**ontogenetic**  Pertaining to the development of an individual person. *Compare* phylogenetic.

**open hospital**  Mental hospital without locked doors or physical restraints.

**operant behavior**  *See* conditioning.

**operant conditioning**  *See* conditioning.

**operational definition**  Means of defining a word so that it is scientifically measurable.

**opiate**  Morphine or other alkaloids derived from opium, an extractable product of the poppy plant *Papaver somniferum* or its variety, *P. album. See also* opioid.

**opiate receptor**  Specific site on a neuronal cell surface that interacts with opiate drugs and mediates their pharmacological actions; presumably, it also mediates the physiological functions of endogenous opioids, such as the enkephalins and endorphins.

**opioid**  Any chemical substance that has morphine-like pharmacological activity; e.g., narcotic analgesics, such as methadone and meperidine, and endogenous opioid peptides, the enkephalins and the endorphins. *See also* opiate.

**opioid peptide**  Peptide that exerts morphine-like actions through interactions with opiate receptors; e.g., endorphin, enkephalin.

**oppositional defiant disorder**  Mental disorder of childhood characterized by pervasive negativism, continuous argumentativeness, and an unwillingness to comply with reasonable suggestions and persuasion.

**oral dyskinesia**  *See* tardive dyskinesia.

**oral phase** Earliest stage in psychosexual development, which lasts through the first 18 months of life. During this period the oral zone is the center of the infant's needs, expression, and pleasurable erotic experiences; it has a strong influence on the organization and development of the child's psyche.

**organic anxiety syndrome** Syndrome characterized by prominent, recurrent panic attacks or generalized anxiety attributable to some clearly defined organic factor; cognitive functioning may be adversely affected as a secondary phenomenon.

**organic brain syndrome (OBS)** ORGANIC MENTAL SYNDROME.

**organic delusional disorder** Disorder characterized by the presence of prominent delusions in a state of full wakefulness and alertness than can be attributed to some clearly defined organic factor.

**organic disorder** Illness that is caused by structural or biochemical pathology. *Compare* functional disorder.

**organic hallucinosis** Disorder characterized by prominent or persistent hallucinations in a state of full wakefulness that can be attributed to some specific organic factor.

**organic mental disorder (OMD)** Mental disorder caused by transient or permanent brain dysfunction attributable to specific organic factors. In DSM-III-R, the organic mental disorders include dementias arising in the senium and presenium, psychoactive substance-induced organic mental disorders, and organic disorders associated with Axis III physical disorders or conditions or whose etiology is unknown. Also called organic psychosis.

**organic mental syndrome (OMS)** Psychologic or behavior abnormality associated with transient or permanent dysfunction of the brain of unknown or unspecified etiology. OMS is characterized by a combination of disorientation to time, place, or person; signs of psychosis, e.g., hallucinations or delusions; and impaired judgment and impulse control. In DSM-III-R, the organic mental syndromes include delirium, dementia, amnestic syndrome, organic delusional syndrome, organic hallucinosis, organic mood syndrome, organic anxiety syndrome, organic personality syndrome, intoxication, and withdrawal; if the cause is known, the condition is called organic mental disorder. Also called organic brain syndrome.

**organic mood syndrome** Disorder characterized by either a depressive or a manic mood attributed to a clearly defined organic factor.

**organic personality syndrome** DSM-III-R term for frontal lobe syndrome.

**organic psychosis** ORGANIC MENTAL DISORDER.

**orgasm** Sexual climax, the peak psychophysiological reaction to sexual stimulation.

**orgasm disorders** One of the major categories of sexual dysfunctions in the sexual disorders section in DSM-III-R.

**orgasmic dysfunction** Failure to achieve orgasm through physical stimulation.

**orgasmic phase** Stage in the human sexual response cycle, as described by Masters and Johnson, in which orgasm occurs.

**orgasmic platform** Outer third of the vagina, which displays marked vasocongestion and contraction in the plateau phase of the female sexual response cycle, as described by Masters and Johnson.

**orientation** State of awareness of oneself and one's surroundings in terms of time, place, and person.

**original thirteen** *See* American Psychiatric Association.

**orphan drug** Any pharmacologic agent that is not economical to produce because the condition for which it is indicated affects relatively few persons.

**orthomolecular psychiatry** Theoretical school of thought proposing that psychiatric illnesses are due to biochemical abnormalities that result in increased requirements for specific substances, such as vitamins.

**orthomolecular treatment** Treatment that entails administration to psychiatric patients of large doses (megadoses) of vitamins (megavitamin therapy), trace elements, or other substances.

**orthopsychiatry** Interdisciplinary approach to the study and practice of maintaining or restoring mental health, involving principles derived from psychiatry, psychology, sociology, social work, medicine, and other fields; particular emphasis is placed on preventive techniques to promote healthy emotional development and growth, especially mental hygiene.

**orthostatic hypotension** Reduction in blood pressure brought about by a shift from a recumbent position to an upright position; observed as a side effect of several psychotropic drugs.

**other-directed person** Person who is readily influenced and guided by the attitudes and values of other people. *Compare* inner-directed person.

**other interpersonal problems** DSM-III-R category describing problems between one or more persons that cause sufficient strain to bring a person into contact with the mental health care system; the stress-inducing circumstances, coping mechanisms, and symptoms that have brought someone to seek consultation or treatment must be individually evaluated.

**other specified family circumstance** DSM-III-R category used when the focus of attention or treatment is not due to a mental disorder or a parent-child or marital problem; may involve in-laws, grandparents, or other family members.

**outcome variable** DEPENDENT VARIABLE.

**outpatient** Ambulatory patient receiving medical care who does not require hospitalization.

**ovarian dysgenesis** TURNER'S SYNDROME.

**overactivity** Abnormality in motor behavior that can manifest itself as psychomotor agitation, hyperactivity (hyperkinesis), tics, sleepwalking, or compulsions.

**overanxious disorder** Anxiety disorder of childhood or adolescence characterized by excessive worrying and fearful behavior grossly disproportionate to the magnitude of the real environmental stress or threat.

**overcompensation** Conscious or unconscious exaggerated correction or compensation for a real or imagined physical or psychological deficit.

**overdetermination** Concept that phenomena such as dreams and neurotic symptoms reflect the operation of multiple causative factors, particularly with regard to symbolic meaning or significance.

**overt homosexuality** Behaviorally expressed homosexuality, as distinct from unexpressed conscious or unconscious homoerotic wishes that are held in check (latent homosexuality).

**overvalued idea** False or unreasonable belief or idea that is sustained with less intensity or duration than is a delusion.

# P

**pain-pleasure principle**  Psychoanalytic concept which states that, in psychic functioning, a person tends to seek pleasure and avoid pain. *See also* pleasure principle.

**panic**  Acute, intense attack of anxiety associated with personality disorganization; the anxiety is overwhelming and accompanied by feelings of impending doom.

**panic attack**  Episode of acute intense anxiety occurring in panic disorder, schizophrenia, major depression, and somatization disorder.

**panic disorder**  DSM-III-R classification of anxiety disorder characterized by attacks of acute intense anxiety, with or without agoraphobia.

**panphobia**  Overwhelming fear of everything.

**pantomime**  Gesticulation; psychodrama without the use of words.

**paradoxical sleep**  REM SLEEP.

**paralogia**  EVASION.

**paralysis agitans**  PARKINSONISM.

**paralytic ileus**  Intestinal obstruction resulting from inhibition of bowel motility, a rare anticholinergic side effect of certain psychoactive drugs. Also called adynamic ileus.

**parameter**  Way of measuring or describing an object or evaluating a subject.

**parametric tests of significance**  Statistical methods used to estimate population parameters, such as the mean and standard deviation; use of these methods requires assumptions about the population characteristics, e.g., that the variable under study is normally distributed within the population from which the sample is drawn.

**paramnesia**  Disturbance of memory in which reality and fantasy are confused. It is observed in dreams and in certain types of schizophrenia and organic mental disorders; includes phenomena such as déjà vu and déjà entendu, which may occur occasionally in normal persons.

**paranoia**  Rare psychiatric syndrome marked by the gradual development of a highly elaborate and complex delusional system, generally involving persecutory or grandiose delusions, with few other signs of personality disorganization or thought disorder.

**paranoiac** Person with paranoia.

**paranoid delusion** Combined delusions of grandeur and persecution.

**paranoid disorder** *See* delusional disorder.

**paranoid ideation** Thinking dominated by suspicious, persecutory, or grandiose content.

**paranoid personality disorder** Personality disorder characterized by rigidity, hypersensitivity, unwarranted suspicion, jealousy, envy, an exaggerated sense of self-importance, and a tendency to blame and ascribe evil motives to others.

**paranoid schizophrenia** Type of schizophrenia characterized by the presence of persecutory or grandiose delusions, often accompanied by hallucinations.

**paraphasia** Abnormal speech in which one word is substituted for another, the irrelevant word generally resembling the required one in its morphology, meaning, or phonetic composition; the inappropriate word may be either a legitimate one used incorrectly, such as "clover" instead of "hand," or a bizarre nonsense expression, such as "treen" instead of "train." Paraphasic speech may be seen in organic aphasias and in mental disorders, such as schizophrenia. *See also* metonymy; word approximation.

**paraphilia** Psychosexual disorder with a sexual dysfunction characterized by persistent and recurrent sexual fantasies, often of an unusual nature, without which imagery erotic arousal or orgasm is not attained; fantasies generally involve themes of suffering, humiliation, sexual activity with nonconsenting partners, or preference for a nonhuman object for sexual arousal. In DSM-III-R, the paraphilias include fetishism, transvestic fetishism, frottage, pedophilia, exhibitionism, voyeurism, sexual masochism, and sexual sadism. Also called sexual deviations.

**paraphrenia** Chronic condition characterized by fantastic and absurd delusions without significant personality deterioration and without the primary disturbances of thought and affect that characterize schizophrenia.

**parapraxis** Faulty act, such as a slip of the tongue or the misplacement of an article. Freud ascribed parapraxes to unconscious motives.

**paraprofessional**   Trained person who works in a mental hospital and may have a degree in the arts or from some professional school other than those serving the mental health group but has not obtained a degree in one of the usual mental health professions.

**parapsychology**   Branch of psychology concerned with extra-normal events and behavioral phenomena not accounted for or explained by the tenets and laws of contemporary science; e.g., clairvoyance, telepathy, psychokinesis. *See also* metapsychology.

**parasomnias**   In DSM-III-R, one of the two major categories of sleep disorders, the other being dyssomnias; dysfunctions associated with sleep, sleep stages, or partial arousals that include sleepwalking, sleeptalking, sleep terror, dream anxiety, and those that are not otherwise specified, such as sleep-related bruxism.

**parasympathetic nervous system**   *See* autonomic nervous system.

**parataxic distortion**   Harry Stack Sullivan's term for distortions in judgment or attitude in interpersonal relations based on patterns set by earlier experience; previously developed ways of coping with significant people in a person's life are applied by the person in later interpersonal integrations.

**parens patriae**   Power of the state to involuntarily hospitalize mentally ill persons in need of care; also called "police power," in that it prevents mentally ill persons from doing harm to themselves or to others.

**parent-child problem**   DSM-III-R category that refers to problems between a parent and a child; e.g., in a family in which the parents are divorced, with either the custodial or the noncustodial parent, and in the remarriage of a divorced or widowed parent.

**paresis**   Weakness or partial paralysis of organic origin.

**paresthesia**   Abnormal spontaneous tactile sensation, such as a burning, tingling, or pins-and-needles sensation.

**parkinsonism**   Extrapyramidal dyskinesia characterized by resting tremor, rigidity, bradykinesia. and postural abnormalities. Parkinsonism is of unknown etiology and occurs in middle or late life, typically with a gradual progression and a prolonged course. Also called paralysis agitans; Parkinson's disease; idiopathic parkinsonism. A parkinsonian syndrome may develop during the course of therapy with antipsychotic phenothiazine or butyrophenone drugs; such drug-induced parkinsonism is reversible when the causative drug is withdrawn or its dosage reduced.

**Parkinson's disease** PARKINSONISM.

**partial hospitalization** System of treating mental illness in which the patient is hospitalized on a part-time basis. *See also* day hospital; night hospital; weekend hospital.

**partial insanity** MONOMANIA.

**passive-aggressive personality disorder** Personality disorder in which the patient manifests aggressive behavior in passive ways, such as obstructionism, pouting, stubbornness, and intentional inefficiency.

**passive-dependent personality** *See* dependent personality disorder.

**pastoral counseling** Use of psychotherapeutic principles by a clergyman in helping parishoners with emotional problems.

**patch amnesia** LOCALIZED AMNESIA.

**pathognomonic** Denoting a sign or symptom specifically diagnostic of a particular disease entity.

**pathological gambling** Compulsion to gamble, one of the disorders of impulse control.

**pathological intoxication** ALCOHOL IDIOSYNCRATIC INTOXICATION.

**pathophobia** Abnormal fear of disease or suffering. Also called nosophobia.

**paucity of speech** Limited use of speech, seen in various pathological states.

**pavlovian conditioning** CLASSICAL CONDITIONING. *See* conditioning.

**Pavlov, Ivan Petrovich** (1849–1936) Russian neurophysiologist famous for his work in conditioning.

**pavor nocturnus** SLEEP TERROR DISORDER.

**PCP** Phencyclidine.

**peccatophobia** Abnormal fear of sinning.

**pecking order** Hierarchy or sequence of authority in an organization or social group.

**pederasty** Anal intercourse between a man and a boy.

**pedophilia** Paraphilia in which a child is the sexual object.

**pedophobia** Abnormal fear of children.

**peer review** Review of physician services by a panel of other physicians.

**Peer Review Organization (PRO)**  Federal review organization for hospitals receiving Medicare funds. In order to promote compliance with federal guidelines for health and hospital care, the PRO conducts independent utilization reviews and quality-of-care studies, validates diagnostic related group (DRG) assignments, and reviews hospital admissions and readmissions. *See also* Professional Standards Review Organization; utilization review committee.

**pellagra**  Deficiency of niacin (nicotinamide) characterized by diarrhea, dermatitis, and mental disturbance.

**penis envy**  Sigmund Freud's concept that the woman envies the man for his possession of a penis; sometimes used to refer to a woman's generalized envy of men.

**perception**  Conscious awareness of elements in the environment by the mental processing of sensory stimuli; sometimes used in a broader sense to refer to the mental process by which all kinds of data, intellectual, emotional, as well as sensory, are meaningfully organized. *See also* apperception.

**perfectionism**  Practice of demanding of others or of oneself a higher quality of performance than is required by the situation.

**period prevalence**  Research term for the total number of cases of a disease known to have existed during a specified time period. *Compare* point prevalence.

**perseveration**  **1.** Pathological repetition of the same response to different stimuli, as in a repetition of the same verbal response to different questions. **2.** Persistent repetition of specific words or concepts in the process of speaking. Seen in organic mental disorders, schizophrenia, and other mental illness. *See also* verbigeration.

**persona**  In Jungian psychology, the outside personality that a person presents to the world, as opposed to his or her inner self (anima).

**personality**  Characteristic configuration of behavior response patterns that each person evolves as a reflection of his or her individual adjustment to life.

**personality disorder**  Mental disorder characterized by inflexible, deeply ingrained, maladaptive patterns of adjustment to life that cause either subjective distress or significant impairment of adaptive functioning; manifestations are generally recognizable in adolescence or earlier. Personality disorders listed in DSM-III-R include paranoid, schizoid, schizotypal, histrionic, narcissistic, antisocial, borderline, avoidant, dependent, obsessive-compulsive, and passive-aggressive.

**personality traits**  Descriptive features of an individual's personality that are within normal limits.

**persuasion**  Supportive psychotherapy in which the patient is encouraged to follow advice; persuasion is directive and limited in its goals.

**pervasive developmental disorder**  Disorder characterized by severe distortions in the development of social skills, language, and contact with reality; e.g., autistic disorder. Many psychological functions are involved, and a child with this disorder displays abnormalities that are not normal for any stage of development. In DSM-III, this condition was known as childhood schizophrenia. *Compare* specific developmental disorder.

**perversion**  Deviation from the expected norm. In psychiatry, it commonly signifies sexual perversion. *See also* psychosexual disorder.

**perverted logic**  EVASION.

**PET**  Positron emission tomography.

**petit mal epilepsy**  Epileptic disorder characterized by recurrent minor, nonconvulsive, momentary lapses of consciousness, commonly beginning in childhood and having a self-limited course. A typical attack involves a sudden transient loss of contact with the environment, during which the patient develops a dazed expression and pauses in what he is doing; this type of seizure has a classical electroencephalographic representation consisting of synchronous, symmetrical spike-and-wave discharges at 3 per second, without cortical localization. Also called absence; minor epilepsy.

**phallic overbearance**  Domination of another person by aggressive means; generally associated with masculinity in its negative aspects.

**phallic phase**  Third stage in psychosexual development, following the anal stage and lasting from about age 2 or 3 to about age 6; resolution of the Oedipus complex is the dominant developmental conflict during this stage. During this period, sexual interest, curiosity, and pleasurable experiences are centered on the penis in boys and the clitoris in girls. Also called oedipal phase.

**phantasy**  Alternative spelling of fantasy.

**phantom limb**   False sensation that an extremity that has been lost is in fact present.

**pharmacokinetics**   Way in which the body processes a drug; its principal divisions are drug absorption, distribution, metabolism, and excretion.

**pharmacotherapy**   PSYCHOPHARMACOLOGY.

**phase of life problem or other life circumstance problem**   DSM-III-R category that refers to problems not severe enough to warrant a psychiatric diagnosis but that interfere with functioning, as arising from marriage, work, change in job, culture shock.

**phencyclidine (PCP)**   Substance of abuse with effects similar to hallucinogens. Also called angel dust.

**phenomenology**   Study of events or happenings in their own right, rather than from the point of view of inferred causes; associated with existential psychiatry and reflects the theory that behavior is determined by the way the person perceives reality, rather than by external reality in objective terms.

**phenothiazine**   One of a class of psychotropic drugs, the prototype of which is chlorpromazine, that are effective in the treatment of psychoses, especially schizophrenia; they exert a favorable influence with regard to the fundamental symptoms of schizophrenia as well as the secondary or accessory symptoms. Their mechanism of action may be related to the blockade of dopamine receptors at critical sites in the central nervous system. *See also* Appendix 2.

**phenotype**   Outward, observable expression of a person's genetic constitution. *Compare* genotype.

**phenylketonuria (PKU)**   Genetic metabolic disorder characterized by the inability to convert the amino acid phenylalanine to tyrosine. If untreated, severe mental retardation results from the accumulation of large concentrations of toxic phenylketones; when detected early in infancy, the condition is treatable by the elimination of phenylalanine from the diet.

**phenylpyruvic oligophrenia**   Former name for phenylketonuria.

**pheromone**   Chemical signal that a person releases into the external environment and that affects the behavior or physiological states of other persons.

**phobia**   Persistent, pathological, unrealistic, intense fear of an object or situation; the phobic person may realize that the fear is irrational but is, nonetheless, unable to dispel it. Some examples are: acarophobia (small objects), acrophobia (high places), agoraphobia (open places, leaving familiar setting of home), aichmophobia (pointed objects), ailurophobia (cats), algophobia (pain), androphobia (men), astraphobia or astrapophobia (thunder and lightning), autophobia (being alone, or of self), bathophobia (depths), claustrophobia (closed or confined places), coprophobia (excreta), cynophobia (dogs), demophobia (crowds), eyrthrophobia (blushing), gynophobia (women), haphcphobia (being touched), hematophobia (sight of blood), hydrophobia (water), hypnophobia (sleep), lalophobia or glossophobia (speaking), mysophobia (dirt, contamination), necrophobia (dead bodies), nyctophobia (darkness, night), panphobia (everything), pathophobia or nosophobia (disease, suffering), peccatophobia (sinning), pedophobia (children), phonophobia (speaking aloud), photophobia (strong light), sitophobia (eating), taphophobia (being buried alive), thanatophobia (death), toxophobia (being poisoned), xenophobia (strangers), zoophobia (animals).

**phobic disorder**  Frequent disorder characterized by a specific fear, which may represent a temptation, a punishment for the forbidden impulse, or a combination of both.

**phobic neurosis**  PHOBIC DISORDER.

**phonophobia**  Abnormal fear of speaking aloud.

**photophobia**  Abnormal fear of strong light.

**phrenology**  Study of the bony conformation of the skull in the now discredited belief that it related to mental faculties and traits.

**phylogenetic**  Pertaining to the development of the species. *Compare* ontogenetic.

**physical dependence**  *See* drug dependence.

**physical disorder**  Disorder of body function whose manifestations are not primarily behavioral or psychological.

**Piaget, Jean** (1896–1980)  Swiss psychologist noted for his research on cognitive development in children; he divided the development of intelligence into three major periods: sensorimotor (birth–2 years), concrete operations (2–12 years), and formal operations (12 years through adult life).

**piblotko**  Culture-specific syndrome seen in Eskimos, usually women, in which the affected person screams, cries, and runs naked through the snow, sometimes with suicidal or homicidal tendencies.

**pica**   Craving and eating of nonfood substances, such as paint and clay.

**Pick's disease**   Rare form of presenile dementia caused by circumscribed cerebral atrophy, with progressive mental deterioration that is indistinguishable clinically from the far more common Alzheimer's disease, in which the pattern of cerebral atrophy is diffuse; in DSM-III-R, classified as presenile dementia not otherwise specified. *See also* primary degenerative dementia of the Alzheimer type.

**pickwickian syndrome**   Condition characterized by obesity, hypoventilation, and hypersomnia.

**Pinel, Philippe** (1746–1826)   French reformer in the field of mental illness known for his work in abolishing physical restraints on hospitalized mental patients.

**piperazine**   Phenothiazine derivative with antipsychotic effects; e.g., fluphenazine (Prolixin). *See* Appendix 1.

**piperidine**   Phenothiazine derivative with antipsychotic effects; e.g., thioridazine (Mellaril). *See* Appendix 1.

**PKU**   Phenylketonuria.

**placebo**   **1.** Inactive substance or preparation that is given as though it were a pharmacologically active medicine; primarily used in controlled studies to determine the efficacy of medicinal preparations; any beneficial or deleterious effects of the placebo may be ascribed to psychological factors. **2.** Any type of treatment that has no specific effects on the particular illness involved.

**placebo effect**   Phenomenon in which a person exhibits a clinically significant response to a pill containing a therapeutically inert substance or a treatment without specific effect on the person's condition. Placebo effects are not limited to subjective reports; physiologic functions may be objectively influenced.

**plaques**   In psychiatry, pathological masses of axons, neurons, and dendrites with a central amyloid core; associated with Alzheimer's disease.

**plasma level**   *See* blood level.

**plasticity**   *See* neuronal plasticity.

**plateau phase**   Stage in the human sexual response cycle, as described by Masters and Johnson, characterized by increased genital blood flow and sense of sexual excitement; it precedes orgasm.

**play therapy**  Type of therapy used with children in which they reveal their problems on a fantasy level with dolls, clay, and other toys; the therapist intervenes opportunely with helpful explanations about the patient's responses and behavior in language geared to the child's comprehension. *See also* activity group therapy.

**pleasure principle**  In psychoanalysis, the principle by which the id seeks immediate tension reduction by either direct or fantasied gratification; developmentally, the pleasure principle antedates the reality principle. Also called the pleasure-pain principle. *See also* reality principle.

**pleonexia**  Psychiatric disorder in which the patient has an excessive desire to acquire wealth or objects.

**pluralism**  In psychiatry, the notion that multiple factors affect behavior.

**point prevalence**  Research term for the total number of cases of a disease known to have existed at a given point in time. *Compare* period prevalence.

**police power**  PARENS PATRIAE.

**polygenic**  Involving the combined action or effects of several genes.

**polymorphous perverse sexuality**  Psychoanalytic conceptualization of sexuality in the human infant, for whom sexual gratification can be achieved by homosexual, heterosexual, or inanimate stimulation of several body zones; all humans, therefore, have the potential to develop sexual perversions in adulthood, depending on how the sexual drives are channeled developmentally.

**polyphagia**  Excessive eating. *See also* bulimia nervosa.

**polysomnography**  Battery of tests that include an electroencephalogram, electrocardiogram, and electromyogram; often given with tests for penile tumescence, blood oxygen saturation, body movement, body temperature, galvanic skin response, and gastric acid. The tests are of assistance in a variety of conditions, such as insomnia, nocturnal myoclonus, sleep apnea, enuresis, somnambulism, seizure disorders, impotence, vascular headache, gastroesophageal reflux, and depression.

**polysubstance dependence**  Disorder characterized by dependence on at least three categories of psychoactive substances.

**population**  Research term for the entire collection of a set of objects.

**porphyria**  Metabolic disorder characterized by excessive urinary excretion of porphyrins (pigments found in hemoglobin and certain cellular enzyme systems) or their precursors; mental symptoms are prominent in the form known as acute intermittent porphyria. Abdominal pain, constipation, and neuromuscular disturbances complete the clinical picture. Attacks may be precipitated by barbiturates.

**positive reinforcement**  *See* reinforcement.

**positive transference**  *See* transference.

**positron emission tomography (PET)**  Imaging technique using short-lived positron-emitting elements of oxygen, carbon, and nitrogen used to label organic compounds (e.g., glucose, amino acids, and neurotransmitters), which are then introduced into the body by injection or inhalation; energy emitted is recorded by scintillation detectors and computer analyzed to construct and display images of transverse sections of tissues, such as the brain. Quantitative data can be assessed in specific areas for such functions as blood flow, oxygen or glucose metabolism, and other complex physiological phenomena; alterations in metabolism associated with disease and the actions of medications can also be monitored in this way.

**postpartum psychosis**  Psychotic reaction, usually depression, after childbirth. Also called atypical psychosis (DSM-III-R); puerperal psychosis.

**post-traumatic stress disorder**  Anxiety disorder that occurs after and as a result of a major, disturbing, out of the ordinary event in a person's life, such as war or rape; may have a delayed onset. *See also* acute situational or stress reaction.

**posturing**  Strange, fixed, and bizarre bodily positions held by a patient for an extended time. *See also* catatonia.

**potency**  Male ability to perform the sexual act; specifically, the capacity to achieve and maintain an erection during coitus.

**poverty of content of speech**  Speech that is quantitatively adequate but qualitatively inadequate because it imparts minimal, vague, or repetitious information.

**poverty of speech**  LACONIC SPEECH.

**PPO**  Preferred Provider Organization.

**practice effect**  Research term referring to the improvement of performance in a task as a result of repeated trials.

**preconscious**  One of three divisions of the psyche in Freud's topographic theory of the mind (the others being the conscious and unconscious), including all mental contents that are not in immediate awareness but that can be consciously recalled with effort.

**predictive value**  Proportion of true-positive or true-negative tests; indicates what percentage of test outcomes are expected to coincide with assigned diagnoses.

**predictor variable**  Test or score used to assess or predict future performance.

**Preferred Provider Organization (PPO)**  Alternative delivery organization that employs a prospective payment system in which a corporation or insurance company forms an agreement with a particular group of community hospitals and doctors to supply health services to PPO members at a previously determined lower rate; patients enrolled in a PPO select their physicians and hospitals from among the list of participants.

**prefrontal lobotomy**  *See* lobotomy.

**pregenital stages**  In psychoanalysis, the first stages of psychosexual development (the oral and anal stages) that occur before the genitals have begun to exert the predominant influence on sexual behavior.

**prejudice**  Preconceived adverse judgment or opinion formed without just grounds or sufficient knowledge; elements of irrational suspicion or hatred are often involved, as in racial prejudice.

**premature ejaculation**  Ejaculation occurring before or immediately after vaginal intromission during coitus; broader definitions take into consideration the ability of a male to delay ejaculation during coitus for a sufficient length of time to satisfy a normally responsive female partner.

**premorbid**  Occurring before the onset of disease.

**presenile dementia**  PRIMARY DEGENERATIVE DEMENTIA OF THE ALZHEIMER TYPE, PRESENILE ONSET.

**presenium**  Period preceding old age, generally ages 55–65.

**pressure of speech, pressured speech**  Increase in the amount of spontaneous speech; rapid, loud, accelerated speech, as occurs in mania, schizophrenia, and organic disorders.

**prevalence**  Total number of cases of a disease existing at a given point in time (point prevalence) or during a specified time period (period prevalence). *See also* incidence.

**prevalence rate**  Number of diagnosed cases of a disease or a condition at a particular point in time; prevalence rate per 1,000 is defined as the cases at a specific point in time, divided by the number of persons in the population at a specific point in time, multiplied by 1,000.

**preventive psychiatry** Branch of preventive medicine concerned with mental disorders. Encompassed within its scope are measures to prevent mental disorders (primary prevention); measures to limit the severity of illness, as through early case finding and treatment (secondary prevention); and measures to reduce disability after a disorder (tertiary prevention).

**primal father** Hypothetical head of a tribe depicted by Sigmund Freud in *Totem and Taboo* as slain by his sons, who subsequently devour him in a cannibalistic rite; later, he is promoted to a god. The son who murders him is the prototype of the tragic hero, and the memory of the crime is perpetuated in the conscience of the individual and of the culture.

**primal scene** In psychoanalysis, the real or fantasied observation by a child of sexual intercourse, particularly between his or her parents.

**primary care physician** Physician who specializes in family medicine, internal medicine, pediatrics, and obstetrics and gynecology; many believe psychiatry should be designated a primary care specialty.

**primary degenerative dementia of the Alzheimer type** DSM-III-R term for a clinical disorder in an elderly patient characterized by a severe loss of intellectual function, for which no other cause is found, and that is progressive and insidious and marked by disorientation as to time, place, and person; senile onset is after age 65 (senile dementia); presenile onset is before age 65 (presenile dementia). Also called Alzheimer's disease. *See also* Pick's disease.

**primary diagnosis** Major emotional disorder for which the patient is treated. Also called principal diagnosis.

**primary gain** Reduction of anxiety achieved by a defense mechanism; relief from tension or conflict through neurotic illness. *Compare* secondary gain.

**primary narcissism** *See* narcissism.

**primary parkinsonism** *See* parkinsonism.

**primary prevention** *See* preventive psychiatry.

**primary process** In psychoanalysis, the mental activity directly related to the functions of the id and characteristic of unconscious mental processes; marked by primitive, prelogical thinking and by the tendency to seek immediate discharge and gratification of instinctual demands. Seen in infancy and in dreams. *Compare* secondary process.

**primary reinforcer**   *See* reinforcement.

**primary retarded ejaculation**   Lifelong inability to ejaculate during coitus. *Compare* secondary ejaculation.

**primitive idealization**   Defense mechanism in which external objects that are viewed as either "all good" or "all bad" are unrealistically endowed with great power; most commonly, the "all good" object is seen as omnipotent, or ideal, while the badness of the "all bad" object is greatly inflated.

**Prince, Morton** (1854–1929)   American neurologist and psychiatrist known for his study of multiple personalities.

**principal diagnosis**   PRIMARY DIAGNOSIS.

**prison neurosis**   *See* chronophobia.

**prison psychosis**   Psychotic reaction to incarceration or to the prospect of incarceration.

**privacy**   **1.** Limiting access of others to one's body or mind, including dreams, fantasies, thoughts, or beliefs. **2.** Freedom from intrusion by the state or third persons. **3.** Restricted areas of personal decision, usually in such matters as personal association, abortion, or bodily integrity.

**privilege**   Legal term referring to the legal right of patients to prevent their physicians from testifying about information obtained in the course of treatment; the legal formulation of the ethical principle of confidentiality. In some states, information obtained in the course of the doctor-patient relationship is considered privileged communication.

**privileged communication**   *See* privilege.

**PRO**   Peer Review Organization.

**probability**   Quantitative statement of the likelihood that an event will occur. A probability of 0 means that the event is certain not to occur; a probability of 1.0 means the event will occur with certainty.

**problem-oriented record**   Method for organizing a patient's clinical chart, consisting of five parts: data base, problem list, treatment plan, progress notes, and discharge summary.

**problem-solving**   Capacity of a person to master a new or novel task.

**process schizophrenia**   Unofficial term for schizophrenia attributed more to endogenous factors than to specific environmental influences. *Compare* reactive schizophrenia.

**prodrome** Early symptom of a disease, often serving as a warning or premonitory sign of the approach of a morbid condition; e.g., the aura preceding an epileptic seizure or classic migraine.

**Professional Standards Review Organization (PSRO)** Organization of physicians in a given region established to review the quality of health care services, particularly with regard to whether the inpatient services rendered are medically necessary. Such an organization has been required by federal law since 1972 in relation to hospital care under Medicare and Medicaid. *See also* peer review organization; utilization review committee.

**profound mental retardation** *See* mental retardation.

**prognosis 1.** Opinion as to the probable future course, extent, and outcome of an illness. **2.** Specific goals of therapy.

**projection** Unconscious defense mechanism in which a person attributes to another those generally unconscious ideas, thoughts, feelings, and impulses that are in himself or herself undesirable or unacceptable as a form of protection from anxiety arising from an inner conflict; by externalizing whatever is unacceptable, the person deals with it as a situation apart from himself or herself. *See also* blind spot.

**projective identification** Defense mechanism in which unwanted aspects of the self are projected onto another person such that the individual projecting feels at one with the object of the projection. It allows one to distance and make oneself understood by exerting pressure on another individual to experience feelings similar to one's own.

**projective test** Psychological test with loosely structured test material that requires the subject to reveal his or her own feelings, personality, or psychopathology; e.g., Rorschach Test, Thematic Apperception Test.

**prolactin** Anterior pituitary hormone that has been studied as a potential index of dopamine activity and receptor sensitivity in studies of central nervous system function in psychiatric patients.

**proprioception** KINESTHETIC SENSE.

**prosopagnosia** Inability to recognize familiar faces that is not due to impaired visual acuity or level of consciousness.

**prospective study** Study based on observing events as they occur.

**prototaxic**   Harry Stack Sullivan's term for primitive illogical thought processes. *See also* primary process.

**pseudoaggression**   Neurotic defense in which a patient denies basic masochistic feelings and displays them, instead, as false aggression.

**pseudoauthenticity**   False or copied expression of thoughts and feelings.

**pseudocollusion**   Sense of closeness, relationship, or cooperation that is not real but is based on transference.

**pseudodementia**   **1.** Dementia-like disorder that can be reversed by appropriate treatment and is not caused by organic brain disease. **2.** Condition in which a patient shows an exaggerated indifference to his or her surroundings in the absence of a mental disorder; also occurs in depression and factitious disorders.

**pseudologia fantastica**   Disorder characterized by uncontrollable lying in which a patient elaborates extensive fantasies that he freely communicates.

**pseudoparkinsonism**   Syndrome that resembles Parkinson's disease, resulting from long-term use of antipsychotic drugs. Also called drug-induced parkinsonism.

**psilocin**   *See* psilocybin.

**psilocybin**   4-Phosphoryloxy-N′,N′-dimethyltryptamine, the active ingredient of various Mexican hallucinogenic mushrooms, which acts as a psychedelic drug producing changes in perception and mood and alterations of consciousness. A variation is called psilocin.

**PSRO**   Professional Standards Review Organization.

**psychalgia**   PSYCHOGENIC PAIN DISORDER.

**psychasthenia**   Obsolete term used by Pierre Janet to describe a syndrome characterized by fears and phobias.

**psyche**   Mind, as divided into conscious, preconscious, and unconscious in Sigmund Freud's topographic model.

**psychedelic**   Denoting drugs that may induce hallucinations and psychotic states. LSD is the prototype; other psychedelic drugs include mescaline, psilocybin, and marijuana.

**psychiatric emergency**   Disturbance in thoughts, feelings, or actions for which immediate treatment is necessary; e.g., suicide intent.

**psychiatric illness**   *See* mental disorder.

**psychiatric nurse** Clinical nurse specialist who functions as part of the mental health team, usually in an institutional setting; often carries out individual, family, and group psychotherapy.

**psychiatric social worker** Skilled professional, trained in social work, who works with psychiatrists, usually in an institutional setting; evaluates family, environmental, and social factors in the patient's illness; may work in intake and reception with new patients; may follow up and counsel after discharge, and also carry out individual, family, and group psychotherapy and participate in community organizations.

**psychiatrist** Medical doctor whose specialty is the study and treatment of mental disorders. After receiving the M.D. degree, a physician spends 4 years as a resident in a hospital setting. When he or she passes the written and oral examinations of the American Board of Psychiatry and Neurology, he or she becomes a diplomate in psychiatry and is said to be Board certified.

**psychiatry** Branch of medicine concerned with the prevention, cause, and treatment of mental disorders.

**psychic determinism** Freudian concept that all mental phenomena have specific antecedent causes, often operating on an unconscious level.

**psychic energizer** Rarely used term for any antidepressant or stimulant drug.

**psychic helplessness** *See* helplessness (2).

**psychic trauma** Psychologically upsetting event that may have lasting consequences on a person's thinking, feeling, or behavior.

**psychoactive drug** PSYCHOTHERAPEUTIC DRUG.

**psychoactive substance abuse** DSM-III-R term for drug abuse.

**psychoactive substance dependence** DSM-III-R term for drug dependence.

**psychoactive substance-induced organic mental disorder** Organic mental disorder caused by the direct effects on the nervous system of a drug or other substance. In DSM-III-R, the substances listed are alcohol; sedatives, hypnotics, or anxiolytics; inhalants; opioids; cocaine; amphetamine or similarly acting sympathomimetics; phencyclidine (PCP) or similarly acting arylcyclohexylamine; hallucinogens; cannabis; nicotine; and caffeine.

**psychoactive substance use disorder** DSM-III-R diagnostic category that involves maladaptive behavior associated with regular use of psychoactive substances; these disorders are further divided into psychoactive substance dependence and psychoactive substance abuse disorders.

**psychoanalysis** Theory of human mental phenomena and behavior, a method of psychic investigation and research, and a form of psychotherapy originally formulated by Sigmund Freud. As a technique for exploring the mental processes, psychoanalysis includes the use of free association and the analysis and interpretation of dreams, resistances, and transferences. As a form of psychotherapy, it uses the investigative technique, guided by Freud's libido and instinct theories and by ego psychology, to gain insight into a person's unconscious motivations, conflicts, and symbols and thus to effect a change in maladaptive behavior. Also called analysis in depth.

**psychoanalyst** Psychotherapist, usually a psychiatrist, who has had training in psychoanalysis and who uses its techniques in a treatment setting.

**psychoanalytic group psychotherapy** Method of group psychotherapy pioneered by Alexander Wolf and based on the operational principles of individual psychoanalytic therapy; analysis and interpretation of a patient's transferences, resistances, and defenses are modified to take place in a group setting.

**psychobiology** Adolf Meyer's term referring to the study of the human being as an integrated unit, incorporating psychological, social, and biological functions.

**psychodrama** Psychotherapy method originated by Jacob Moreno in which personality makeup, interpersonal relationships, conflicts, and emotional problems are expressed and explored through dramatization. Therapeutic dramatization of emotional problems includes: (1) protagonist or patient, the person who presents and acts out his or her emotional problems with the help of (2) auxiliary egos, persons trained to act and dramatize the different aspects of the patient that are called for in a particular scene in order to help the patient express feelings, and (3) the director, leader, or therapist, who guides those involved in the drama for a fruitful and therapeutic session.

**psychodynamics** Science of mental forces and motivations that influence human behavior and mental activity; the role of unconscious motivation in the causation of human behavior is emphasized.

**psychoendocrinology** Study of the role of hormones on thinking, behavior, and emotional disorder.

**psychogenic** Produced or caused by mental factors, rather than organic factors; usually refers to a symptom or an illness.

**psychogenic amnesia** DSM-III-R classification of dissociative disorder characterized by the sudden inability to recall information stored in memory in the absence of an underlying organic mental disorder; when associated with travel to another locale and the assumption of a new identity, the condition is called psychogenic fugue.

**psychogenic fugue** DSM-III-R classification of dissociative disorder characterized by periods of total amnesia in which one travels and assumes a new identity. *See also* fugue; psychogenic amnesia.

**psychogenic pain disorder** Condition in which there is a preoccupation with pain for at least six months in the absence of organic pathology to account for the pain. Also called psychalgia; somatoform pain disorder in DSM-III-R.

**psychohistory** Approach to history that examines events within a psychological framework; attempts to connect individual and collective ideas and emotions with wider historical currents.

**psychoimmunology** Study of the relationship between the immune system and emotions.

**psychokinesis** Parapsychological phenomenon in which directed thought processes influence physical events.

**psycholinguistics** Exploration of the psychological factors involved in the development and use of language.

**psychological defense system** *See* defense mechanism.

**psychological factor affecting physical condition** Disorder characterized by physical symptoms partially caused or affected by psychological factors; physiological and organic changes stem in part from a sustained emotional disturbance; e.g., atopic dermatitis, migraine, ulcer. Also called psychophysiological disorder; psychosomatic disorder.

**psychologist** Person trained in psychology, usually with a graduate degree (M.A., Ph.D.).

**psychology** Study and profession concerned with mental processes and behavior.

**psychometry** Science of testing and measuring mental and psychological functioning.

**psychomotor**   Relating to combined physical and mental activity.

**psychomotor agitation**   Physical and mental overactivity associated with a feeling of inner turmoil, as seen in agitated depression.

**psychomotor epilepsy**   COMPLEX PARTIAL SEIZURE.

**psychomotor retardation**   Slowing of mental and physical activity, common in depression.

**psychomotor stimulant**   Drug that arouses the patient through its central excitatory properties; e.g., amphetamine, methylphenidate (Ritalin). Also called analeptic.

**psychoneuroimmunology**   Study of psychological factors as causes of diseases or their effect on the course of disease, particularly as it relates to the immune system. *See also* psychoimmunology.

**psychoneurosis**   NEUROSIS.

**psycho-oncology**   Study of the role of emotions and their relation to cancer in terms of prevention, diagnosis, and treatment.

**psychopathic personality**   Former term for the personality characteristic of antisocial personality disorder.

**psychopathological**   Denoting abnormal, maladaptive behavioral or mental activity.

**psychopathology**   **1.** Study of mental disorders. **2.** Abnormal, maladaptive behavioral or mental activity.

**psychopharmacology**   Study of the mental and behavioral effects of drugs. *See also* pharmacokinetics.

**psychophysiological disorder**   PSYCHOLOGICAL FACTOR AFFECTING PHYSICAL CONDITION.

**psychopolitics**   **1.** Psychological dimensions of political behavior, such as the reciprocal influence on persons of political environments and their societies. **2.** Specific tactics of politicians that are intended to yield benefits to them through the use of psychological strategies.

**psychosexual development**   **1.** Broadly, the maturation and development of the sexuality of a person throughout the life cycle. **2.** More specifically, in psychoanalysis, series of dynamic and crucial developmental stages that each person passes through and that influence basic personality characteristics in later life; the stages or phases are oral, anal, phallic, latency, and genital.

**psychosexual disorder**   Disorder of sexual functioning, desire, or performance that is caused, wholly or partly, by psychological factors. Also called sexual disorder in DSM-III-R.

**psychosis** Mental disorder in which a person's thoughts, affective response, ability to recognize reality, and ability to communicate and relate to others are sufficiently impaired to grossly interfere with his or her capacity to deal with reality; the classical characteristics of psychosis are impaired reality testing, hallucinations, delusions, and illusions.

**psychosocial deprivation** Deprivation of social and intellectual stimulation; believed to be a causative factor in mental retardation and emotional disorders in children.

**psychosocial development** Developmental progress of a person with regard to social relations and social reality, as primarily described by Erik Erikson. Specific developmental tasks characterize successive chronological periods from infancy through maturity: trust versus mistrust (infancy), autonomy versus doubt (toddler), initiative versus guilt (preschool), industry versus inferiority (school age), identity versus identity diffusion (adolescence), intimacy versus isolation (young adulthood), generativity versus self-absorption (adulthood), and integrity versus despair (mature age).

**psychosocial dwarfism** Syndrome usually first manifested in children 2 to 3 years of age, who typically are unusually short, have frequent growth hormone abnormalities, and have severe behavioral disturbances; all of these symptoms are the result of an inimical caretaker-child relationship and resolve without any medical or psychiatric treatment upon being placed in a more favorable domicile. Also called psychosocially determined short stature.

**psychosocially determined short stature** PSYCHOSOCIAL DWARFISM.

**psychosocial stressor** STRESS.

**psychosomatic disorder** PSYCHOLOGICAL FACTOR AFFECTING PHYSICAL CONDITION.

**psychosurgery** Neurosurgical intervention to treat a mental disorder that involves destruction or ablation of brain tissue.

**psychotherapeutic drug** Drug used to alter abnormal thinking, feelings, or behavior; traditionally divided into classes of antipsychotic, antidepressant, antimanic, and antianxiety (anxiolytic) drugs. Also called psychoactive drug; psychotropic drug. *See also* Appendix 1.

**psychotherapist** Person trained to treat mental, emotional, and behavioral disorders. For types of therapist, see the specific term.

**psychotherapy** Treatment for mental illness and behavioral disturbances in which a trained person establishes a professional contract with the patient and through definite therapeutic communication, both verbal and nonverbal, attempts to alleviate the emotional disturbance, reverse or change maladaptive patterns of behavior, and encourage personality growth and development; distinguished from other forms of psychiatric treatment such as the somatic therapies, e.g., drug and convulsive therapies.

**psychotic** 1. Person suffering from a psychosis. 2. Denoting or characteristic of a psychosis.

**psychotic depressive reaction** Psychosis distinguished by depressed mood precipitated by some event, usually in a person who had not previously demonstrated severe depression. Also called major depressive disorder, single episode, with mood-congruent psychotic features, in DSM-III-R.

**psychotomimetic drug** Drug that produces psychic and behavioral changes that resemble psychosis; unlike other drugs that can produce organic psychosis as a toxic reaction (e.g., hallucinogenic and psychedelic drugs such as LSD, marijuana, mescaline), a psychotomimetic drug does not produce gross confusion, delirium, or overt memory impairment.

**psychotropic drug** PSYCHOTHERAPEUTIC DRUG.

**puerperal psychosis** POSTPARTUM PSYCHOSIS.

**punishment** Presentation of an aversive stimulus contingent on an operant response, resulting in a decreased probability of that response recurring. *See also* reinforcement.

**pyromania** Compulsion to set fires.

# Q

**q-sort** Technique of personality assessment based on the degree to which a standard set of descriptive statements are believed to describe a particular person.

**quadrangular therapy** Marital therapy that involves four people, the married pair and each spouse's therapist.

**quality assurance** Measurement and evaluation of medical and other related services provided with regard to their effectiveness, efficiency, appropriateness, and acceptability; such evaluation will trigger corrective or remedial action for services not meeting the desired standards.

**quantitative variable** Experimental factor that can be measured.

# R

**random**   Statistical term that means occurring by chance or without attention to selection or planning.

**random sample**   In a given population, a group of subjects selected in such a manner that each member of the population has an equal probability of being selected for the sample.

**random variable**   Variable for which the variation is determined by chance.

**range**   Statistical measure of the variability of a set of values, defined as the difference between the largest value and the smallest value.

**Rank, Otto** (1884–1939)   Austrian psychoanalyst, long-time secretary and recorder of the minutes of the Vienna Psychoanalytic Society, and one of Sigmund Freud's earliest followers, who split with him on the significance of the birth trauma, which Rank used as a basis of brief psychotherapy. Rank's works include *The Trauma of Birth* and *The Myth of the Birth of the Hero*.

**rape**   Sexual intercourse without the person's consent and against his or her will, chiefly by force; usually heterosexual but may be homosexual.

**rapid eye movement**   *See* REM latency; REM sleep.

**rapport**   Conscious feeling of harmonious accord, sympathy, and mutual responsiveness between two or more persons; contributes to an effective therapeutic process in both group and individual settings.

**rapture-of-the-deep syndrome**   Psychosis, seen in scuba and deep-sea divers, characterized by disorientation and loss of judgment and skill, and associated with excessive blood nitrogen levels; sensory deprivation may also contribute to this acute, self-limited mental disorder. Also called nitrogen narcosis.

**rationalization**   Ernest Jones's term for an unconscious defense mechanism in which irrational or unacceptable behavior, motives, or feelings are logically justified or made consciously tolerable by plausible means.

**Ray, Isaac** (1807–1881)   One of the original 13 founders of the American Psychiatric Association, known for his *Treatise on Medical Jurisprudence of Insanity* (1837).

**rCBF**   Regional cerebral blood flow.

**reaction formation**   Unconscious defense mechanism in which a person develops a socialized attitude or interest that is the direct antithesis of some infantile wish or impulse that is harbored either consciously or unconsciously. One of the earliest and most unstable defense mechanisms, closely related to repression; both are defenses against impulses or urges that are unacceptable to the ego.

**reactive attachment disorder of infancy or early childhood**   Severe impairment of the ability to relate, beginning before age 5.

**reactive depression**   Mental disorder characterized by depression developing in reaction to some precipitating life event or circumstance.

**reactive disorder**   Mental disorder judged to be a reaction to one or more life events or circumstances, without which the disorder would not have occurred. *See also* brief reactive psychosis; reactive depression; reactive schizophrenia.

**reactive schizophrenia**   Unofficial term for schizophrenia attributed primarily to predisposing or precipitating environmental factors. *Compare* process schizophrenia.

**reality**   Totality of objective things and factual events; includes everything that is perceived by a person's special senses and is validated by other people.

**reality principle**   In psychoanalysis, ego processes that modify the demands of the pleasure principle to meet the inescapable demands and requirements of the outside world; net result is behavior that gratifies id impulses within realistic limits. *See also* pleasure principle.

**reality testing**   Fundamental ego function that consists of tentative actions that test and objectively evaluate the nature and the limits of the environment; includes the ability to differentiate between the external world and the internal world and to accurately judge the relation between the self and the environment.

**recall**   Process of bringing stored memories into consciousness. *See* memory.

**receiver operating characteristic (ROC)**   Special statistical method, recently used in psychiatry, that gives a balance between sensitivity and specificity for a diagnostic test, e.g., Dexamethasone Suppression Test. The method was derived from signal detection theory as a way to determine how well an electronic receiver was able to distinguish signal from noise.

**receptive dysphasia**  Difficulty in comprehending oral language; the impairment involves both comprehension and production of language.

**receptors**  Proteins in the neuronal membrane that are exposed in part to the extracellular fluid and specifically recognize neuromessengers; stimulation of receptors generally causes a biologic response to occur.

**reciprocal inhibition and desensitization**  Behavior therapy in which a person is conditioned to associate comfortable, supportive surroundings with anxiety-producing stimuli, thus decreasing the anxiety associated with those stimuli.

**refractory period**  Temporary state of psychophysiological resistance to sexual stimulation immediately after orgasm in the human sexual response cycle, as described by Masters and Johnson.

**reframing**  Technique used in family therapy whereby a problem or conflict is viewed by the therapist in an entirely different and sometimes startling perspective, thus enabling the family members to achieve objectivity.

**regional cerebral blood flow (rCBF)**  Test using xenon-133, a low energy gamma ray-emitting isotope, to determine blood flow in the brain; useful for studying diseases that have a decrease in the amount of brain tissue, e.g., dementia, ischemia, atrophy.

**registration**  *See* memory.

**regression**  Unconscious defense mechanism in which a person undergoes a partial or total return to earlier patterns of adaptation; observed in many psychiatric conditions, particularly schizophrenia.

**regressive-reconstructive approach**  Psychotherapeutic procedure in which regression is made an integral element of the treatment process; an original traumatic situation is reproduced to gain new insight and to effect personality change and emotional maturation.

**rehabilitation**  All methods and techniques used in an attempt to achieve maximal function and optimal adjustment in a given patient; the physical, mental, social, and vocational preparation of a patient for the fullest possible life compatible with his or her abilities and disabilities. Inasmuch as the process aims also to prevent relapses or recurrences of the patient's condition, it is sometimes called tertiary prevention.

**Reich, Wilhelm** (1897–1957) Austrian psychoanalyst who emigrated to the U.S. in 1939. He coined the term "orgone," a kind of universally pervasive physical and biological energy that was typified by the pent-up libidinal energy that sought free expression and release through orgasm.

**Reik, Theodor** (1888–1969) Psychoanalyst and early follower of Sigmund Freud, who considered Reik one of his most brilliant pupils; Freud's book, *The Question of Lay Analysis,* was written to defend Reik's ability to practice psychoanalysis without medical training. Reik made many valuable contributions to psychoanalysis on the subjects of religion, masochism, and therapeutic technique.

**reinforcement** *Positive reinforcement* refers to the process by which certain consequences of behavior increase the probability that the behavior will occur again. Positive reinforcers tend to be viewed as pleasant. *Negative reinforcement* describes the process by which behavior that leads to the removal of an unpleasant event strengthens that behavior. Negative reinforcers tend to be viewed as unpleasant. Stimuli that possess inherent reinforcing characteristics are called *primary reinforcers*, e.g., food. Stimuli that acquire reinforcing characteristics by being paired with primary reinforcers are called *conditioned reinforcers*, e.g., money. *See also* conditioning.

**reinforcer** Reinforcing stimulus. *See* reinforcement.

**relatedness** Sense of sympathy and empathy with regard to others; sense of oneness with others. *Compare* isolation; alienation.

**relative frequency** *See* frequency.

**relative risk** Epidemiologic measure of the risk of developing a disorder in a specified subset of the population as compared with the total population or a different subset of it. Comparison is usually made between groups exposed and groups not exposed to a particular hereditary or environmental factor to gain information about the role of that factor in the disorder in question. Relative risk is then expressed as a ratio of the frequency of the disorder in exposed persons to its frequency in those not exposed.

**Relative Value Scale** Payment scale for medical services developed at Harvard University that reimburses physicians in terms of time spent with patients, office overhead expenses, years of training, and cognitive skills; under the program, surgeons would receive less money and internists would receive more money from third-party (insurance) carriers than under previous payment scale programs. Also called Resource-Based Relative Value Scale (RBRVS).

**reliability** Research term meaning replicability, i.e., the degree to which a test result or experimental finding can be confirmed by repetition. *See also* validity.

**religious delusion** Delusion involving the Deity or theological themes.

**reminiscence** Recall or recollection of past experiences, with alternations of remembering an apparently lost memory and forgetting one that was just there.

**remission** Significant improvement or recovery from a disorder, which may or may not be permanent. *Compare* intermission.

**remote memory** LONG-TERM MEMORY.

**remotivation** Group treatment technique used with withdrawn patients in mental hospitals to encourage them to develop social and vocational skills.

**REM (rapid eye movement) latency** First REM episode of the night, about 90 minutes after sleep onset; shortening of REM latency frequency occurs with disorders such as depression and narcolepsy.

**REM (rapid eye movement) sleep** Stage of sleep during which dreaming occurs and the sleeper exhibits coordinated rapid eye movement (REM). The electroencephalogram demonstrates a desynchronized pattern of cerebral activity. It accounts for one-fourth to one-fifth of total sleep time. Also called paradoxical sleep.

**repetition compulsion** Psychoanalytic concept of an impulse to repeat earlier experiences and situations.

**repetitive pattern** Continual attitude or mode of behavior characteristic of a person and performed mechanically or unconsciously.

**repression** Freud's term for an unconscious defense mechanism in which unacceptable mental contents are banished or kept out of consciousness; important in both normal psychological development and in neurotic and psychotic symptom formation. Freud recognized two kinds of repression: (1) repression proper, in which the repressed material was once in the conscious domain; (2) primal repression, in which the repressed material was never in the conscious realm. *Compare* suppression.

**repressive-inspirational group psychotherapy** Group therapy in which discussion is intended to bolster the patients' morale and help them avoid undesired feelings; used primarily with large groups of seriously regressed patients in institutional settings.

**reserpine**  Alkaloid extracted from the *Rauwolfia serpentina* plant, formerly used as an antipsychotic agent because of its sedative effects but currently used primarily as an antihypertensive agent, although this use has declined partly because of its potential to produce a considerable incidence of nightmares and suicidal depression; that untoward effect may be related to reserpine's depletion of catecholamines at critical sites in the central nervous system.

**resident**  **1.** In psychiatry, a patient living in a treatment center for a prescribed period of time. **2.** In medicine, a physician in postgraduate training after graduation from medical school; four years of residency training are necessary to become a psychiatrist.

**residential treatment facility**  Center where patients live and receive treatment appropriate for their particular needs; a children's residential treatment facility ideally furnishes both educational and therapeutic experiences for the emotionally disturbed child.

**residual**  Denoting a condition in which a person's acute mental symptoms have subsided.

**residual schizophrenia**  Schizophrenia in which the patient no longer is psychotic but does have some remaining signs of the illness.

**resistance**  Conscious or unconscious opposition to the uncovering of unconscious material; linked to underlying psychological defense mechanisms against impulses from the id that are threatening to the ego.

**resistant attachment**  As described by Mary Ainsworth, a child's simultaneous yet antithetical wish for and avoidance of his or her mother's approach. *Compare* avoidant attachment; secure attachment.

**resolution phase**  Final stage in the human sexual response cycle, as described by Masters and Johnson, during which the sexual system returns to its normal, nonexcited state following orgasm.

**respondent conditioning**  CLASSICAL CONDITIONING. *See* conditioning.

**restricted affect**  Affective expression characterized by a reduction in range and intensity.

**retardation**  Reduction or slowing down of mental and physical activity, as often observed in depression. *See also* mental retardation.

**retarded ejaculation**  INHIBITED MALE ORGASM.

**retention**  *See* memory.

**retroflexion**  Psychoanalytic term used notably by Sandor Rado to describe the turning of rage onto oneself.

**retrograde amnesia**  Loss of memory for events preceding the onset of the amnesia. *Compare* anterograde amnesia.

**retrospective falsification**  Unconscious distortion of memories of past experiences.

**retrospective study**  Investigation based on past data or past events, such as a case control study or a case history study.

**reversal**  In psychoanalysis, an impulse's change from passive to active or from active to passive, as when a destructive impulse changes from masochism to sadism or vice versa.

**right to refuse treatment**  Legal doctrine that holds that a person cannot be forced to have treatment against his or her will unless it is a life-and-death emergency.

**right to treatment**  Legal principle that a facility that has assumed the responsibility of providing treatment is legally obligated to provide adequate treatment for a patient.

**rigidity**  In psychiatry, a person's resistance to change.

**risk factor**  Factor that accounts for the increased risk of a disorder. *See also* attributable risk; relative risk.

**ritual**  **1.** Formalized activity practiced by a person to reduce anxiety, as in obsessive-compulsive disorder. **2.** Ceremonial activity of cultural origin.

**ritualistic behavior**  Automatic behavior of cultural or psychogenic origin.

**ROC**  Receiver operating characteristics.

**Rogers, Carl R.** (1902–1987)  American psychologist who developed person-centered or client-centered theory of personality and psychotherapy, utilizing the concepts of self-actualization and self-direction; emphasized subjective experiential life of people and considered the self as a primary entity in both adjustment and maladjustment in people.

**role**  Pattern or type of behavior developed under the influence of significant people in the person's environment. When the behavior pattern conforms with the expectations and demands of other people, it is said to be a complementary role; if it does not, it is known as a noncomplementary role. *See also* alternating role.

**role playing** Psychodrama technique in which persons are trained to function more effectively in their real-life roles. In the therapeutic setting of psychodrama, protagonists are free to try and to fail in their roles, for they are given the opportunity to try again until they succeed; new approaches to feared situations can thus be learned and applied outside the therapeutic setting.

**Romberg's sign** Markedly increased swaying of the body or falling when a person stands erect with heels together and closes the eyes; typically indicates dysfunction of the dorsal column proprioceptive system, but it may also be seen in hysteria.

**Rorschach Test** Projective test, developed by Hermann Rorschach, in which the person is asked for associations in response to a series of inkblot pictures.

**rumination** Constant preoccupation with and thinking about a single idea or theme, as in obsessive-compulsive disorder.

**rumination disorder of infancy** Rare eating disorder of early childhood characterized by recurrent regurgitation of food in the absence of nausea, retching, or associated gastrointestinal disorder; regurgitated food is either ejected from the mouth or rechewed and reswallowed. Also called merycism.

**Rush, Benjamin** (1745–1813) Father of American psychiatry whose book, *Medical Inquiries and Observations upon the Diseases of the Mind* (1812), was the only American textbook on psychiatry until the end of the 19th century.

# S

**SAD**  Seasonal affective disorder.

**sadism**  Paraphilia in which sexual gratification is achieved by inflicting pain or humiliation on a partner; first described by the French writer the Marquis de Sade (1740–1814). *See also* masochism; sadomasochistic relationship.

**sadistic personality disorder**  Disorder in which a person shows a pervasive pattern of cruel, demeaning, and aggressive behavior whereby physical cruelty or violence is used to inflict pain on others and not to achieve some goal; such a person is fascinated by violence, weapons, injury, or torture. In DSM-III-R, this is a proposed diagnostic category requiring further study.

**sadomasochistic relationship**  Relationship in which the enjoyment of suffering by one person (masochism) and the enjoyment of inflicting pain by the other person (sadism) are important and complementary attractions in their ongoing interaction.

**sample**  Research term for a subset of observations selected from a population.

**sanatorium**  Institution where patients are treated for chronic physical or mental diseases or where they are attended to during a period of recuperation.

**satyriasis**  Morbid, insatiable sexual needs or desires in a male; may be caused by organic or psychiatric factors. *Compare* nymphomania.

**schedule of reinforcement**  Scheme of intermittent reinforcement in which a response is not reinforced every time it occurs. Four broad classes of intermittent schedules are based on either the number of responses required before an opportunity for reinforcement is presented or the passage of a certain amount of time before a given performance is reinforced: (1) *fixed-ratio schedule,* in which reinforcement is delivered after a specified number of responses have occurred, e.g., after every tenth response; (2) *variable-ratio schedule,* in which reinforcement is delivered on a schedule randomly changing around a given ratio, e.g., after the third, sixth, then second response, and so on; (3) *fixed-interval schedule,* in which reinforcement is delivered contingent on the first required response after the elapse of a specified interval of time, e.g., after every 10 minutes; and (4) *variable-interval schedule,* in which reinforcement is delivered after variable intervals of time have elapsed, e.g., after 3, 6, then 2 hours, and so on. *See also* reinforcement.

**schizoaffective disorder** Psychotic disorder with signs and symptoms compatible with both a mood disorder and schizophrenia.

**schizoid fantasy** Through fantasy, indulgence by a person in autistic retreat to resolve conflict and to obtain gratification; interpersonal intimacy is avoided and eccentricity serves to repel others. The individual does not fully believe in or insist on acting out the fantasies.

**schizoid personality disorder** Diagnostic category in DSM-III-R for persons with defects in the capacity to form social relationships but without other striking communicative or behavioral eccentricities. Also called introverted personality disorder.

**schizophrenia** Term introduced by Eugen Bleuler for a psychotic mental disorder of unknown etiology characterized by disturbances in thinking, mood, and behavior. The thinking disturbance is manifested by a distortion of reality, sometimes with delusions and hallucinations, accompanied by a fragmentation of associations that results in characteristic disturbances of speech; the mood disturbance includes ambivalence and inappropriate or constricted affective responses; the behavior disturbance may be manifested by apathetic withdrawal or bizarre activity. Types of schizophrenia listed in DSM-III-R include disorganized, catatonic, paranoid, undifferentiated, and residual. Formerly called dementia praecox.

**schizophreniform disorder** In DSM-III-R, a disorder similar to schizophrenia except that it lasts less than 6 months but more than 1 month.

**schizotypal personality disorder** Diagnostic category in DSM-III-R for persons who exhibit various eccentricities in communication or behavior, coupled with defects in the capacity to form social relationships; the term emphasizes a possible relationship with schizophrenia.

**schneiderian first rank symptoms** Symptoms that Kurt Schneider, a German psychiatrist (1887–1967), considered to be of great pragmatic value in making a diagnosis of schizophrenia, including audible thoughts, arguing voices, thought withdrawal and insertion, delusions, and flat affect.

**school phobia**  Young child's sudden fear of and refusal to attend school, usually considered a manifestation of separation anxiety but also may be a symptom of depression.

**Schreber case**  One of Sigmund Freud's cases. Daniel Paul Schreber's published autobiographical account, entitled *Memoirs of a Neurotic* (1903), was analyzed by Freud (1911) and allowed him to decipher the fundamental meaning of paranoid processes and ideas, especially the relationship between repressed homosexuality and projective defenses.

**scopophilia**  Sexual deviation in which a person achieves sexual gratification by viewing sexual acts or the genitals of others. *Compare* voyeurism.

**scotoma**  **1.** In psychiatry, a figurative blind spot in a person's psychological awareness. *See also* blind spot. **2.** In neurology, a localized visual field defect.

**screening**  Initial patient evaluation that includes medical and psychiatric history, mental status evaluation, and diagnostic formulation to determine the patient's suitability for a particular treatment modality.

**screen memory**  Memory that serves as a cover-up for an associated painful memory.

**SCT**  Sentence Completion Test.

**SD**  Standard deviation.

**SDS**  Zung Self-Rating Depression Scale.

**seasonal affective disorder (SAD)**  Mood disorder subtype characterized by depression, psychomotor slowing, hypersomnia, and hyperphagia that develops in autumn or winter and improves in spring and summer. Also called mood disorder, seasonal pattern, in DSM-III-R.

**seasonal pattern**  *See* seasonal affective disorder.

**secondary gain**  Obvious advantage that a person gains from an illness, such as gifts, attention, and release from responsibility. *Compare* primary gain.

**secondary narcissism**  *See* narcissism.

**secondary prevention**  *See* preventive psychiatry.

**secondary process**  In psychoanalysis, the form of thinking that is logical, organized, reality-oriented, and influenced by the demands of the environment; characterizes the mental activity of the ego. *Compare* primary process.

**secondary retarded ejaculation** After previous normal sexual functioning, the inability to ejaculate during coitus. *Compare* primary retarded ejaculation.

**secondary sexual characteristics** Physical characteristics, other than the external sexual organs, that distinguish male from female.

**secure attachment** As described by Mary Ainsworth, the positive, happy responses of a child following the mother's appearance.

**sedative** Drug that produces a calming or relaxing effect through central nervous system depression; e.g, barbiturates, chloral hydrate, paraldehyde, and benzodiazepines. *Compare* hypnotic.

**selection bias** Nonrepresentative sampling resulting in erroneous conclusions.

**selective inattention** Harry Stack Sullivan's term for inattentiveness to anxiety-generating areas.

**self** Psychophysical total of a person at any given moment, including conscious and unconscious attributes. *See also* identity.

**self-actualization** Abraham Maslow's term for the inborn capacity of people to direct themselves in the healthiest way, toward a level of completeness.

**self-analysis** Investigation of one's own psychic components, which plays a part in all analysis, although to a limited extent, since few people are capable of sustaining independent and detached attitudes to the degree necessary for this approach to be therapeutic.

**self-awareness** Sense of knowing oneself, particularly in terms of insight into one's own psychodynamics; a major goal of most psychotherapies.

**self-defeating personality disorder** Disorder in which persons avoid or undermine pleasurable experiences and are drawn to situations or relationships in which they will suffer, even when better options are available; positive personal events are responded to with guilt or depression, reasonable offers of assistance from others are rejected, and anger or rejecting responses from others are invited, leaving them feeling hurt or humiliated. In DSM-III-R, this is a proposed diagnostic category requiring further study.

**self-discovery** In psychoanalysis, the freeing of the repressed ego in a person who has been brought up to submit to the wishes of the significant others around him.

**self-fulfilling prophecy** Situation in which one predicts a type of behavior that eventually one carries out.

**self-help groups** Groups composed of persons who want to cope with a specific problem or life crisis; characterized by homogeneity and cohesion.

**self-image** One's conception of one's own identity, personality, and worth as a person.

**self-reference** Denoting a person's repeatedly referring the subject under discussion back to himself.

**self-system** Harry Stack Sullivan's term for a personality system designed to ward off anxiety and preserve a positive view of the self.

**SEM** Standard error of the mean.

**senescence** Aging, as determined by inherent or hereditary factors.

**senile dementia** Dementia secondary to diffuse cerebral atrophy associated with advancing age; onset is insidious, progression is slow and gradual, and no specific therapy is known. Also called primary degenerative dementia of the Alzheimer type, senile onset, in DSM-III-R.

**senium** Period of old age, generally after age 65.

**sensate focus learning** In the treatment of sexual disorders, exercises that focus on heightening sensory awareness to touch, sight, sound, and smell.

**sensation** Feeling or impression when the sensory nerve endings of any of the six senses (taste, touch, smell, sight, kinesthesia, and sound) are stimulated.

**sense of self** One's feeling of individuality, uniqueness, and self-direction.

**sensitivity** In research, the probability of a positive test result in one who has the disorder. *Compare* specificity.

**sensitivity training group** Group in which members seek to develop self-awareness and an understanding of group processes, rather than to gain relief from an emotional disturbance. *See also* encounter group; T-group.

**sensorimotor period** *See* Piaget, Jean.

**sensorium** Hypothetical sensory center in the brain that is involved with clarity of awareness about oneself and one's surroundings, including the ability to perceive and process ongoing events in light of past experiences, future options, and current circumstances; sometimes used interchangeably with consciousness.

**sensory deprivation** Lack of external stimuli and the opportunity for the usual perceptions; may be produced experimentally or may occur in real-life contexts (e.g., deep-sea diving, solitary confinement, loss of hearing or eyesight), leading to hallucinations, panic, delusions, and disorganized thinking. *See also* emotional deprivation.

**sensory extinction** Neurological sign operationally defined as failure to report one of two simultaneously presented sensory stimuli, despite the fact that either stimulus alone is correctly reported. Also called sensory inattention.

**sensory inattention** SENSORY EXTINCTION.

**Sentence Completion Test (SCT)** Test designed to tap patients' conscious associations to areas of functioning in which the clinician may be interested; it is composed of a series (usually 75–100) of sentence stems, such as "I like . . . ," "Sometimes I wish . . . ," that patients are asked to complete in their own words.

**separation anxiety** Reaction expressed in a child who is isolated or separated from the mother, such as tearfulness, irritability.

**separation anxiety disorder** In DSM-III-R, an anxiety disorder characterized by an infant's or child's fear and apprehension on being removed from the parent or parent figure.

**separation-individuation** As elaborated by Margaret Mahler, the phase during which the child perceives itself as distinct from the mother; as the child separates, it becomes more independent and aware of its physical and psychological autonomy and can endure separation from the mother.

**serotonin** 5-Hydroxytryptamine (5-HT), an endogenous indolamine synthesized from dietary tryptophan and found in the gastrointestinal tract, the platelets, and the central nervous system. Evidence indicates that this monoamine serves as a neurotransmitter substance in the central nervous system and may play an important role in such diverse functions as sleep, sexual behavior, aggressiveness, motor activity, perception (particularly pain), and mood; dysfunction in central serotonergic systems has been proposed as a cause or factor in various mental disorders, including schizophrenia and the mood disorders.

**serum levels** *See* blood serum levels.

**severe mental retardation** *See* mental retardation.

**sexual aberration** Deviation from usual sexual practices. For types of sexual aberrations, see the specific term.

**sexual arousal disorders** Sexual dysfunction characterized by an inability to achieve a degree of sexual excitement sufficient to engage in coitus. Formerly called inhibited sexual excitement.

**sexual aversion disorder**   Sexual desire disorder characterized by a disgust and/or avoidance of genital contact with a sexual partner.

**sexual delusion**   Delusion centering on sexual identity, appearances, practices, or ideas.

**sexual desire disorder**   Dysfunction characterized by a diminished or hypoactive sexual drive. Formerly called inhibited sexual desire. *See also* hypoactive sexual desire disorder; sexual aversion disorder.

**sexual deviation**   PARAPHILIA.

**sexual disorder**   DSM-III-R term for psychosexual disorder.

**sexual drive**   One of the two primal drives or instincts (the other is the aggressive drive) in Freud's dual-instinct psychoanalytic theory. It operates under the pleasure-unpleasure (pleasure-pain) principle, with its main goal being the preservation and maintenance of life, in contrast to the aggressive drive that follows the repetition-compulsion principle; its unconscious psychic energy is known as libido. Also known as life instinct; Eros.

**sexual dysfunction**   Class of sexual disorders characterized by inhibitions in sexual desire or the psychophysiologic changes that characterize the sexual response cycle.

**sexual identity**   Biologically determined sexual state. *Compare* gender identity.

**sexualization**   Endowment of an object or function with a sexual significance that it previously did not have, or possessed to a lesser degree, in order to ward off anxieties associated with prohibited impulses or their derivatives.

**sexual masochism**   *See* masochism.

**sexual orientation distress**   DSM-III-R term for a sexual disorder characterized by persistent and marked distress about one's sexual orientation; most often characterized by a desire to acquire heterosexual rather than homosexual arousal.

**sexual pain disorders**   Sexual dysfunction characterized by pain during coitus, such as dyspareunia and vaginismus.

**sexual reassignment**   *See* transsexualism.

**sexual sadism**   *See* sadism.

**shaman**   Healer in a primitive tribe who uses supernatural or spiritual powers to cure the sick.

**shame**   *See* guilt.

**shaping**   Operant conditioning technique, used in behavior therapy, in which a behavioral goal is reached in stepwise fashion through selective reinforcement of closer and closer approximations of the desired behavior.

**shared paranoid disorder**   DSM-III-R term for induced psychotic disorder.

**shell shock**   Obsolete World War I term for an acute mental disorder arising as a consequence of combat experience. *See* post-traumatic stress disorder.

**shock treatment**   Obsolete term for convulsive therapy.

**short-term memory**   Reproduction, recognition, or recall of per-ceived material within seconds to minutes after the initial presentation; Also called immediate memory. *Compare* long-term memory.

**shyness disorder**   AVOIDANT DISORDER OF CHILDHOOD OR ADOLES-CENCE.

**sibling**   One of two or more individuals having one common parent.

**sibling rivalry**   Competition among siblings for the attention, affection, and esteem of their parents or for other recognition or reward.

**sick role**   Use of illness or complaints about bodily functioning as a means of escaping personal failure and the expectation to succeed, or as a way of avoiding other social responsibilities. *See also* hypochondriasis.

**side effect**   Action of a drug other than the desired therapeutic effect.

**sign**   Objective evidence of a disease or disorder. *Compare* symptom.

**signal anxiety**   Sigmund Freud's term describing a type of anxiety characteristic of the psychoneuroses, in which a child learns to anticipate and react to the possibility of a traumatic situation before it becomes traumatic.

**significant differences**   *See* statistical significance.

**simple phobia**   Phobic disorder characterized by fear and avoidance of an object or situation not included in agoraphobia or social phobia.

**simultanagnosia**   Impairment in the perception or integration of visual stimuli appearing simultaneously.

**sitophobia**   Abnormal fear of eating.

**Skinner, B. F.** (1904–1990)   American behavioral psychologist and author noted for his work on operant conditioning.

**sleep**   Recurrent temporary period of relative unconsciousness, characterized by a reversible cessation of waking sensorimotor activity and accompanied by characteristic electroencephalographic changes; divided into REM (rapid eye movement) and non-REM (NREM) sleep.

**sleep disorder**   Abnormality of the sleep-waking cycle. Sleep disorders include dyssomnias (insomnia disorder, primary insomnia, hypersomnia disorder, sleep-wake schedule disorder) and parasomnias (dream anxiety disorder, sleepwalking disorder, sleep terror disorder).

**sleep terror disorder**   Sleep disorder in which there are repeated episodes of abrupt awakenings from sleep, usually beginning with a panicky scream; characterized by verbalizations, confusion, autonomic activity, and poor recall of the dream. Also called pavor nocturnus; night terror.

**sleep-wake schedule disorder**   Sleep disorder in which persons cannot sleep when they wish to sleep, but are able to sleep at other times; correspondingly, they cannot be fully awake when they want to be fully awake, but they are able to be awake at other times. A tentative classification in DSM-III-R.

**sleepwalking disorder**   DSM-III-R term for somnambulism.

**slow-wave sleep (SWS)**   Non-REM sleep stages 3 and 4; so termed because of the characteristic wave appearance on the electroencephalogram (EEG) record. Also called delta sleep.

**social adaptation**   Adjustment to the whole complex of interpersonal relationships; the ability to live and express oneself in accordance with society's restrictions and cultural demands. *See also* adaptational approach.

**social breakdown syndrome**   Signs and symptoms indicating that the long-term institutionalization of a mental patient has itself contributed to the patient's symptoms; e.g., development of progressive social and vocational incompetence, excessive passivity, learning the chronic sick role.

**social control**   Influence exerted on a person or a group of persons to conform to the demands or expectations of a society or any of its representative institutions, agencies, or organizations.

**social instinct**   *See* herd instinct.

**socialization**   Process through which an individual becomes a competent member of society; the condition in which inner impulses, i.e., instincts, are expressed in conformity with cultural demands of the environment.

**social learning theory**    Approach to behavior therapy that incorporates the elements of respondent and operant conditioning, but views cognitive processes as important mediators in such learning; relies on role modeling, identification, and human interactions.

**social network therapy**    Type of therapy in which the therapist assembles all persons (relatives, friends, social relations, work relations) who have emotional or functional significance in the patient's life to provide feedback and support to the patient; all or some of the social network may be assembled at any given time. *See also* extended-family therapy.

**social phobia**    Any of a variety of phobic disorders characterized by a fear of being observed by others; e.g., fear of public speaking, blushing, eating in public, writing in front of others, using public lavatories.

**social psychiatry**    Branch of psychiatry concerned with ecological, sociological, and cultural variables that engender, intensify, or complicate maladaptive patterns of behavior and their treatment.

**social therapy**    Rehabilitation therapy used with psychiatric patients to improve social functioning; e.g., occupational therapy, therapeutic community, recreational therapy, milieu therapy, attitude therapy.

**sociobiology**    Systematic study of the biological basis of social behavior, pioneered by E. O. Wilson.

**sociology**    scientific study of group behavior and social organization.

**sociometry**    study and measurement of the interpersonal psychological structure of a group or society.

**sociopath**    Obsolete term for a person with an antisocial personality disorder.

**sociopathic behavior**    Former term for antisocial behavior.

**sociotherapy**    Any treatment modality whose primary emphasis is on socioenvironmental and interpersonal factors; e.g., the therapeutic community.

**sodomy**    Anal intercourse. Legally, the term may include other sexual deviations as well, such as bestiality.

**soldier's heart**    DACOSTA'S SYNDROME.

**soma**    The body.

**somatic delusion**  Delusion pertaining to the functioning of one's body.

**somatic hallucination**  Hallucination involving the perception of a physical experience localized within the body.

**somatic therapy**  Treatment of psychiatric disorders with biological, organic, or physical treatments.

**somatization disorder**  Somatoform disorder characterized by recurrent and multiple physical complaints with no apparent physical cause. Also called Briquet's syndrome.

**somatoform disorders**  Mental disorders characterized by a marked preoccupation with the body and fears of disease; production of the symptoms is linked to psychological factors or conflicts but is not under voluntary control. In DSM-III-R, somatoform disorders include somatization disorder, conversion disorder, body dysmorphic disorder, somatoform pain disorder, and hypochondriasis. *See also* factitious disorder; malingering; Munchausen syndrome.

**somatoform pain disorder**  DSM-III-R term for psychogenic pain disorder.

**somatotype**  Physical build and structure of a person; one's physique.

**somnambulism**  Repeated episodes of arising from bed during sleep, usually during the first third of the night during non-REM (stages 3 and 4 sleep); on awakening, the person has amnesia for the episodes. More frequently seen in males than in females, most commonly in children who generally outgrow it; in adults, often associated with other psychiatric disturbances, such as schizoid personality disorder and schizophrenia. Also called sleepwalking disorder in DSM-III-R.

**somnolence**  Pathological sleepiness or drowsiness from which one can be aroused to a normal state of consciousness.

**spatial agnosia**  Inability to recognize spatial relations.

**specific developmental disorder**  Disorder characterized by delays in the development of specific psychological functions involved in social skills and language; children with a specific developmental disorder act as though they were passing through a developmental stage later than is appropriate for their years. In DSM-III-R, specific developmental disorders include academic skills disorders (developmental arithmetic disorder, developmental expressive writing disorder, developmental reading disorder), language and speech disorders (developmental articulation disorder, developmental expressive language disorder, developmental receptive language disorder), and motor skills disorder (developmental coordination disorder). *Compare* pervasive developmental disorder.

**specificity**   In research, the probability of a negative test result in one who does not have the disorder.

**specific reading disability**   DEVELOPMENTAL READING DISORDER.

**speech disturbance**   Any of a variety of language and communication disorders not due to impaired function of speech muscles or organs of articulation.

**splitting**   Defense mechanism in which external objects are divided into "all good" and "all bad," accompanied by the abrupt shifting of an object from one extreme category to the other.

**stammering**   STUTTERING.

**standard deviation (SD)**   Statistical measure of variability within a set of values so defined that, for a normal distribution, about 68% of the values fall within one SD of the mean, and about 95% lie within two SDs of the mean; sometimes represented by the Greek letter sigma ($\sigma$).

**standard error of the mean (SEM)**   Statistical measure of how variable, i.e., how reliable, a mean value calculated on the basis of a given sample is as an estimate of the the mean of the population from which the sample was selected; obtained by dividing the standard deviation of the population by the square root of the number of measures in the sample.

**standardized score**   Deviation of a score from its group mean expressed in standard deviation units. Also called z-score.

**Stanford-Binet Intelligence Scale**   Primarily a verbal test of intellectual functioning, administered individually to children and adults, that emphasizes problem solving; one of the most widely used I.Q. tests.

**startle reaction**   Reflex response to a sudden intense stimulus, consisting of a diffuse motor response involving flexion movements of the trunk and extremities and associated with a sudden increase in alertness; occurs in normal persons and in anxiety disorders.

**state-dependent learning or memory**   Facilitated recall of information when one is in the same internal state (e.g., drug state) or external environment that the information was first acquired.

**statistical inference**   Research term used to make a general statement about a study based on a small group or to decide whether to attribute differences between two groups to chance or to nonchance factors.

**statistical significance**  Research term referring to an experimental result, based on a sample of observations, that demonstrates an outcome or effect of sufficient magnitude such that the probability of that result being due to chance alone is less than 5%. *See also* Type 1 error.

**status epilepticus**  Continuous epileptic seizures. *See also* epilepsy.

**stereotypy**  Continuous mechanical repetition of speech or physical activities; observed in cases of catatonic schizophrenia.

**stereotypy and habit disorder**  Disorder in which there are intentional and repetitive behaviors that are nonfunctional, i.e., serve no constructive, socially acceptable purpose; e.g., body-rocking, head-banging, face-slapping.

**stilted speech**  Excessively formal, stiff, stylized, or pompous speech; overly polite, distant, or antiquated speech.

**stimulant**  Drug that stimulates the central nervous system to produce increased psychomotor activity; e.g., methylphenidate (Ritalin), caffeine, amphetamines.

**stimulus**  Any event, internal or external to the person, that elicits some kind of nervous system activity or response.

**Stockholm syndrome**  Syndrome in which captives identify with, and have sympathy for, their captors on whom they are dependent for survival; seen in terrorist-hostage situations. The major defense mechanism, as described by Anna Freud, was known as identification with the aggressor.

**STP**  Slang name for 2,5-dimethoxy-4-methylamphetamine.

**street drugs**  Readily available, illegally acquired psychoactive substances; e.g., marijuana, heroin, cocaine, crack. *See* Appendix 2.

**strephosymbolia**  Reading and writing disability characterized by confusion between similarly formed but oppositely oriented letters (as in b and d, p and q), with tendency to reverse the order of letters and words.

**stress**  Circumstance in a person's life that causes tension or dysphoria. Stressors may be mild (e.g., termination of a friendship) or catastrophic (e.g., suicide of a spouse). DSM-III-R contains a Severity of Psychosocial Stressor Scale for children, adolescents, and adults. Also called psychosocial stressor.

**stress immunity**   Failure to react to emotional stress.

**stress reaction**   Disturbed psychologic or physiologic functioning encountered when strong, involuntary, often unconscious internal impulses press for action that conflicts with one's conscious, reality-oriented behavior.

**stroke**   CEREBROVASCULAR ACCIDENT.

**structured interactional group psychotherapy**   Group therapy developed by Harold Kaplan and Benjamin Sadock, in which the therapist provides a structural matrix for the group's interactions, the most important of which is that a different member of the group is the focus of the interaction in each session.

**structured interview**   **1.** Interview in which the same questions are asked of all patients. **2.** Interview in which the interviewer asks specific questions about specific topics.

***Studies on Hysteria***   Title of a book by Josef Breuer and Sigmund Freud (1895) that described the cathartic method of treatment and the beginnings of psychoanalysis; demonstrated the psychological origins of hysterical symptoms and the possibility of effecting a cure through psychotherapy.

**stupor**   **1.** State of decreased reactivity to stimuli and less than full awareness of one's surroundings; as a disturbance of consciousness, it indicates a condition of partial coma or semicoma. **2.** In psychiatry, used synonymously with mutism and does not necessarily imply a disturbance of consciousness; in catatonic stupor, patients are ordinarily well aware of their surroundings.

**stuttering**   Speech disorder characterized by repetitions or prolongations of sounds, syllables, or words or by hesitations and pauses that disrupt the flow of speech. Also called stammering.

**subcoma therapy**   *See* insulin coma therapy.

**subconscious**   Obsolete term for the preconscious and the unconscious.

**subjectivity**   State in which evaluation and interpretation are influenced by one's own feelings and thinking.

**sublimation**   Unconscious defense mechanism in which the energy associated with unacceptable impulses or drives is diverted into personally and socially acceptable channels; unlike other defense mechanisms, it offers some minimal gratification of the instinctual drive or impulse.

**substance abuse**   *See* drug abuse; psychoactive substance abuse.

**substance withdrawal**  Cessation or reduction of intake of a substance regularly used to induce a state of intoxication.

**substitution**  Unconscious defense mechanism in which a person replaces an unacceptable wish, drive, emotion, or goal with one that is more acceptable.

**succinylcholine**  Powerful skeletal muscle relaxant used in anesthesia and as a muscle relaxant in electroconvulsive treatment.

**suggestibility**  State of uncritical compliance with influence or of uncritical acceptance of an idea, belief, or attitude; commonly observed among persons with hysterical traits.

**suggestion**  Process of influencing a person to the point of uncritical acceptance of an idea, belief, or other cognitive process.

**suicide**  Act of taking one's own life. Although the underlying factors that lead a person to take his or her own life may not necessarily be fully understood by that person, the act of suicide is considered to be both voluntary and intentional.

**suicide cluster**  *See* cluster suicide.

**Sullivan, Harry Stack**  (1892–1949) American psychiatrist and psychoanalyst best known for his interpersonal theory of psychiatry.

**sundowner's syndrome**  SUNDOWNING.

**sundowning**  Syndrome in the elderly that usually occurs at night and is characterized by drowsiness, confusion, ataxia, and falling as the result of being overly sedated with medications. Also called sundowner's syndrome.

**superego**  One of the three components of the psychic apparatus in the freudian structural framework, the others being the ego and id. It represents the internalized values, ideals, and moral attitudes of society and has psychic functions that are expressed in guilt, self-criticism, and conscience. It develops through the child's identification with his parents, and the severity of its prohibitions or demands is said to be related to the intensity and extent of resolution of the Oedipus complex. *See also* conscience.

**supportive psychotherapy**  Psychotherapy that seeks to strengthen patients' defenses and to provide them with reassurance, rather than to probe deeply into their conflicts.

**suppression**  Conscious act of controlling and inhibiting an unacceptable impulse, emotion, or idea; differentiated from repression in that repression is an unconscious process.

**surrogate**  One who takes the place of another; a substitute.

**susto**  Culture-specific mental syndrome seen in Latin America; characterized by an intense fear of evil supernatural forces.

**SWS**  Slow-wave sleep.

**symbiosis**  Dependent, mutually reinforcing relationship between two persons. Generally a normal, constructive characteristic of the infant-mother relationship, it can also occur in a destructive context, as between two mentally ill persons who reinforce each other's pathology or in a mother-infant relationship that induces in the child an intense separation anxiety, autism, and severe regression (symbiotic psychosis).

**symbiotic psychosis**  Disorder in children characterized by an inability to separate psychologically or physically from the mother; such children experience confusion, intense separation anxiety, and an inability to function.

**symbolization**  Unconscious defense mechanism in which one idea or object comes to stand for another because of some common aspect or quality in both; based on similarity and association; the symbols formed protect the person from the anxiety that may be attached to the original idea or object.

**sympathetic nervous system**  The part of the autonomic nervous system innervating the viscera by outflow from thoracolumbar segments of the spinal cord. Its physiological effects (e.g., tachycardia, peripheral vasoconstriction, pupillary dilation, decreased bowel motility) are predominantly adrenergic, and they characterize the fight-or-flight reaction that occurs in response to dangerous or threatening situations.

**sympathomimetic drug**  Drug whose effects mimic the responses to stimulation of the sympathetic nervous system; e.g., amphetamine, epinephrine.

**sympathy**  Compassion for or sharing of another person's feelings, ideas, and experiences. *Compare* empathy.

**symptom**  Any abnormality indicative of a mental or physical disorder experienced by the patient but not observable by a physician. *Compare* sign.

**symptomatic psychosis**  Brain dysfunction as a result of some general physical disease, the most common feature of which is a delirious state; may occur in the course of an acute infectious disease, such as pneumonia, influenza, or pelvic infections following childbirth.

**symptom formation** Unconscious psychic process in which a repressed impulse is indirectly released and manifested through a symptom; may be regarded as a kind of compromise reflecting a partial satisfaction of both the forbidden impulse and the ego reaction against it.

**symptom substitution** Phenomenon in which a set of symptoms that are removed directly in therapy, without regard for the unconscious conflicts responsible for their formation, are replaced by new symptoms. It has constituted a theoretical objection to such modalities as behavior therapy and hypnotherapy.

**synapse** Specialized structure at which one neuron makes contacts with the receptor elements in the adjacent neuron.

**syncretic thought** Jean Piaget's term for the prelogical, egocentric, solipsistic thinking that characterizes early childhood mentation. *See also* primary process.

**synesthesia** Condition in which the stimulation of one sensory modality is perceived as sensation in a different modality, as when a sound produces a sensation of color.

**syntactical (central) aphasia** Aphasia characterized by difficulty in understanding spoken speech, associated with gross disorder of thought and expression.

**syntaxic mode of experience** Harry Stack Sullivan's term denoting the highest level of interpersonal communication, which is based entirely on reality and which is considered the desirable outcome of healthy development. *See also* secondary process.

**syntropy** Adolf Meyer's term characterizing healthy or wholesome relationships.

**systematic desensitization** Form of behavior therapy developed by Joseph Wolpe and others in which anxiety-evoking stimuli are presented to a patient in a state of deep muscle relaxation in an attempt to weaken the bond between the stimuli and the anxiety; particularly useful in the treatment of phobias. *See also* reciprocal inhibition and desensitization.

**systematized delusion** Group of elaborate delusions related to a single event or theme.

# T

**taboo**  Restrictions or prohibitions on behavior imposed by a culture, usually involving a dangerous, forbidden, or unclean entity.

**tachylogia**  LOGORRHEA.

**tactile amnesia**  *See* neurological amnesia.

**tactile hallucination**  Hallucination primarily involving the sense of touch. Also called haptic hallucination.

**talion**  Retaliation; the fear that all bad deeds, intentional or accidental, will be punished in kind; i.e., an eye for an eye and a tooth for a tooth. In psychoanalysis, the fear of castration or punishment for oedipal strivings, as in the Oedipus complex.

**tangentiality**  Disturbance in which the person replies to a question in an oblique, digressive, or even irrelevant manner and the central idea is not communicated; failure to communicate the central idea distinguishes tangentiality from circumstantiality, in which the goal idea is reached in a delayed or indirect manner. The term has also been used synonymously with loosening of associations and speech derailment.

**taphophobia**  Abnormal fear of being buried alive.

**Tarasoff decision**  California Supreme Court decision that a physician or psychotherapist who has reason to believe that a patient may injure or kill someone must notify the potential victim, his or her relatives or friends, or the authorities.

**tardive dyskinesia**  Late-appearing extrapyramidal syndrome associated with antipsychotic drug use and characterized by stereotyped involuntary movements of the lips, jaw, and tongue (tardive oral dyskinesia) and by other involuntary dyskinetic movements; symptoms may remit eventually or persist indefinitely after discontinuation of the medication, and the condition does not respond to treatment with antiparkinsonism drugs.

**TAT**  Thematic Apperception Test.

**telepathy**  Extrasensory perception of the mental activities of another person.

**temperament**  Inherent, constitutional predisposition to react in a certain way to stimuli; variations in temperament are evident very early in life.

**temporal lobe epilepsy**   COMPLEX PARTIAL SEIZURE.

**temporary admission**   Hospitalization in which a person is admitted on the recommendation of one physician (which must be confirmed by a psychiatrist, upon admittance), for no more than 15 days if against his or her will; applies to patients who are so senile or confused that they require hospitalization and are not able to make decisions on their own, or so acutely disturbed that they must be immediately admitted to a psychiatric hospital on an emergency basis.

**tension**   Physiological or psychic arousal, uneasiness, or pressure toward action; an unpleasurable alteration in mental or physical state that seeks relief through action.

**terminal insomnia**   Early morning awakening or waking up at least two hours before planning to. *Compare* initial insomnia; middle insomnia.

**tertiary prevention**   *See* preventive psychiatry.

**testamentary capacity**   One's competency to make a will. Three psychological abilities are necessary to demonstrate this competency: (1) the nature and extent of their bounty (property); (2) that they are making a will; and (3) who their natural beneficiaries are, e.g., their spouse, children, and other relatives.

**testimonial privilege**   Right to maintain secrecy or confidentiality in the face of a subpoena. Privilege belongs to the patient, not to the physician.

**test of significance**   Statistical test used to determine whether a difference in the data obtained is due to chance or is meaningfully related to some specific factor or variable (statistically significant).

**tetrahydrocannabinol (THC)**   Chemical substance produced by the Indian hemp plant (*Cannabis sativa*), believed to be responsible for most of the characteristic psychological effects of marijuana. Street drugs alleged to be THC frequently contain phencyclidine (PCP), a veterinary tranquilizer that may produce extreme excitement, visual disturbances, and delirium.

**T (training)-group**   Group that emphasizes training in self-awareness and group dynamics.

**thanatology**   Study of death and matters leading up to and following it.

**thanatophobia**   Abnormal fear of death.

**Thanatos**   AGGRESSIVE DRIVE.

**THC**   Tetrahydrocannabinol.

**Thematic Apperception Test (TAT)**   Projective psychological test in which subjects supply interpretations of a series of ambiguous life situation drawings, based on their own feelings and attitudes and reflecting their unconscious conflicts and defensive structures.

**theory**   Plausible or scientifically acceptable general principle or body of principles offered to explain phenomena.

**therapeutic agent**   Anything that promotes healing, such as a substance, person, or apparatus.

**therapeutic alliance**   Conscious contractual relationship between therapist and patient in which each implicitly agrees that they need to work together to help the patient with his or her problems; involves a therapeutic splitting of the patient's ego into observing and experiencing parts. A good therapeutic alliance is especially necessary for the continuation of treatment during phases of strong negative transference.

**therapeutic atmosphere**   All therapeutic, maturational, and growth-supporting agents, i.e., cultural, social, and medical.

**therapeutic community**   Institutional treatment setting designed with an emphasis on the importance of socioenvironmental and interpersonal influences in the therapy, management, and rehabilitation of the hospitalized mental patient. *See also* milieu therapy.

**therapeutic group**   Group of patients joined together under the leadership of a therapist for the purpose of working together for psychotherapeutic ends; specifically, for the treatment of each patient's mental disorders.

**therapeutic role**   Position in which one aims to treat, bring about an improvement, or provide alleviation of a distressing condition or state.

**therapeutic window**   Range of blood plasma levels of a drug within which optimal therapeutic effects occur, based on such factors as age, sex, race, genetic makeup, and concurrent medications.

**therapist**   *See* psychotherapist.

**thinking** *See* cognition.

**thinking compulsion**   INTELLECTUALIZATION.

**thioxanthene derivative**   One of a class of antipsychotic drugs closely related, both structurally and pharmacologically, to the phenothiazines; e.g., chlorprothixene (Taractan), thiothixene (Navane). *See also* Appendix 1.

**third ear**  Ability to make use of intuition, sensitivity, and awareness of subliminal cues to interpret clinical observations of individual and group patients; a term introduced by the German philosopher Friedrich Nietzsche and later used in analytic psychotherapy by Theodor Reik.

**third party payer**  Health or medical care insurer.

**thought broadcasting**  Feeling that one's thoughts are being broadcast or projected into the environment. *See also* thought withdrawal.

**thought control**  *See* delusion of control.

**thought deprivation**  BLOCKING.

**thought disorder**  Any disturbance of thinking that affects language, communication, or thought content; the hallmark feature of schizophrenia. Manifestations range from simple blocking and mild circumstantiality to profound loosening of associations, incoherence, and delusions; characterized by a failure to follow semantic and syntactic rules which is inconsistent with the person's education, intelligence, or cultural background.

**thought insertion**  Delusion that thoughts are being implanted in one's mind by other people or forces.

**thought process disorder**  Symptom of schizophrenia, involving the intellectual functions, manifested by irrelevance and incoherence of verbal productions; ranges from simple blocking and mild circumstantiality to total loosening of associations, as in word salad.

**thought withdrawal**  Delusion that one's thoughts are being removed from one's mind by other people or forces. *See also* thought broadcasting.

**three-cornered therapy**  CO-THERAPY.

***Three Essays on the Theory of Sexuality***  Title of a book by Sigmund Freud (1905) in which the libido theory was applied to the successive phases of psychosexual maturation in the infant, child, and adolescent; made possible the integration of a vast diversity of clinical observations and promoted the direct observation of child development.

**tic disorders**  Predominantly psychogenic disorders characterized by involuntary, spasmodic, stereotyped movement of a small group of muscles; seen most prominently in moments of stress or anxiety, rarely as a result of organic disease. *See also* Tourette's disorder.

**timidity** Inability to assert oneself for fear of some fancied reprisal, even in the absence of objective evidence of potential harm.

**tinnitus** Noises in one or both ears, such as ringing, buzzing, or clicking; a rare side effect of some tricyclic antidepressant drugs.

**tobacco dependence** *See* nicotine dependence.

**toilet training** Program of teaching a child to control bladder and bowel functions; attitudes of both parent and child during the period may have important psychological implications for the child's later development.

**token economy** Program applying principles of operant conditioning to the management of an institutional setting, such as a ward or a classroom, during which reinforcement of desirable behavior is provided in the form of tokens or credits (conditioned reinforcers) that may be exchanged for a variety of positive reinforcers, such as food, television time, or a weekend pass.

**tolerance** Phenomenon in which, after repeated administration, a given dose of a drug produces a decreased effect or increasingly larger doses must be administered to obtain the effect observed with the original dose. *Compare* drug dependence.

**tomography** *See* computed tomography; positron emission tomography.

**topectomy** Psychosurgical procedure involving ablation of a small and specific area of the frontal cortex for treatment of a chronic psychotic patient.

**Totem and Taboo** Title of a book by Sigmund Freud (1913) in which he applied his psychoanalytic concepts to the data of anthropology. He was able to afford much insight into the meaning of tribal organizations and customs, especially by invoking the Oedipus complex and the characteristics of magical thought as discovered from his studies of the unconscious.

**Tourette's disorder** or **syndrome** Rare illness, first described by a Paris physician, Gilles de la Tourette, that has its onset in childhood and is characterized by involuntary muscular movements (tics) and motor incoordination, accompanied by echolalia and coprolalia.

**toxicity** State of being poisonous.

**toxic psychosis** Psychosis caused by toxic substances produced by the body or introduced into it in the form of chemicals or drugs.

**toxophobia** Abnormal fear of being poisoned.

**trailing phenomenon** Perceptual abnormality associated with hallucinogenic drugs in which moving objects are seen as a series of discrete and discontinuous images.

**trainable** Capable of achieving a certain degree of self-care and social adjustment at home and vocational usefulness in a closely supervised setting; describes the moderately mentally retarded (I.Q. of 35–40 to 50–55). *Compare* educable.

**training group** *See* T-group.

**trait** Distinguishing quality as an observed or measured characteristic of an individual.

**trance** Sleep-like state of reduced consciousness and activity.

**tranquilizer** Psychotropic drug that induces tranquility by decreasing anxiety or agitation, usually without clouding consciousness; formerly classified as major and minor tranquilizers which are now called antipsychotic and antianxiety agents, respectively. *See also* Appendix 1.

**transactional analysis** Eric Berne's system of psychodynamic psychotherapy that focuses on the interactions (transactions) between the patient and the therapist in the treatment session and between the patient and others in a social environment; used in both individual and group psychotherapy. The system includes four components: (1) structural analysis of intrapsychic phenomena; (2) transactional analysis proper, the determination of the currently dominant ego state (parent, child, or adult) of each participant; (3) game analysis, identification of the games played in their interactions and of the gratifications provided; and (4) script analysis, uncovering of the causes of the patient's emotional problems.

**transcultural psychiatry** Branch of psychiatry concerned with the mental health of members of different cultures, i.e., what may be considered normal for one culture may be unacceptable in another.

**transference** Unconscious tendency of a person to assign to others in the present and immediate environment those feelings and attitudes originally linked with significant figures in the person's early life, e.g., identification of the therapist with a parent; the transference may be negative (hostile) or positive (affectionate). Analysis of transference phenomena is used as a major therapeutic tool in both individual therapy and group therapy to help patients better understand and gain insight into their behavior and its origins. *See also* countertransference; transference neurosis.

**transference neurosis**  Phenomenon occurring in psychoanalysis in which the patient develops a strong emotional attachment to the therapist as a symbolized nuclear familial figure; repetition and the depth of that misperception or symbolization characterize it as a transference neurosis.

**transsexualism**  Gender identity disorder in which a person has a desire to be of the opposite sex. Some transsexuals, many of whom have adopted the role of the opposite sex since childhood, have successfully undergone sex-changing surgical procedures, accompanied by intensive hormonal therapy and psychotherapy. *Compare* transvestism.

**transvestism, transvestitism**  Paraphilia characterized by dressing in the clothing of the opposite sex for the purpose of sexual arousal; usually seen in men with a strong desire to appear as women. Also called cross dressing. *Compare* transsexualism.

**trauma**  In psychiatry, a significant, upsetting experience or event that may precipitate or aggravate a mental disorder.

**traumatic neurosis**  *See* post-traumatic stress disorder.

**treated prevalence**  Number of persons being treated for a disorder in a defined geographic area.

**trend of thought**  Thinking that centers on a particular idea associated with an affective tone.

**triad**  Interactional relationship among three persons. Its prototype, the father-mother-child relationship, may evolve projectively in group therapy.

**triadic therapy, triangular therapy**  CONJOINT THERAPY.

**trichotillomania**  Compulsion to pull out one's hair.

**tricyclic drug**  One of a group of antidepressant drugs so named because of their three-ringed structure; currently the most widely used drugs for the treatment of depression, although anticholinergic side effects are prominent; e.g., imipramine (Tofranil), amitriptyline (Elavil).

**trisomy**  Chromosomal aberration in which there are three chromosomes of one type instead of the usual two in an otherwise diploid cell, as in Down's syndrome.

**trisomy 21 syndrome**  DOWN'S SYNDROME.

**true insight**  Understanding of the objective reality of a situation coupled with the motivational and emotional impetus to master the situation or change behavior.

**t-test**   Statistical procedure designed to compare two sets of observations.

**Tuke, William** (1732–1822)   British pioneer in the treatment of mental patients without the use of physical restraints.

**Turner's syndrome**   Disorder secondary to a chromosomal anomaly in which affected females typically have an XO sex chromosome constitution (instead of the usual XX) and a total of 45 chromosomes (instead of the usual 46). Classical somatic features include short stature, webbed neck, distinctive facies, sexual infantilism, and cubitus valgus. The incidence of mental retardation is not increased and severe psychopathic manifestations are uncommon, in contrast to the increased frequency of those disorders in XXY males. Also called ovarian dysgenesis; gonadal dysgenesis. *See also* Klinefelter's syndrome.

**twilight state**   Disturbed consciousness with hallucinations.

**twin studies**   Studies that are useful in separating genetic and environmental influences and in looking for protective and precipitating factors.

**Type 1 error**   Research term referring to the rejection of the null hypothesis when it should have been retained. When the statistically calculated probability ($p$ value) of making a Type 1 error on the basis of an experimental result is less than 0.05, the result is considered statistically significant; that type of error and the arbitrarily chosen 0.05 level of significance are sometimes called alpha ($\alpha$) error. *Compare* Type 2 error.

**Type 2 error**   Research term referring to the failure to reject a false null hypothesis, i.e., concluding that any difference or effect demonstrated in an experiment is no greater than that expected by chance alone when, in fact, there is an actual difference or effect. Also called beta ($\beta$) error. *Compare* Type 1 error.

**Type A personality**   As defined by Meyer Friedman and Ray Rosenman, cardiologists, an action-oriented individual who struggles to achieve poorly identifiable goals by means of competitive hostility; has increased amounts of low-density lipoprotein, serum cholesterol, triglycerides, and 17-hydroxycorticosteroids; and tends to develop coronary heart disease.

**Type B personality**   As defined by Meyer Friedman and Ray Rosenman, cardiologists, a relaxed and less-aggressive individual (than Type A) who tends to strive less vigorously to achieve goals.

**tyramine** Sympathomimetic amine that acts by displacing stored transmitter from adrenergic axonal terminals; its degradation is normally aided by monoamine oxidase (MAO). Ingestion of food containing tyramine (e.g., cheese, beer, wine, yeast) by a patient on MAO inhibitors can provoke a potentially fatal hypertensive crisis.

# U

**UCR**  Unconditioned response or reflex.

**UCS**  Unconditioned stimulus.

**ultradian rhythm**  *See* biological rhythm.

**ululation**  Incoherent crying of a psychotic or hysterical patient.

**unconditioned response, unconditioned reflex (UCR)**  *See* conditioning.

**unconditioned stimulus (UCS)**  *See* conditioning.

**unconscious**  **1.** One of three divisions of Sigmund Freud's topographic theory of the mind (the others being the conscious and preconscious) in which the psychic material is not readily accessible to conscious awareness by ordinary means; its existence may be manifested in symptom formation, in dreams, or under the influence of drugs. **2.** In popular but more ambiguous usage, any mental material not in the immediate field of awareness. **3.** Denoting a state of unawareness, with lack of response to external stimuli, as in a coma.

**underachiever**  One who fails to perform at the level of his or her known potential or capability.

**undersocialized**  Characterized by the absence of adequate social bonds to others, as a type of conduct disorder.

**undifferentiated schizophrenia**  Schizophrenic disorder in which the psychotic symptoms are prominent but do not fall into the other schizophrenic subtypes.

**undoing**  Unconscious primitive defense mechanism, repetitive in nature, by which a person symbolically acts out in reverse something unacceptable that has already been done or against which the ego must defend itself; a form of magical expiatory action, commonly observed in obsessive-compulsive disorder.

**unio mystica**  Feeling of mystic unity with an infinite power.

**unipolar psychosis**  Mood disorder characterized by recurrent episodes of depression or, much more rarely, recurrent manic states. *Compare* bipolar disorder.

**universality**  Total effect produced when all group therapy members share specific symptoms or problems.

**unstructured interview**  **1.** Interview in which the interviewer chooses questions based on clinical judgment. **2.** Interview in which questions are related to what the patient brings up spontaneously.

**urolagnia**  Paraphilia in which sexual pleasure is derived from urinating on someone else, being urinated on, or drinking urine.

**utilitarian principle**   In policy and ethical decisions, a choice that is determined by whatever promises the greatest advantage to the common good.

**utilization review committee**   Hospital committee that reviews the quality of services rendered, with particular attention to the appropriate use of facilities.

# V

**vagina dentata**   Sigmund Freud's theory that an unconscious fantasy exists in certain persons who are afraid of women and who believe that there are "biting teeth" in the vagina.

**vaginismus**   Painful vaginal spasm, usually psychogenic, that occurs during coitus, causing dyspareunia; may have its onset during preparation for intercourse, making penile insertion impossible.

**validity**   Degree to which a test measures what it claims to measure; the degree to which an experimental design yields data truly applicable to the phenomenon under investigation. *See also* reliability.

**variable**   In research, any characteristic or factor that may assume different values. The terms "independent variable" and "dependent variable" indicate a relationship of cause and of effect, respectively.

**variable-interval schedule**   *See* schedule of reinforcement.

**variable-ratio schedule**   *See* schedule of reinforcement.

**variance**   Statistical measure of the variability within a set of observations, defined as the sum of the squared deviations from the mean divided by the number of observations; it equals the standard deviation squared. *See also* analysis of variance.

**variation**   Statistical term referring to the manner in which persons in a population vary among themselves with respect to a given quality or trait; variability of persons also affects the precision of sample estimates. Three common measures of variation are the range, the variance, and the standard deviation. A knowledge of variation in a population is important because it indicates how useful the mean value is as a representative figure.

**vegetative**   **1.** Pertaining to autonomic functions that are largely physiological or concerned with the growth, nutrition, or general physical health and homeostasis of the organism. **2.** In depression, denoting characteristic symptoms such as sleep disturbance (especially early morning awakening), decreased appetite, constipation, weight loss, and loss of sexual response.

**vegetative nervous system**   Obsolete term for autonomic nervous system.

**verbal amnesia**  *See* neurological amnesia.

**verbigeration**  Meaningless and stereotyped repetition of words or phrases as seen in schizophrenia. Also called cataphasia. *See also* perseveration.

**verbiomania**  LOGORRHEA.

**vertigo**  Sensation that one or the world around one is spinning or revolving; a hallmark symptom of vestibular dysfunction, not to be confused with dizziness.

**visceral learning**  *See* biofeedback; learned autonomic control.

**visual agnosia**  Inability to recognize objects or persons.

**visual amnesia**  *See* neurological amnesia.

**visual hallucination**  Hallucination primarily involving the sense of sight.

**visual motor gestalt test**  BENDER-GESTALT TEST.

**vitamin therapy**  *See* orthomolecular psychiatry.

**volitional**  Self-initiated.

**volubility**  LOGORRHEA.

**voluntary admission**  Hospitalization in which patients apply in writing for admission to a psychiatric hospital and are admitted if psychiatric examination reveals such need.

**voluntary control**  Deliberate bringing about of an activity or refraining from an activity. The person exercising the control is aware of the nature of the activities and of the end to be achieved.

**volunteer bias**  Sampling bias of persons who volunteer to take part in an experiment; such persons are not truly representative of the population and may tend to skew the results of the study, e.g., the subjects may be more cooperative.

**von Domarus principle**  Theory proposed by Eilhard von Domarus (1946) to explain schizophrenic thinking, which is characterized by the idea that two things are identical merely because they have identical predicates or properties.

**voyeurism**  Paraphilia in which sexual excitement, frequently with orgasm, is obtained by looking at others naked, disrobing, or engaging in sexual activity. *Compare* scopophilia.

# W

**WAIS**   Wechsler Adult Intelligence Scale.

**Watson, John B.**   (1878–1958)   American psychologist who used Ivan Pavlov's theory of classical conditioning to explain human behavior. *See also* Little Albert.

**waxy flexibility**   CATALEPSY.

**Wechsler Adult Intelligence Scale (WAIS)**   Intelligence test that assesses intellectual functioning in adults.

**Wechsler Intelligence Scale for Children (WISC)**   Intelligence test that assess intellectual functioning in children aged 5 to 15.

**Wechsler Preschool and Primary Scale of Intelligence (WPPSI)**   Intelligence test that assesses intellectual functioning in children aged 4 to 6.

**Wednesday Evening Society**   Small group of Sigmund Freud's followers who in 1902 started meeting with him informally on Wednesday evenings to receive instructions in psychoanalysis; as the society grew in numbers and importance, it evolved in 1910 into the Vienna Psychoanalytic Society.

**weekend hospital**   Partial hospitalization in which the patient spends only weekends in the hospital and functions in the outside world during the week. *Compare* day hospital; night hospital.

**Wernicke-Korsakoff syndrome**   Thiamine deficiency seen in Korsakoff's psychosis (alcohol amnestic syndrome). Also called alcohol dementia. *See also* Wernicke's fluent encephalopathy; Korsakoff's psychosis.

**Wernicke's aphasia**   FLUENT APHASIA.

**Wernicke's fluent encephalopathy**   Neurological disorder caused by nutritional deficiency of thiamine (vitamin B) as seen in chronic alcoholism, with hallmark clinical features of ophthalmoplegia, ataxia, and confusion; some patients show disorders of short-term memory and other cognitive functions characteristic of Korsakoff's psychosis (alcohol amnestic disorder), which has come to be regarded as a more advanced and chronic stage of the same disease process. Wernicke's encephalopathy responds dramatically to the administration of thiamine, which may also prevent progression into the largely irreversible Korsakoff's psychosis.

**Weyer, Johann** (1515–1588)  Dutch physician considered by some to be the first psychiatrist, whose interest in human behavior led to his writing *De Praestigiis Daemonum* (1563), a landmark in the history of psychiatry.

**white-out syndrome**  Psychosis that occurs in Arctic explorers and mountaineers who are exposed to a lack of diverse stimuli in the snow-clad environment.

**WHO**  World Health Organization.

**windigo**  Culture-specific syndrome seen in Canadian Indians, characterized by a delusion of transformation into or possession by a windigo (wihtigo), a feared supernatural cannibalistic monster.

**WISC**  Wechsler Intelligence Scale for Children.

**withdrawal**  **1.** Pathological retreat from interpersonal contact and social involvement; extreme decrease of intellectual and emotional interest in the environment. It may be seen in schizophrenia and depression. **2.** *See* substance withdrawal.

**withdrawal syndrome**  Stereotyped constellation of signs and symptoms that appears when a person stops taking a drug or chemical substance on which he or she has become physically dependent. It is more likely to appear immediately after abrupt discontinuation, but may also appear a few days later; specific clinical features are characteristic for the particular drug or substance. Also called abstinence syndrome.

**word approximation**  Use of conventional words in an unconventional or inappropriate way (metonymy) or of new words that are developed by conventional rules of word formation (e.g., "handshoes" for gloves and "time measure" for clock); distinguished from a neologism, which is a new word whose derivation cannot be understood. *See also* paraphasia.

**word association technique**  Technique devised by Carl Jung, who presented stimulus words to patients and had them respond with the first word that came to mind; it gives insight into persons' unconscious or subconscious thinking.

**word blindness**  Obsolete word for alexia.

**word salad**  Incoherent, essentially incomprehensible mixture of words and phrases commonly seen in far-advanced cases of schizophrenia. *See also* incoherence.

**working through**  In psychoanalysis, the repeated and varied examination of a conflict, neurotic trend, or other problem for the purpose of increasing insight into unconscious processes and effecting adaptive personality changes; constitutes a fundamental facet of the psychoanalytic process.

**World Health Organization (WHO)** Specialized agency of the United Nations, established in 1948, governed by the World Health Assembly. Technical committees and regional organizations further the purpose of the WHO: "the attainment by all people of the highest level of health." It publishes the *International Classification of Diseases* (ICD).

**World Psychiatric Association (WPA)** International association, encompassing psychiatric associations from 75 countries throughout the world, whose objectives are to strengthen and promote international cooperation in psychiatry and among psychiatrists working in different fields and to encourage the exchange of information concerning psychiatric disorders.

**WPA** World Psychiatric Association.

**WPPSI** Wechsler Preschool and Primary Scale of Intelligence.

# X—Y—Z

**xenophobia** Abnormal fear of strangers.

**yohimbine**  Drug that blocks adrenergic α-receptors; because of its parasympathetic effect that causes vasodilatation, it has been used as an agent to help induce penile erection.

**York retreat**  One of the earliest hospitals for the mentally ill, founded in 1792 in York, England, by William Tuke and other Quakers.

**yttrium-90**  Radioisotope that has been implanted experimentally in the brain to destroy certain tracts and areas in an effort to improve severe mental disorder.

**zeitgeist**  German word for the general intellectual, moral, and cultural climate of an era.

**zoophilia**  Paraphilia in which animals are used to produce sexual excitement. *See also* bestiality.

**zoophobia**  Abnormal fear of animals.

**z-score**  STANDARDIZED SCORE.

**Zung Self-Rating Depression Scale (SDS)**  Twenty-item report in which the patient answers questions about symptoms of depressive disorders such as sleep patterns, appetite disturbance, libido, irritability, and hopelessness.

**zygote**  Fertilized egg produced by the union of two cells (sperm and ovum) to form a diploid cell in sexual reproduction.

**zygotic**  Pertaining to a zygote or to the individual developing from such a fertilized egg.

# Psychotherapeutic Drug Identification Guide

This guide contains color reproductions of some commonly prescribed major psychotherapeutic drugs. This guide mainly illustrates tablets and capsules. A † symbol preceding the name of the drug indicates that other doses are available. Check directly with the manufacturer. *(Although the photos are intended as accurate reproductions of the drug, this guide should be used only as a quick identification aid.)*

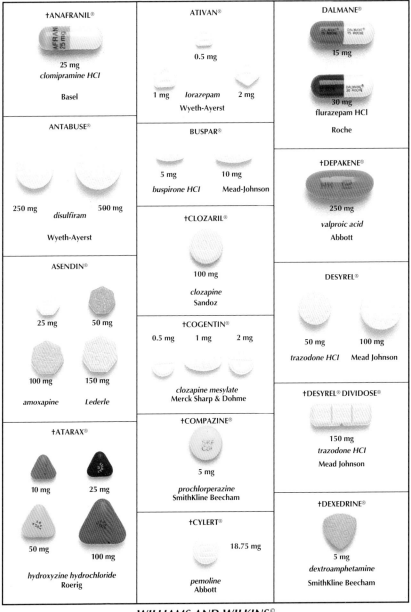

**†ANAFRANIL®**
25 mg
*clomipramine HCl*
Basel

**ANTABUSE®**
250 mg   500 mg
*disulfiram*
Wyeth-Ayerst

**ASENDIN®**
25 mg   50 mg
100 mg   150 mg
*amoxapine*   Lederle

**†ATARAX®**
10 mg   25 mg
50 mg   100 mg
*hydroxyzine hydrochloride*
Roerig

**ATIVAN®**
0.5 mg
1 mg   *lorazepam*   2 mg
Wyeth-Ayerst

**BUSPAR®**
5 mg   10 mg
*buspirone HCl*   Mead-Johnson

**†CLOZARIL®**
100 mg
*clozapine*
Sandoz

**†COGENTIN®**
0.5 mg   1 mg   2 mg
*clozapine mesylate*
Merck Sharp & Dohme

**†COMPAZINE®**
5 mg
*prochlorperazine*
SmithKline Beecham

**†CYLERT®**
18.75 mg
*pemoline*
Abbott

**DALMANE®**
15 mg
30 mg
*flurazepam HCl*
Roche

**†DEPAKENE®**
250 mg
*valproic acid*
Abbott

**DESYREL®**
50 mg   100 mg
*trazodone HCl*   Mead Johnson

**†DESYREL® DIVIDOSE®**
150 mg
*trazodone HCl*
Mead Johnson

**†DEXEDRINE®**
5 mg
*dextroamphetamine*
SmithKline Beecham

*WILLIAMS AND WILKINS©*

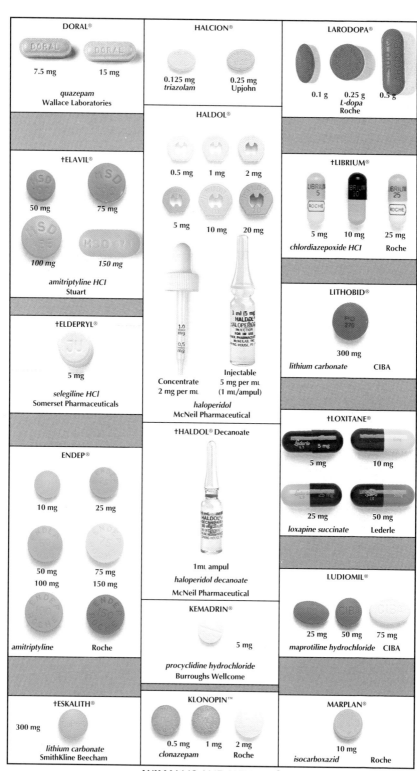

**DORAL®**

7.5 mg　　　15 mg

*quazepam*
Wallace Laboratories

**†ELAVIL®**

50 mg　　　75 mg

*100 mg*　　　*150 mg*

*amitriptyline HCI*
Stuart

**†ELDEPRYL®**

5 mg

*selegiline HCI*
Somerset Pharmaceuticals

**ENDEP®**

10 mg　　　25 mg

50 mg　　　75 mg
100 mg　　150 mg

*amitriptyline*　　　Roche

**†ESKALITH®**

300 mg

*lithium carbonate*
SmithKline Beecham

**HALCION®**

0.125 mg　　　0.25 mg
*triazolam*　　　Upjohn

**HALDOL®**

0.5 mg　　1 mg　　2 mg

5 mg　　10 mg　　20 mg

1.0 mg
0.5 mg

1 ml (5 mg)
HALDOL
HALOPERIDOL
INJECTION
FOR I.M. USE
McNEIL PHARMACEUTICAL
SPRING HOUSE, PA

Concentrate
2 mg per mL

Injectable
5 mg per mL
(1 mL/ampul)

*haloperidol*
McNeil Pharmaceutical

**†HALDOL® Decanoate**

1 mL ampul
*haloperidol decanoate*
McNeil Pharmaceutical

**KEMADRIN®**

5 mg

*procyclidine hydrochloride*
Burroughs Wellcome

**KLONOPIN™**

0.5 mg　　1 mg　　2 mg
*clonazepam*　　　Roche

**LARODOPA®**

0.1 g　　0.25 g　　0.5 g
*L-dopa*
Roche

**†LIBRIUM®**

LIBRIUM 5
ROCHE

LIBRIUM 10

LIBRIUM 25
ROCHE

5 mg　　10 mg　　25 mg

*chlordiazepoxide HCI*　　　Roche

**LITHOBID®**

300 mg

*lithium carbonate*　　　CIBA

**†LOXITANE®**

5 mg　　　10 mg

25 mg　　　50 mg
*loxapine succinate*　　　Lederle

**LUDIOMIL®**

25 mg　　50 mg　　75 mg
*maprotiline hydrochloride*　　CIBA

**MARPLAN®**

10 mg
*isocarboxazid*　　　Roche

## WILLIAMS AND WILKINS©

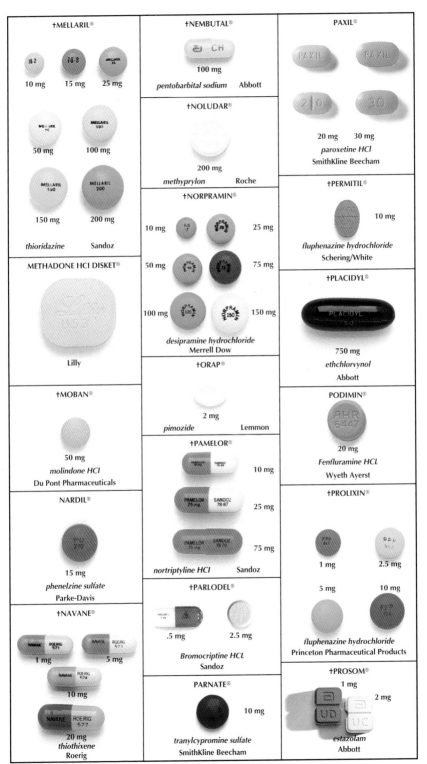

†MELLARIL®

10 mg  15 mg  25 mg

50 mg  100 mg

150 mg  200 mg

*thioridazine*    Sandoz

METHADONE HCl DISKET®

Lilly

†MOBAN®

50 mg

*molindone HCl*
Du Pont Pharmaceuticals

NARDIL®

15 mg

*phenelzine sulfate*
Parke-Davis

†NAVANE®

1 mg  5 mg

10 mg

20 mg
*thiothixene*
Roerig

†NEMBUTAL®

100 mg

*pentobarbital sodium*    Abbott

†NOLUDAR®

200 mg

*methyprylon*    Roche

†NORPRAMIN®

10 mg  25 mg

50 mg  75 mg

100 mg  150 mg

*desipramine hydrochloride*
Merrell Dow

†ORAP®

2 mg

*pimozide*    Lemmon

†PAMELOR®

10 mg

25 mg

75 mg

*nortriptyline HCl*    Sandoz

†PARLODEL®

.5 mg  2.5 mg

*Bromocriptine HCL*
Sandoz

PARNATE®

10 mg

*tranylcypromine sulfate*
SmithKline Beecham

PAXIL®

20 mg  30 mg

*paroxetine HCl*
SmithKline Beecham

†PERMITIL®

10 mg

*fluphenazine hydrochloride*
Schering/White

†PLACIDYL®

750 mg

*ethchlorvynol*
Abbott

PODIMIN®

20 mg

*Fenfluramine HCL*
Wyeth Ayerst

†PROLIXIN®

1 mg  2.5 mg

5 mg  10 mg

*fluphenazine hydrochloride*
Princeton Pharmaceutical Products

†PROSOM®

1 mg

2 mg

*estazolam*
Abbott

*WILLIAMS AND WILKINS*©

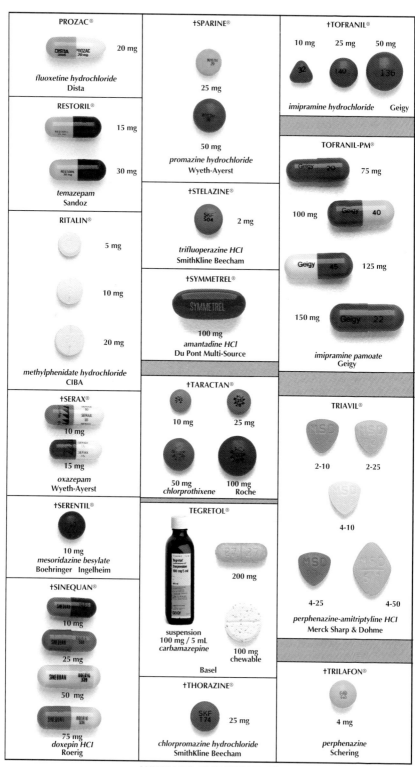

**PROZAC®**

20 mg

*fluoxetine hydrochloride*
Dista

**RESTORIL®**

15 mg

30 mg

*temazepam*
Sandoz

**RITALIN®**

5 mg

10 mg

20 mg

*methylphenidate hydrochloride*
CIBA

**†SERAX®**

10 mg

15 mg

*oxazepam*
Wyeth-Ayerst

**†SERENTIL®**

10 mg
*mesoridazine besylate*
Boehringer Ingelheim

**†SINEQUAN®**

10 mg

25 mg

50 mg

75 mg
*doxepin HCl*
Roerig

**†SPARINE®**

25 mg

50 mg
*promazine hydrochloride*
Wyeth-Ayerst

**†STELAZINE®**

2 mg

*trifluoperazine HCl*
SmithKline Beecham

**†SYMMETREL®**

100 mg
*amantadine HCl*
Du Pont Multi-Source

**†TARACTAN®**

10 mg          25 mg

50 mg          100 mg
*chlorprothixene*          Roche

**TEGRETOL®**

200 mg

suspension
100 mg / 5 mL
*carbamazepine*

100 mg
chewable

Basel

**†THORAZINE®**

25 mg

*chlorpromazine hydrochloride*
SmithKline Beecham

**†TOFRANIL®**

10 mg    25 mg    50 mg

*imipramine hydrochloride*    Geigy

**TOFRANIL-PM®**

75 mg

100 mg    40

125 mg

150 mg

*imipramine pamoate*
Geigy

**TRIAVIL®**

2-10          2-25

4-10

4-25          4-50

*perphenazine-amitriptyline HCl*
Merck Sharp & Dohme

**†TRILAFON®**

4 mg

*perphenazine*
Schering

**WILLIAMS AND WILKINS©**

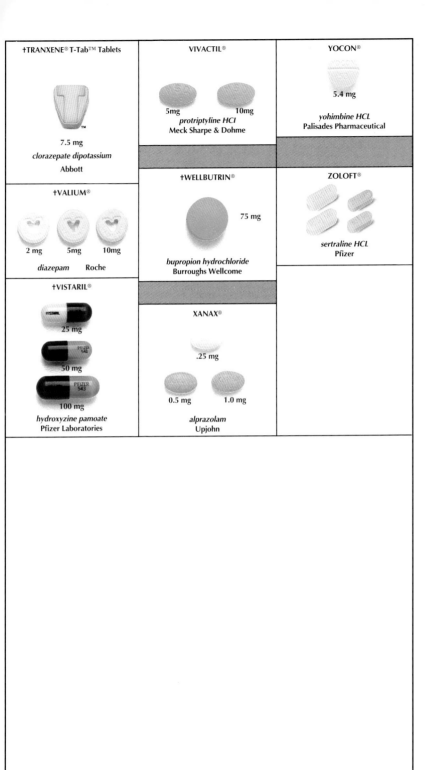

†TRANXENE® T-Tab™ Tablets

7.5 mg

*clorazepate dipotassium*
Abbott

†VALIUM®

2 mg    5mg    10mg

*diazepam*    Roche

†VISTARIL®

25 mg

50 mg

100 mg

*hydroxyzine pamoate*
Pfizer Laboratories

VIVACTIL®

5mg    10mg

*protriptyline HCl*
Meck Sharpe & Dohme

†WELLBUTRIN®

75 mg

*bupropion hydrochloride*
Burroughs Wellcome

XANAX®

.25 mg

0.5 mg    1.0 mg

*alprazolam*
Upjohn

YOCON®

5.4 mg

*yohimbine HCL*
Palisades Pharmaceutical

ZOLOFT®

*sertraline HCL*
Pfizer

# NOTES

# NOTES

# NOTES

# Appendix 1
## Classification of Drugs Used in Psychiatry

**Antianxiety Drugs**   The drugs of choice for the treatment of anxiety are the benzodiazepines and buspirone. These compounds offer a wide margin of safety. There are 14 benzodiazepines available for clinical use in the U.S. They are widely prescribed, with at least 10% of the population using one of these drugs each year. *See* Tables 1 and 2.

TABLE 1
**Currently Marketed Benzodiazepines According to Primary Approved Indication**

| Anxiety | Insomnia | Other |
|---|---|---|
| alprazolam (Xanax) | flurazepam (Dalmane) | clonazepam (Klonopin) |
| chlordiazepoxide (Librium) | quazepam (Doral) | midazolam (Versed) |
| clorazepate (Tranxene) | temazepam (Restoril) | |
| diazepam (Valium) | triazolam (Halcion) | |
| halazepam (Paxipam) | | |
| lorazepam (Ativan) | | |
| oxazepam (Serax) | | |
| prazepam (Centrax) | | |

TABLE 2
## Comments on Individual Antianxiety Drugs

| Drug | Comments |
| --- | --- |
| alprazolam | Effective in blocking panic attacks. May need doses up to 8 mg/day for treating panic disorder. Due to short half-life, may need to be given three times/day (TID) or four times/day (QID). Major problem is difficulty discontinuing treatment because of withdrawal syndrome. |
| buspirone | Not a benzodiazepine. First anxiolytic of azapirone class. Therapeutic effect seen after 3-4 weeks. No sedative or hypnotic effects. Lack of sedation and no potential for abuse or physical dependence. Can be used with benzodiazepines. |
| chlordiazepoxide | Slower onset of action minimizes abuse potential. Main use today is in the management of alcohol withdrawal and, with caution, treatment of anxiety in alcoholic patients. Due to long half-life, accumulates with daily use. |
| clonazepam | Not officially an anxiolytic, but now widely used in treating panic disorder. Its half-life range of 18–54 hours may permit QID or two times/day (BID) dosing. May carry higher risk of causing depression than other benzodiazepines. |
| clorazepate | Absorption may be delayed when ingested with antacids. Due to long half-life, accumulates with daily use. |
| diazepam | Rapidly and completely absorbed. Also very lipid soluble. Result is rapid onset of action. May account for some abuse potential. Due to long half-life, accumulates with daily use. |
| flurazepam | Long half-life produces significant residual sedation, particularly with repeated use. Increased risk of falls in the elderly. Only advantage is a less severe withdrawal syndrome. |
| halazepam | Similar to clorazepate but more reliably absorbed. Due to long half-life, accumulates with daily use. |
| lorazepam | Wide range of elimination half-life (8–25 hours) means that duration of effects varies from person to person. Reliably absorbed IM. Metabolized mainly by conjugation. Risk of amnesia present. May be effective in treating panic disorder. |
| oxazepam | Narrow range of elimination half-life (5–13 hours) assures short duration of action. Slowly absorbed. Metabolized mainly by conjugation. |
| midazolam | Three to four times the sedative potency of diazepam. Only available in aqueous injectable form. Used for induction of anesthesia with sedative, anxiolytic and amnesic action occurring within 1–5 minutes after IV administration. |
| prazepam | Similar to clorazepate but more reliably absorbed. Due to long half-life, accumulates with daily use. |
| quazepam | Similar to flurazepam. Claim by the manufacturer that Quazepam has relative preference for benzodiazepine type-1 receptors in the brain has not been conclusively demonstrated. |
| temazepam | Intermediate half-life results in minimal residual sedation. May find some morning sedation. Only hypnotic metabolized by conjugation. |
| triazolam | Very short half-life results in virtually no next-day sedation. Extremely potent so very low doses should be used. At higher doses, amnesia becomes a possibility. Rebound insomnia a potential problem when drug is stopped. |

**Appendix 1**

**Antipsychotic Drugs**  These drugs are used mainly to treat schizophrenia but are also useful for other severe disorders including mania, organic psychosis, and Tourette's disorder. *See* Table 3.

TABLE 3
**Currently Used Antipsychotic Drugs**

| | |
|---|---|
| *butyrophenone*<br>    haloperidol (Haldol) | *phenothiazine*<br>    **aliphatic**<br>        chlorpromazine (Thorazine) |
| *dibenzoxazepine*<br>    loxapine (Loxitane) |         triflupromazine (Vesprin)<br>    **piperazine** |
| *diboroxazepine*<br>    clozapine (Clozaril) |         acetophenazine (Tindal)<br>        fluphenazine (Prolixin)<br>        perphenazine (Trilafon) |
| *diphenybutylpiperidine*<br>    pimozide (Orap) |         trifluoperazine (Stelazine)<br>    **piperidine**<br>        thioridazine (Mellaril) |
| *indolone*<br>    molindone (Moban) | *thioxanthene*<br>    thiothixene (Navane)<br>    chlorprothixene (Taractin) |

**Antidepressant Drugs** There are five broad categories of antidepressant drugs: standard tricyclic compounds, tetracyclic compounds, serotonergic agents, atypical agents, and monoamine oxidase inhibitors (MAOIs). *See* Table 4.

TABLE 4
## Currently Used Antidepressant Drugs

**Tricyclics**
    amitriptyline (Elavil)
    clomipramine* (Anafranil)
    doxepin (Sinequan)
    imipramine (Tofranil)
    trimipramine (Surmontil)

    desipramine (Norpramin)
    nortriptyline (Pamelor)
    protriptyline (Vivactil)

**Tetracyclics**
    amoxapine (Asendin)
    maprotiline (Ludiomil)

**Serotonergic Agents**
    fluoxetine (Prozac)
    sertraline (Zoloft)

**Atypical Agents**
    alprazolam (Xanax)
    bupropion (Wellbutrin)
    trazodone (Desyrel)

**Monoamine Oxidase Inhibitors (MAOIs)**
    isocarboxazid (Marplan)
    phenelzine (Nardil)
    tranylcypromine (Parnate)

*Approved in the U.S. for treatment of obsessive-compulsive disorder.

**Other Drugs**   Other drugs that are used to treat psychotic and manic conditions are listed in Table 5.

TABLE 5
**Other Drugs Used in Treatment of Psychosis and Mania**

| | |
|---|---|
| beta-adrenergic blockers (Inderal) | Beta-adrenergic blockers may be effective in treating aggressive behavior or rage in schizophrenic patients. |
| carbamazepine (Tegretol) | Some patients get worse with antipsychotic drugs. It is thought they may have atypical psychoses that respond to carbamazepine and other anticonvulsants. Manic psychosis also responds to carbamazepine. |
| lithium (Eskalith) | Apart from reducing manic symptoms, lithium also has been reported to be useful in treating refractory schizophrenic patients when given in conjunction with antipsychotic drugs. |
| reserpine (Serpasil) | Acts as a presynaptic dopamine depleter. Slow onset, marginal efficacy, and risk of depression and suicide. No longer used in schizophrenia. |

# Appendix 2
## Table of Commonly Abused Drugs

| Class | Trade Name* (or Source) | Street Names |
|---|---|---|
| **Opioids** | | |
| morphine | morphine sulfate | dope, M, Miss Emma, morpho, white stuff |
| heroin | none | H, junk, skag, smack, boy, hard stuff, horse |
| hydromorphone | Dilaudid | DL's |
| oxymorphone | Numorphan | blues |
| oxycodone | Percodan, Percocet | Percs |
| meperidine | Demerol | |
| methadone hydrochloride | Dolophine | dollys, done |
| pentazocine | Talwin | |
| tincture of opium | paregoric | PG, licorice |
| cough preparations with codeine | Elixir terpin hydrate, Robitussin A-C | schoolboy, blue velvet, Robby |
| hydrocodone | Hycodan | |
| **Non-narcotic Analgesics** | | |
| propoxyphene | Darvon | |
| **Benzodiazepines** | | |
| diazepam | Valium | |
| chlordiazepoxide | Librium | |
| alprazolam | Xanax | |
| oxazepam | Serax | |
| lorazepam | Ativan | |
| **Barbiturates** | | barbs, candy, dolls, goofers, peanuts, sleeping pill, downers |
| secobarbital | Seconal | pink lady, red devils, red, seccy, pinks |
| amobarbital | Amytal | blue angels, bluebirds, blue devils, blues, lilly |
| pentobarbital | Nembutal | nebbies, yellow bullets, yellow dolls |
| phenobarbital | Luminal | phennies, purple hearts |
| amobarbital/secobarbital | Tuinal | Christmas trees, double-trouble, rainbows, tooies |
| **Other Sedative-Hypnotics** | | |
| methaqualone | Quaalude | sopors, ludes |
| glutethimide | Doriden | CIBA's, packs (with codeine) |
| methyprylon | Noludar | |

| Class | Trade Name* (or Source) | Street Names |
|---|---|---|
| ethchlorvynol | Placidyl | |
| chloral hydrate | Noctec | |
| paraldehyde | Paral | |
| meprobamate | Miltown | |
| scopolamine aminoxide | Sominex | truth serum |
| **Central Nervous System Stimulants** | | |
| cocaine hydrochloride | cocaine | coke, blow, toot, girl, snow-flake, uptown, happy dust, baseball, roxane |
| cocaine freebase | | crack, rock, base |
| dextroamphetamine | Biphetamine | black beauties |
| amphetamine sulfate | Benzedrine | A's, beans, bennies, cart-wheels, crossroads, jelly beans, hearts, peaches, whites |
| dextroamphetamine sulfate/ amobarbital | Dexamyl | greenies |
| dextroamphetamine sulfate | Dexedrine | brownies, Christmas trees, dexies, hearts, wakeups, uppers |
| methamphetamine hydro-chloride | Methedrine | bombit, crank, crystal, meth, speed |
| **Drugs with Hallucinogenic Properties** | | |
| lysergic acid diethylamide (LSD) | synthetic deriva-tive (ergot fungus) | acid, pink wedges, sandos, sugar cubes, dots, window-panes, blotters |
| psilocin/psilocybin | mushroom (*Psilocybe mexicana*) | magic mushroom |
| dimethyltryptamine (DMT) | synthetic | DMT, DET, DPT, business man's acid |
| morning glory seeds | bindweed (*Rivea corymbosa*) | flower power, heavenly blue, pearly gates |
| mescaline | peyote cactus | barf tea, big chief, buttons, cactus, mesc |
| dimethoxymethylam-phetamine (DOM) | synthetic (derivative) | STP |
| myristicin | nutmeg | MMDA |
| muscarine | mushroom (*Amanita muscaria*) | fly |
| phencyclidine (PCP) | | angel dust, dust, PCP, crystal, hog |
| **Tetrahydrocannabinoids** | | |
| marijuana | *Cannabis sativa* (leaves, flow-ers) | grass, hay, joints, Mary Jane, pot, reefer, rope, smoke, tea, weed |
| hashish | *Cannabis sativa* (resin) | hash |

| Class | Trade Name*<br>(or Source) | Street Name |
|---|---|---|
| **Volatile Solvents and Gases** | | |
| benzine | gasoline | |
| tuluol | glue vapor | |
| carbon tetrachloride | cleaning fluid | |
| naphtha | cleaning fluid | scrubwoman's kick |
| amyl nitrite | amyl nitrite | amys, pears, snapper,<br>poppers |
| butyl/isobutyl nitrate | perfume,<br>incense, room<br>deodorizers | rush, lockerroom, jock,<br>sweat, hardware |
| nitrous oxide | nitrous oxide | laughing gas, nitrous |

Table adapted from *American Psychiatric Glossary*, American Psychiatric Press, Inc., 1988, with permission.
*Many of these drugs are sold under a variety of trade names; only a single popular example is used for each.

# Appendix 3
## Drug Enforcement Administration (DEA) Schedule of Drugs According to Abuse Potential

| DEA Control Level (Schedule) | Characteristics of Drug at Each Control Level | Examples of Drugs at Each Control Level |
|---|---|---|
| 1 | High abuse potential<br>No accepted use in medical treatment in the U.S. at the present time and therefore not for prescription use<br>Can be used for research | LSD, heroin, marijuana, peyote, PCP, mescaline, psilocybin, tetrahydrocannabinols, nicocodeine, nicomorphine, and others |
| II | High abuse potential<br>Severe physical dependence liability<br>Severe psychological dependence liability<br>No refills: no telephone prescriptions | Amphetamine, methamphetamine, opium, morphine, codeine, hydromorphine, phenmetrazine, cocaine, amobarbital, secobarbital, pentobarbital, methylphenidate, and others |
| III | Abuse potential less than levels I and II<br>Moderate or low physical dependence liability<br>High psychological liability<br>Prescriptions must be rewritten after 6 months or 5 refills | Glutethimide, methyprylon, nalorphine, sulfonmethane, benzphetamine, phendimetrazine, clortermine, mazindol, chlorphentermine, compounds containing codeine, morphine, opium, hydrocodone, dihydrocodeine, naltrexone, diethylpropion, and others |
| IV | Low abuse potential<br>Limited physical dependence liability<br>Limited psychological dependence liability<br>Prescriptions must be rewritten after 6 months or 5 refills | Phenobarbital, benzodiazepines,* chloral hydrate, ethchlorvynol, ethinamate, meprobamate, paraldehyde, and others |
| V | Lowest abuse potential of all controlled substances | Narcotic preparations containing limited amounts of nonnarcotic active medicinal ingredients |

*In New York State, benzodiazepines are treated as Schedule II substances, which require a triplicate prescription for a maximum of 1 month's supply.